The Children's Crusade

Clothbound edition ISBN 0 88778 048 2
Paperbound edition ISBN 0 88778 049 0

Library of Congress Catalog Card Number: 70-141801

Printed in Canada by Alger Press Limited

Peter Martin Associates Limited, 17 Inkerman Street, Toronto 5, Ontario

The Children's Crusade

The Story of the Company of Young Canadians

by Ian Hamilton

Peter Martin Associates Limited

Introduction

The Company of Young Canadians leaves scars on people. It was, and probably still is, an organization driven by emotion, with personality pitted against personality. It was an organization where battles to the death were an everyday occurrence, where compromise showed weakness — a view typical of the civil service.

Very few people managed to leave the Company in the same shape they entered it. Some were destroyed. Others emerged with new strength. The majority left, muddled and confused, still looking for something that the Company had promised, but had never provided.

I suffered and bled with the CYC for more than two years. I too was changed by the time I left. Instead of being calm and mild, I found myself edgy, attuned to crisis situations, and used to fighting — continuous fighting.

My role in the Company was an odd one. During Alan Clarke's regime I was kept at a distance, involved in higher planning only when necessary. I knew about most of the things that went on, however, as most Company people were notoriously bad at keeping secrets. When Stewart Goodings took over the Company, I moved into the inner circle. When Claude Vidal took over, I became entrenched there.

This book is a review of the Company I saw and knew. It is, I believe, the real Company with the illusions and rumours stripped away. In many ways the reality of the Company is more frightening than the illusion.

During my time with the CYC, I was directly involved in

nearly every scandal and crisis the Company went through. I explained over and over again the role of the Company: to the press, to the public, to the MPs and to fellow Company people. I was the front man — the talker.

My name is not mentioned in the book. My role is not revealed directly. I am there all the same — sitting beside Vidal at the parliamentary inquiry; writing his speeches; writing briefs; working for Jerry Gambill; for Goodings; and for Clarke. I was consulted by them and gave them advice. With some of them I helped to form strategies and policies.

I left, finally, because I was tired, beaten and frustrated. I had worked, like others, for the kind of Company I wanted. Time and time again that Company was denied us. With the emergence of the Company in its final form, the anti-volunteer body that I had unwillingly helped to create, I could no longer hope and could no longer stay.

In this book I judge my colleagues. It is only fair that I should judge myself as well. With the Company I made my share of mistakes. I was wrong on some issues. I didn't foresee the results of some incidents. I also had my successes and perhaps in a small way I helped the Company to survive for as long as it did.

In the end, I suppose that I was no better and no worse than most of the people I worked with. We all had our faults and our virtues. One virtue that cannot be denied us is the simple fact that we cared.

Contents

Contents

Dedication:

To my wife, Lynn.

Acknowledgements:

There were four people who helped me through this thing.
Joseph A.P. Clark, a kind man who understands the Company's generation. Bernie Muzeen, who lent me his files
and best wishes. Dale Seddon, who was just plain cheery.
And Bev Lawrence, editor and friend.

1
The Beginning

No one is sure when the idea for the Company of Young Canadians first began to circulate and catch hold of official Ottawa. An educated guess is that sometime in the winter of 1964-65, someone thought of creating a Canadian volunteer body. Canada will never know who the originator was. Some people claim it was an agent for Russian Intelligence. Others, less dramatic, say it was a senior civil servant. Whoever it was, though, is lying low at present and saying nothing and most people can sympathize with the reluctance of the Company's father to come forward.

The idea did, however, strike a responsive chord and throughout the early months of 1965, other people picked it up and began to expand on it, to Canadianize it. The leading advocates were John Turner, Judy LaMarsh and Duncan Edmonds, all three of whom would later harshly repudiate the child they had helped bring into the world. Turner and LaMarsh were both cabinet ministers at the time; Edmonds was executive assistant to Paul Martin. Edmonds was a go-getter and his enthusiasm for the volunteer-body idea was soon bubbling over to anyone nearby.

The bubbling was effective. In the Speech from the Throne, April, 1965, the name, the Company of Young Canadians, was heard for the first time. No real explanation was given, but everyone fell in love with the name—it had been contributed by Miss LaMarsh.

The next step was the establishing of an organizing committee, with Dr. F. Leddy as its chairman. Duncan Edmonds was rewarded for his enthusiasm by being named secretary to the committee. He quickly brought in an assistant secretary named Stewart Goodings.

The committee was detailed to hammer out a blueprint for the Company of Young Canadians and attempted to do that over the next six months. During this time, the quietest in the Company's history, the committee held an endless parade of meetings with only one real element missing—youth. When the Leddy Report was produced in November, it turned out to be a giant anti-climax. There was no blueprint for the CYC. Instead, the government received what it considered to be rhetoric in the form of pious statements of principle, and waffly statements at that. After the report was received, official Ottawa was quiet for two months, causing some to complain that the government was trying to hold the CYC back. In December, the government's plans were announced.

The Company of Young Canadians was going to be a revolutionary body. The first of its kind in the world. The government had decided to gamble. It was going all the way with youth.

It was a strange move for the Pearson government to make, and a move for which it should be given credit. The Leddy report had been a major disappointment.
This is the reason for the two-month delay. Contrary to common myth, which contends that the government tried to play down radicalism, the government took the revolutionary spirit upon itself and became bold. Within two months, it discussed, designed, approved and announced the concept of the CYC. The youth of the country played a minor role in compiling the report. One senior civil servant claims that not one articulate brief from the young people of Canadian society was ever presented to the committee. The radicals were, incredibly, the government officials.

The concept of the CYC was an exciting one and it was hoped that it would be a forerunner in the field of government legislation. The Company was to be set up separately from other government departments. It would report to Parliament for its funds through a minister, but that was its only obligation. It was to be governed by a council of fifteen members — ten of whom would be elected by volunteers. The council was to determine all the policies of the Company, including programmes and finances. The executive director would run the Company on a day-to-day basis, but would be directly responsible to the council. He would be responsible for all professional staff, but would have no real authority over volunteers.

Beyond these structural points, the Company grew even more revolutionary. The government wanted a Company of young people who would disrupt the establishment. The act was to read, "The objects of the Company are to support, encourage and develop programs for social, economic and community development in Canada or abroad through voluntary service". Those objects gave the Company a free hand. It could sponsor a social revolution or help old ladies across the street. In the main it opted for the former, but this is what the government expected, or should have expected.

There were many other volunteer agencies in the world in 1965, the best known being the Peace Corps in the United States. But not one of them had ever been given this kind of freedom, either structurally or operationally. The Peace Corps was under tight government control, as were all other volunteer agencies. The Corps was directed by a Presidential nominee. Its policies were decided by the government. The volunteers were told where to work, with whom to work and how to work. There would be no boat-rocking in the Peace Corps. It is difficult to know why the Canadian government broke with this accepted form. It may just have wanted an organization different from the Peace Corps, or it may have sincerely believed in giving young people the chance to develop their own ideas. In any event that is what it did – it turned over total control of the Company, theoretically, and gave the youth of Canada a chance to put their idealism into practice, a chance to change the shape of Canadian society.

The Prime Minister publicly announced the guiding principles of the CYC in December and the Company was then left to itself. The staff, initially just Edmonds and Goodings, began to grow and the Company's first executive director was appointed early in 1966. He was William McWhinney. McWhinney's credentials in the field of volunteer service were impressive, as he had previously been executive secretary of Canadian University Services Overseas (CUSO), Canada's elite volunteer body at the time. His appointment was on an interim basis.

All through the early months of 1966, the staff worked on plans for recruiting volunteers while, at the same time, working out a pilot program. They were also guiding the drafting of the legislation that would bring the Company into legal existence. The legislation went slowly and there was some criticism that the Company was being held back once more by the government. No one seemed to realize that the Company had been included in the 1965-66 estimates under the Appropriations Act, which was all the legal basis it really needed.

On April 14th, the government took another step in the formation of the Company. It appointed an 18-member Interim Advisory Council to manage the Company. The government had decided to slow down the process by which the volunteers would have control of the CYC and, consequently, the volunteers would not be represented on the council. However, assurances were given that a volunteer-controlled body would come into existence when the volunteers had sufficient experience.

The appointed council was an attempt to be non-political and, to an extent, it was successful. Several members were suspect politically, namely Marc Lalonde, Duncan Edmonds and R.A.J. Phillips. But it was felt that they were balanced by a group that was obviously not political in the traditional sense. This group included Arthur Pape, Alan Clarke, Douglas Ward and Richard Thompson.

The chairman of the council was Ward, 27, of Toronto. At the time, he was president-elect of the Canadian Union of Students. He had extensive experience in youth and student organizations, including a stint as president of the Students' Council at the University of Toronto. Also listed as credits were his experiences as a detached youth worker in Toronto and as a student minister in Western Canada.

Ward would serve as chairman of the council until September, 1969, a longer occupancy than anyone had ever imagined. Ward remains as much a mystery as anyone who ever worked with the Company. As chairman of the governing council, it could be expected that he should share part of the blame for events that took place during his tenure. But, things did not develop that way and he managed to escape with an almost clean sheet. The clean sheet was, however, only in the eyes of the public. Within the Company, like everyone else, Ward had his share of detractors as well as admirers.

The vice-chairman was Lalonde. There was no question that Lalonde was an extremely able man. He had his Master's degree in law and had been a professor of commercial law and economics at the University of Montreal. Following that, he was special assistant to E. Davie Fulton for one year of the B.C. Tory's tenure as Minister of Justice. Lalonde began to practice law in 1960, but later left to become a mainstay in Prime Minister Pearson's Ottawa office. The difficulty for Lalonde would be to keep the interests of the Liberal Party of Canada out of the CYC.

The other sixteen council members were an unbelievable mixture. The radicals were represented by Pape, 24, a former national staff member of the Student Union for Peace Action, and Thompson, 23, who was working on the infamous Neestow Partnership Project in Green Lake, Saskatchewan, an Indian-Métis community. Business was represented by Maurice Strong, 36, of Montreal, president and director of the Power Corporation of Canada Ltd. and by Lloyd Shaw, 52, of Halifax, general manager of L.R. Shaw Ltd. Even the clergy got into the act with Reverend Roland Soucie, dean of the school of psychology and education at the University of Moncton. Then there were in-betweeners, men like Tim Reid, a former football player and a Liberal candidate in the 1965 federal election, who was then lecturing in economics at Toronto's York University, and Alan Clarke, 36, executive director of the Canadian Citizenship Council.

As a group, the council was impossible to define politically or socially. D.G. Poole of the Company made a valiant effort in May, 1966, when he wrote: "In Ottawa, staff and council meetings are far from peaceful. Represented in both bodies are pigeons, inclined to see the world in pigeon-hole terms, born bureaucrats, eager to get the show on the road, and political diplomats concerned that the CYC be a credit to the government. There are also a number of young men and women who have chosen to forego the advantages of career and the rewards of competitive effort in the hope of discovering more meaningful objectives."

The council began to meet almost immediately. Its meetings were gruelling marathons. They usually lasted for three days and each day ran between 12 and 18 hours. There was a difficult job to do. Policies were non-existent, but expectations were high. The government had talked of 2,000 volunteers in the field within two years. The Company itself, through the words of Poole, settled on 250. The Company in its first year decided to treat that year as a pilot project open for experiment.

The pressure on the council was enormous. Two pilot projects were to be started by the end of spring and the first full training session in Antigonish was to be held in late June, yet the Company had no policies.

The council decided not to yield to the pressures to rush into policy-making. Meetings were taken up with soul-searching discussions on the Company's mission in life and little time was spent on the small nitty-gritties.

There was a definite split on the council, a left-to-right split that was further complicated by differing opinions on priorities. This split never clearly crystallized, but was observed on several issues. The first was the matter of service projects. Some council members, like Edmonds, maintained that service projects should play a large role in the Company. Others, like Pape, talked of social action. They had little tolerance for the service-oriented people. Service was do-gooding and the Company, in their eyes, was set up as an alternative to do-gooding. The bleeding hearts, as represented by the United Appeal and the YMCA, had always taken care of themselves. Now was the time for real action and change to take place. The debate went on endlessly. Boy Scouts or activists, which role for the CYC? The activists won. The CYC would be radical.

This was clearly pointed out in the Aims and Principles of the Company as adopted by the council. That document reads in part:

> In looking at the needs which have led to the forma-
> tion of the Company, it is impossible to ignore some
> of the major themes which appear to be significant to
> all people. These factors, which we attempt to describe
> below, provide the framework, or the context, for
> political and social change in the sixties . . . .
> . . . . it does not appear that any decisions are taken
> at all. And yet, by apparently failing to take decisions
> one can end up with a situation far more dangerous
> and damaging to the human condition, than if certain

drastic decisions were taken. Ordinary people are often powerless in the face of such bureaucratic juggernauts and of the experts who service them . . . .

The ten-page, typewritten paper then goes on to state the aims of the Company as simply: "We are seeking a society in which people are in charge of their own destinies. Second, we seek a society in which diversity and variety are at the basis of human life."

The twelve operational principles were then outlined:

1. The Company has been established in response to the economic, social and cultural needs of communities and to the desire of Canadians to volunteer their time and talents for constructive social change at home and abroad;

2. The dominant goal of the Company is to help people and communities better their situations and tackle their own problems;

3. The volunteers will work and live with those groups or communities who are their hosts. They will work with and not on behalf of these people;

4. People in any situation have the right to make decisions about their lives and to evaluate their own positions. Company volunteers will respect this right.

5. Volunteers will be partners with their hosts in a mutual learning and acting experience.

6. Volunteers are not "professional helpers" and will not seek to impose their own solutions on people or communities. They will assist other people in articulating their own problems and in working on them.

7. Where projects conform to the spirit and criteria of the Company, there will be no hesitation on the Company's part in seeking volunteers, whether the project is submitted by a governmental department, a private group or any other community organization.

8. The Company council and its staff will support its

volunteers, but it will not identify itself with issues in which volunteers are involved.

9. The volunteer should be the primary decision-maker in the Company of Young Canadians.

10. The project should allow the volunteer a maximum degree of freedom in deciding his own techniques and in using his own initiative and independence.

11. The Company will support projects which will hopefully help to alleviate the causes of problems and will not simply "bandage" a symptom.

12. Volunteers in the Company will choose their own assignments in consultation with the staff.

The Aims and Principles were readily agreed to by the entire council. The document (only parts have been quoted) is designed to inspire action. In the rhetoric of the left, it slams at the liberals (do-gooders) and at the agencies (the bandage boys). It sets up the framework for participatory democracy and self-determination, major catchwords for the left in 1966. All in all, the Aims and Principles are a credit to the Company. They are over-wordy and at times the rhetoric is self-indulgent, but the meaning, the intent and feeling behind the paper are clear. The Company was out to create change.

The tragedy of the Aims and Principles is that they were never taken seriously. They were sent to every volunteer applicant, but were hardly looked at in Ottawa. The 12 operational principles became, in effect, the verbal shield that the Company used to deflect the arrows from the government, the press and the public. Certainly, some people in the Company believed in them, and certainly some followed them, but generally, they became meaningless.

It is difficult, for example, to look at principles eight and nine with anything but cynicism. The support that was so rashly promised has never existed. Since the day the first volunteers went into the field, the one constant complaint has been lack of support. As for being the primary decision-makers, volunteers in the Company have had to threaten, blackmail and connive to get even basic consideration.

If this reduces the Aims and Principles to an artificial, verbal level, then perhaps this is where they belong.

There can be no questioning, in the beginning at least, the morals and intentions of the 18 people who sat on the council. They were basically honest people trying to set up a two-million dollar organization under tremendous handicaps. They had too much on their plate and too little time to digest it. They were also hampered by an undermanned administrative staff, and one that seemed to regard administration as a trap, as an evil of the establishment.

That was one of the first fatal mistakes of the council, and of the Company. Administration got short shrift at council meetings. Its leprous bedfellow was communications. Usually placed at the end of agendas, these topics sometimes didn't get discussed at all and, if they did, it was usually only for a short time. The talk was of aims and principles, philosophy of recruitment, methods for achieving change. All important, of course, but administration and communications were no less important.

The pressure for more emphasis on administration and communications came from Duncan Edmonds and Bob Phillips. But they were both suspect; Edmonds because of his political ties and Phillips because he was a civil servant.

"The council wanted their staff to be people with exciting ideas. They forgot all about the accountants. Many people on council and in the Company were romanticists or anarchists. They regarded administration as infringement on their freedom," a council member later said.

Whether they did or not is immaterial. The facts are that the council never adequately looked at administration until it was too late, until indeed, the government, press and public had walked over the Company wearing cleats.

One of the first rules in a business as controversial as social change is to keep your books clean. Make them come after you on the issues.

But the Company was new and open for experimentation and not concerned with books. One of the first experiments was lack of structure. The philosophy was seen in action at council meetings. Doug Ward was never a gavel man. He let discussions take their course and rarely interfered. This philosophy spilled over into such a simple thing as council meetings starting on time. They never did. At one particular session, the meeting the night before had lasted until midnight, but everyone agreed to meet the next morning at nine a.m. By the time the council had enough people for a quorum it was eleven a.m. Unimportant as this may seem, it was two hours lost that might have been spent on administration.

The other large hole in the Company was communications. This turned out to be another cancer that was never removed.

"You have to communicate with the public," Phillips told the council in 1966. He belonged to a hopeless minority, mainly the discredited followers of liberalism.

The majority said: "We want to talk to our constituents," which seemed to have meant the people who agreed with them.

From this philosophy came many problems for the Company. The CYC was never really understood and when it came under attack and finally went to the public for support, it was too late. Everything was tried between 1967 and 1969 to gain at least the understanding of the Canadian public. All efforts failed. If the attempt had been made when the Company was a showpiece, shiny and new, the reaction might have been quite different.

It is important to say that the council's initial desire to experiment, to try new methods, did not cause the majority of the CYC's problems. Many of the experiments worked, and even some that failed ended up producing some valuable information. It was not the gambling that caused the Company to suffer, it was lack of foresight, and a tendency to put realism behind idealism.

But, these were the first days of the Company and no one could foresee what would happen in the future. The Company was just beginning. The council was laying the foundation. The first volunteers were preparing to be parachuted into the field. The staff was growing at an unbelievable rate. The first training session was being set up. And, finally, the act creating the Company of Young Canadians was passed by Parliament.

It was assented to on July 11th, 1966 and it was a glorious day. Liberals, NDP'ers, Tories, Creditistes — they all sang the praises of the Company, of the magnificent future it had, of the great deeds it would do. The act was passed unanimously.

The MPs should, however, have listened to David McDonald, the young Tory from PEI, when he added his voice to those voting yeah. "I say to you, Mr. Speaker, that some of the most glorious things that may happen under this program will be not its successes, but its failures, because it will be willing to take the risks in the projects put forward that no other agency or group is willing to take — and that will be all to its credit. We must consider that the Company of Young Canadians may be most responsible when they are taking some of the greatest risks."

2

Antigonish

If the Company of Young Canadians had tried to arrange a worse debut than its first training session in Antigonish, Nova Scotia, it undoubtedly would have failed. It wasn't intended to be a flop, but the Company managed to plan a training session that is still painfully vivid in the minds of nearly everyone who went through it, near it, or even heard of it.

The session wasn't actually held in Antigonish. A much more dramatic setting was discovered some eight miles away amid rich, green highland, complete with a lagoon and beaches. Crystal Cliffs had been an exclusive resort at one time, but it now consisted of some huts, an old farm house, a barn and a dining centre. It was owned by St. Francis Xavier University. The university was slightly concerned about the session and issued a two-page welcome release with a long list of do's and don'ts.

A good deal of planning had gone on in preparation for the training of the Company's first volunteers. It was essential that the Company start off on the right foot, and so it was essential that the training session be a success. The aims of the session were understated quite simply in a document entitled, *The Company of Young Canadians Invites You.*

"There will be special training in human relations and community development; in methods of instruction and the communication of knowledge and skills," it read. "Trainees will learn about the areas in which they will be serving, about the problems they will encounter and the institutions already working on them. Part of the training may be given in co-operation with local sponsoring organizations."

By June 27th, nearly all of the 56 young people invited to the session had arrived and had been billeted. They were an odd assortment. A good many of them were straight, middle-class products such as Torben Angelo, a Danish immigrant well adjusted to the ways of Canada after living for nine years in Toronto; Harvey Stevens, 21, of Port Colborne, a devout Christian; Bernard Muzeen, an English war orphan with years of experience in service organizations in Oshawa; Maeve Hancey from Sudbury, a graduate of St. Patrick's University in Ottawa; and Ross Eadie, a young high school graduate from a small town south of Ottawa.

There was another group that came from more diverse backgrounds, men and women who had been through other than normal experiences. There was Dorothy Hill, a 27-year old nurse from near Niagara Falls; Roy Daniels, an Indian; Joan Jones, a black from Halifax, and wife of the militant Rocky Jones; Carole Pickles, a Toronto girl who had been Miss Bicks' Pickles and who thought of herself as a folksinger; and Robert Davis, who had his masters in education from Cambridge University and dreamed about a better kind of educational system.

Added to these two groups was a group that was difficult to define. Some called them hippies, others thought they were just kooks. But, the only way to look at them is as individuals. Al Burger was one — "a cheerful anarchist" was one way he was described. Peter Mussalem was another. Mussalem was a forerunner of the generation of 1970 — drug-aware, verbally brilliant, but somewhat detached. The leader, Lynn Curtis, was a young man of 24 who disrupted and upset the group but was inevitably a centre of attraction. The *Globe and Mail* described him as looking like Jesus Christ, due no doubt to his gentle face, his beard and his soft voice. His reasons for coming to Antigonish were quite unique.

"When I came here and found this was a group of middle-class 18-year-olds, I attempted to destroy it. Then I found out they were dedicated . . . . If I hadn't come, this would have turned out to be an organization favorable to the government," the *Globe* quotes him as saying. "There are 5,000 people in Canada like me, of radical identification. Three of them came here. CYC has been boycotted by the radicals. They say its a big snow-job. I was convinced it was a big snow-job myself, but I wanted to see it," he continued.

The training session started with a small speech from Stewart Goodings, now an executive staff member with the Company.

"The Company is yours," the young people were told, "you will run it." And in a way, they were expected to start at Antigonish.

The first ten days were taken up with a human relations laboratory run by psychiatrist Dr. Noel Murphy. Participation was a key word and this was to be the start of it. The 56 people, from their variety of backgrounds, were to be thrown into five groups. The groups were to be unstructured — no authority or supervision and from this, the young people, nearly all between 18 and 22 years of age, were to try to build some sort of cohesive community which would function through consensus.

The press was present at these sessions and Michael Valpy of the *Globe and Mail*, who later joined the CYC, commented: "Such a task could be a big order for a unit as small as a family of four. But for a group of 56, many fresh out of high school, whose whole lives had been chock full of authority figures and discipline, it turned out to be a nerve-stretching experience."

These T-group sessions were one major part of the first ten days; the other was a full Company meeting which was held to hash out community problems such as what time to have breakfast on Sunday mornings.

"Those volunteer assemblies never really worked," said Bernie Muzeen afterward. "Philosophies of life used to be discussed and then immovable positions were taken. I was regarded as being right wing. Curtis and Mussalem were on the left. Burger was the anarchist. The group never agreed on anything, but they sure as hell knew how to apply group pressure."

It was the T-group sessions that held the attention of the press though, and would later result in Antigonish being cursed.

The sessions were highly intensive and personal. Words and actions would be analyzed or attacked.

In later years, a small skit was worked up from the Antigonish experience. The key figure is a young man getting up from a session.

"Where are you going?" he would be asked.

"To the bathroom," was the reply.

"Why?"

"Why does anyone want to go to the bathroom?"

"Why do you want to go?"

"To have a leak!"

"I don't believe you," said his analyzer.

"Why not?"

"I think you're copping out. I think you're uncomfortable and just want an excuse for cutting out, or else you want to masturbate."

"Okay, I want to masturbate. Now, can I go?"

As playful as that may seem, the sessions were not games. The volunteers were never told what was going on and as they looked about daily, they could see who the latest crack-up had been. Seven people left the session for a variety of emotional and psychiatric reasons. One trainee was hospitalized. Another 15 trainees were left floating, either for further training or for psychiatric assistance. Indeed, it was no game.

Some of the crack-ups were pitiful. Valpy reported several of them in detail. One involved a young married woman who was there with her husband and their four-year old child. Lynn Curtis, who had by this time become convinced that some of the people at Crystal Cliffs were planted (by the RCMP presumably) to disrupt the training session, told the girl that there was LSD in her food. She took him seriously.

The repercussions started with her staring at people in a vampish way, and then asking if she made them have strong sexual responses. This was followed by her belief that she could make people have diarrhea simply by staring at them.

At three a.m. the next morning, the husband, convinced that his child could be harmed by a longer stay at Crystal Cliffs, left with his family. They walked off into the night.

A day prior to this there had been a series of rattling emotional explosions that resulted in one girl being hospitalized and two others, a man and a woman, being asked to leave. It was recommended that the man have outpatient psychiatric treatment for three months at the expense of the CYC.

There were other unreported incidents. One involved a man who became convinced he was a lighthouse. He would stand in the middle of a room moving his head back and forth while making appropriate sounds.

The Crystal Cliffs Rumour, a small newsletter turned out by the trainees, spoke of another incident. "Is it true that Alice and Elaine tried to committ suicide the other night by jumping off the Manor House Roof?"

Dr. Murphy was calm.

"It was a time for problems to come out," he said. "And when they do, defenses fall and all sorts of insecurities are made apparent. I should point out that the psychiatric problems held by anyone taking this course would have come out eventually, either here or later."

Not everyone was cracking-up of course, and some people were gaining some insight through the experience, but all were over-shadowed by the personal tragedies of the rest.

The sensitivity training lasted for ten days officially, unofficially it went on for six weeks. The feelings that had emerged during the ten days could not evaporate when the time for community development theory rolled around. This was an important subject, perhaps the most important.

It was expected that when these young people had finished their training they would be posted to projects across the country. The communities in which they would work would be entirely different from anything most of them had ever experienced — the middle-class kids would find themselves in Cabbagetown in Toronto, in Indian communities, in poverty-stricken Maritime towns and hamlets — and they were expected to function in these communities. Function is a bad word because it does not suggest progress — to be catalytic is closer to the truth. It was a daring experiment and the theory, when simplified to its barest essentials, could be stated as follows:

A volunteer is put into a community with no specific purpose, other than to eventually help to cause change. He spends his first months establishing himself, talking to people, trying to identify problems that the community presents. Eventually some problems will become constant and the volunteer will have an idea about community needs. His job is then to help the community organize itself around the problems it has observed, and to help the community arrive at solutions to its own problems. The volunteer at this point can move from being a catalyst to being a source of information. Once a strong, indigenous community group has established itself and solved some community problems, theoretically, there should be no further need for the volunteer and he can move on.

The volunteer was to perform this task for a monthly salary of $35, plus room and board, a yearly $100 clothing allowance, and an honorarium of $50 a month.

The job of community development is not an easy one. Professionals, trained in its intricacies, have had as many failures as successes. Turning young, inexperienced people loose on such a job may seem ludicrous, but this is not quite the case.

In 1966, nearly all community development officers were employed by governments. This usually limited the activities they could become involved in, the issues they could tackle and the solutions they could arrive at. How could an employee of the Saskatchewan government who was working with Indians organize the Indians to fight the policies of the very government he was working for?

The volunteers with the Company had none of these restrictions. The activities, issues and solutions were all wide open. They could, in reality, do as the community wished. In addition, volunteers had the boundless enthusiasm that many community development officers seemed to have lost, perhaps through constant compromise with their employers. They would have a commitment to the community and little else. They were expected to live in the community and work with it 24 hours a day. Another vital factor was the concern of the volunteers. The people who came to Antigonish came because they cared, because they wanted to help. They could expect little, if any, financial return and had no assurance of professional status when they finished.

It was thus hoped that the lack of restrictions (the freedom), the enthusiasm, the dedication, the concern, the capacity to learn and grow in a community, plus the smattering of community development theory would make the volunteers effective. To some, it seemed like a mad dream. To others, it was quite plausible.

The first part of the training, the sensitivity, had been designed to supply the concern and the awareness of self and others. Professor Desmond Connor of St. Francis Xavier, a social scientist and community development expert, was to supply the technical know-how.

For a stretch of ten days, the volunteers were thrust into Connor's vital world. He had four aims in the course: to teach the volunteers to be community observers, to teach them how to diagnose community problems, to teach them strategy in community development, and to teach them how to stimulate community development.

"When I start, I have a group of school teachers, social workers, experts from other fields. What I try to finish up with is a crystallized single unit.

"In the strategy of community development, the volunteers must become a resource to any community which requests them.

"The volunteers can't go into communities like college boys — great talkers and paper men. Often they will have to prove themselves by working along with the people they want to help.

"In community stimulus, they've got to avoid becoming too involved in middle class methods. If you want to get information to a community, you don't put out a mimeographed news letter. You use individual contact — the corner store, or an older woman in the community who might serve as a clearing house for information."

Connor's lectures were not well attended, but those who did attend listened and pursued the topic outside of classes. The theory of community development excited some of them, and all they were receiving were the barest of bones.

When their time came to go into the community they would add to it. Some would succeed with it, others would fail, but those who tried to go without it were almost certain to end up on the list of CYC dropouts.

The time now came for the selection of projects by the trainees. An interviewing, selection body had been set up and the original 56 was now narrowed down to about 45. The 45 had no inkling as to what projects were available. They had been asking throughout the training session, but were put off until less than two weeks before the conclusion. By this time they were in a state of hyper-excitement.

One late July morning they were called to the barn. In the barn they found sheets of green paper neatly stacked in rows. Each piece of paper contained information about certain projects — basically, where the project was located, what job was envisioned, what community group had requested volunteer help, and what kind of volunteer was needed. In most cases, all the information was condensed onto one sheet. Each volunteer was allowed to take three project descriptions, from these three he or she would have to decide the one they wanted. It didn't turn out to be that simple.

Sensitivity had taken its price. A great many volunteers had formed admiration for some of their cohorts and a deep dislike for others. The next two or three days were spent on bartering, forming alliances and character assassinations. Great plots were hatched to keep people off some projects and to get them on others. This rather primitive form of selection ended when P.C. Mackie arrived from Ottawa. Mackie was director of domestic programmes and he personally talked to nearly every volunteer about his or her choice. Few were changed. A few days later, the volunteers left for their projects, via Ottawa and a visit with head office staff. They left for their projects, armed with their sheet of green paper and the experiences of sensitivity and community development theory, to do battle with the villains.

The main villain, of course, was the mysterious establishment. It was very real in the minds of some of the volunteers. This was part of the change they underwent during their time at Crystal Cliffs. The change would be expressed in many individual ways during coming months.

Lynn Curtis noticed it.

"Of the middle class types here, one-quarter of them will resent their backgrounds for the rest of their lives. I may have been instrumental in this," he said.

Douglas Fisher, the former NDP MP, visited Crystal Cliffs in late July and came away noticeably upset. In his syndicated column on July 30th he wrote: " . . . the Company has been captured by the spirit and methods of the New Left. It's an impressive victory . . . .

"Politics, even more, politicians, are anathema to the volunteers. Most of them seem to have been amused or disgusted with the Commons debate which has led to the creation of their Company.

"A further belief of the volunteers is that the sickness of society is more manifest in the exploiters than in the exploited. Who are the exploiters? The middle class, the politicians, the men and women who staff schools and government departments – all bureaucrats . . . . "

This indeed is what happened to many of the young people. Their concept of society may have been imperfect before their training, because they were young and had been sheltered. At the end of six weeks at Crystal Cliffs, it was just as imperfect. For, instead of seeing everything through rose-colored glasses, as they had before, they were now looking through black-colored glasses. The middle-ground had been wiped out. Words like tolerance were demolished.

What can one say, for example, about the following passage from Fisher's column: "When I asked one young lady, who will be working with Indians and Eskimos, if she had talked with any experts in the field she wrinkled her nose and said: "Never, they've been oppressing the Indians and Eskimos for a century. They'll be my enemy."

This attitude was actually encouraged at the session. It would lead to problems later for those who took it seriously. The formal training had consisted of sensitivity, community development theory, a few lessons in native languages and lore, plus reading documents that were passed out. The informal training was radical rhetoric.

Looking back at that first session and arriving at one conclusion is difficult. Of the original 56 who arrived for training, 45 eventually made it into the field. This is a failure rate of close to 20 per cent. Canadian University Services Overseas counted on a failure rate of four per cent. Of the 45 who made it into the field, less than 10 completed their two-year contracts. This is a failure rate of 75 per cent. But figures can be misleading since they judge only quantity. In qualitative terms, that training session unleashed, in a small number of people, a desire to help create change and this they managed to accomplish in a way no one else had ever been able to match.

The volunteers who went through the process had their own opinions. Some, like Maeva Hancey, regarded it as valuable. Others, like Bernie Muzeen, have rather bitter memories. Jeremy Ashton, a volunteer, put his thoughts down in a critique of the session.

"There is a conflict between sensitivity training and factual, practical training. At Crystal Cliffs, many were too hung-up on personal staff and group problems to concentrate. However, there was much success in role-playing of projected CD problems. Even in this, some opted out; for them it was useless. The sensitivity was incomplete; therefore the Company meetings were garbled and chaotic; vacillating from deep concentration on realities to bickering, to monopolizing drones, power struggles, picking on Bernie (Muzeen) etc. . . . " wrote Ashton.

If the volunteers were split on their opinions, the staff seemed not to be. Crystal Cliffs was treated as an unmitigated disaster. The general feeling was that the session had flopped, the volunteers were doomed to failure and the Company itself would disappear from sight as soon as its incompetence was realized.

Michael Valpy rather graphically noted the depth of the staff's despondency in the *Globe and Mail:* "There are senior staff members, deeply committed to the Company, who have tended to don sackcloth and heap guilt and blame upon themselves. Bill McWhinney, CYC's director, tried to resign and the volunteers who straggled into Ottawa a couple of weeks ago came with complaints of what has gone on so far and fears of what lies ahead."

The situation was considered grave enough that several unlikely proposals came into being. The first was a suggestion that the volunteers be brought together again for a seminar on how unprepared they were for their projects. The second was that the volunteers do nothing for the following six months except plant themselves in their project communities and observe.

Valpy pointed out that the staff members, the supposed cool professionals, didn't hesitate to discuss their worries with the volunteers. The result was a spreading of the fears from the staff to the volunteers.

He concluded his article with: "Yet it would appear as if the CYC staff is hesitant to send the volunteers out because of the risk of failure. Perhaps it would be helpful if there was a little less self-recrimination and renting of garments and more positive support for the young people who have committed themselves to serve for the next two years."

And so in August, 1966, the Company of Young Canadians sent its first large contingent of volunteers into the field. The launching had not been planned in this manner. The unfortunate people were the volunteers. They had just come through a mind-shattering six weeks, from which some of them would never recover, and were faced with a staff that had little confidence in them. One wonders what confidence the volunteers had in the staff. In addition to these problems, the volunteers were going into strange communities to practice a new brand of magic. They were out to change the shape of life in Canada. Waiting for them was their regional staff; anxious communities; the press; and the enemies. Watching them was the government, the first seeds of doubt already planted at Antigonish.

3

The First Signs
of Confusion

The graduates of Antigonish were not the first CYC volunteers to go into the field, although they were the first batch of any size. Even before Antigonish began, the CYC had three volunteers at work — Dal Brodhead and Helen Kwok on the west coast, and Bill Poole on the Eskasoni Indian Reserve on Cape Breton Island. The choice of these three people was a wise one. Poole and Brodhead would complete their two-year contracts and perform admirably. Helen Kwok would resign within a year, but contribute significantly during her stay in Alert Bay, B.C.

It had been decided to place these three to get the program rolling and to give other volunteers something to measure themselves against. Brodhead, in addition to being a resource to his community, was expected to be a guinea pig for the Company.

Helen, 27, and Dal, 25, met each other in mid-May, 1966, in Ottawa and for the next couple of weeks were put through tests and briefing sessions. In early June it was decided they were ready to tackle the Company's first project. The two of them were flown into Alert Bay, a community one mile northeast of Vancouver Island, and dumped. The only person there to greet them was Arthur Tinney, principal of the local school, and he was there by coincidence. The two volunteers then searched for their own accommodation and ended up boarding at separate ends of town — Dal with an Indian family, Helen with a white family.

Dal was the all-Canadian kid — polite, a conservative dresser, a careful speaker, a product of English-speaking

Montreal and a graduate of McGill University in political science. To be shifted across the country to deal with a different life style must have been a frightening experience for him, but he recovered well, perhaps because he had so few misconceptions about his own abilities, and about the plight of the people with whom he was to work. He was also willing to go slow and was an extremely likeable person.

He spent the first eight weeks getting to know the community of 1,500 people, but still trying to remain out of its mainstream. "We like to have a finger in as many places in the community as possible. But, we have to be careful or we'll become a real part of the community," he said. "People are beginning to get used to us, but there's still a fair amount of skepticism about our work because people can't comprehend that we don't have anything to sell — we want to help and serve the community wherever and whenever we are able."

The work of Dal and Helen was remarkably unexciting. She babysat, ironed clothes, washed dishes, and ran a recreational program for children. Dal became a home-made probation officer and parole chief, a bookkeeper, a welfare worker and a dance organizer. Unexciting as it seemed, those chores helped them to fit into Alert Bay and the two volunteers were determined to gain the trust and friendship of the community. If and when the time came for more radical things, the two of them would be part of it, a natural and accepted part.

Meanwhile, the Antigonish group was not faring so well. Most of them had visited the head office in Ottawa and were now dispersing to projects that took in every province except Prince Edward Island. A smaller group headed for Camp Redstone for further sensitivity training. This group consisted of 10 volunteers and for all of them Redstone was a shock. The camp is part of the Brown Camp's organization. Brown was the head of Warrendale, the home for emotionally disturbed children. The camp was an arm of Warrendale. It seemed like a strange place to send volunteers, and during the first five days there the volunteers had the same thoughts. The volunteers were regimented into the schedule of the children — up at 7:30, breakfast, clean-up, games, then lunch etc., with the day ending at 11 p.m. They followed the schedule until they were told to go to bed by a staff member at the camp, they then usually rebelled and stayed up for hours. The last two days of their visit was spent in discussion with Brown. They then left for their projects, feeling better equipped to handle themselves.

The 30 or so others whe were straggling into the field found things less easy to handle than had been imagined. Within a month of the official start of the program, complaints began to flow into the Ottawa office. The first concerned lack of communiciations.

One volunteer wrote from Outreach, British Columbia: " . . . can we ever expect to receive the mail which was forwarded from Crystal Cliffs? Please forward anything you find lying around . . . even an advertisement would help . . . . "

" . . . the basic problem is non-communication between Ottawa and the rest of the world," wrote Lynn Curtis.

After only a month in the field, the volunteers were pointing out this problem — one that would continue to haunt the Company. In reply to their demands, the volunteers in Ottawa started a newsletter, the *Impromptu*, and in its first edition mentioned some other problems that were developing. One was the lack of money for some volunteers and the apparent lack of concern of the Ottawa staff. Darby Eddy, a volunteer in Halifax, wanted to visit his home town before getting settled on his project. This was a procedure carried out by nearly every other volunteer. The money never arrived from the Company and volunteers in Ottawa met and raised the money themselves. The general feeling was that the guaranteed source, the CYC, had let the volunteers down. The feeling was soon repeated when Katy Barlow and Barb Hall, both also in the Maritimes, had money difficulties.

Then complaints began to filter in about the training process. From Glace Bay, Nova Scotia, volunteer Pat Ross wrote: "I feel that we should have started out with a little more strategy (perhaps more concentrated areawise) and since we didn't, a lot depends on projects." "Who in the Company knows beans about Canada? Who can do research or interpret available research? Who can point to strategic areas?"

The first doubt about the capability of the volunteers had been raised, and by a volunteer.

It was not all complaints about loneliness, money and lack of preparation, however. Some volunteers were swiftly integrating themselves with their new ways of life. In British Columbia, the Outreach team arrived in Vancouver and began to look around. Maeve Hancey headed straight for Skeena Terrace and her work with single-parent families and public housing. Dorothy Hill was going to run the third Vancouver project, one which centred around widows and deserted mothers. Ross Eadie was getting settled in Haney, near the penitentiary where he hoped to work. Lynn Curtis, as usual, had come up with something different than had been intended.

" . . . am concentrating on the high school and university population . . . there may be a need for a new type of volunteer committment . . . most projects are orientated towards results of poverty . . . may be an opportunity to place volunteer or two into white, middle class establishment orientated Victoria community to fulfill some kind of awareness producing role . . . . "

On the Prairies, Al Burger and Jeremy Ashton were working their way towards Lesser Slave Lake in Alberta, via Vancouver. Maureen Corcoran, and Kippy Murphy were casing Prince Albert, Saskatchewan. The Selkirk (Manitoba) Mental Hospital even had a volunteer — John Cooper. Bernie Muzeen and Carole Pickles were both in Calgary, but neither knew the other was there until a week after their almost simultaneous arrivals. Doreen Jarvis and Harvey Stevens were moving into the Logan Street area of Winnipeg.

Ontario was a bit quieter. Marg Whyte and John Earnshaw were starting their association with Deep River, the nuclear capital of Canada. Bryan Wooltorton was establishing himself in Keelerville.

There was no word from Quebec, as the Company at this time was an almost totally English-speaking volunteer community.

Gerry and Rose Fatels, and their two children, were setting up house in St. John, New Brunswick. Ron McKay and Don Clarke had volunteered for Brig Bay, Newfoundland.

At this stage, no one knew quite what to expect from the volunteers. Brodhead, Kwok and Poole were having their successes four thousand miles apart, but they hadn't gone through Antigonish. That first training session had badly shaken the Ottawa staff. There was another training session scheduled for September in Moncton with Dr. Guy Beaugrand-Champagne as chief trainer. Jacques Noel, the leading French-speaking staff member, had no intention of it becoming another Antigonish — Antigonish, no! Moncton, si!, was his battlecry. The cry would turn out to be somewhat futile. Meanwhile, plans were afoot for a regrouping of the Antigonish survivors. It was finally decided that the reunion would be held October 31st to November 6th in Orillia, Ontario. By then, the Company would have a new director and would be well on its way to accepting the philosophy of the New Left as its official doctrine.

4

Enter Alan Clarke

The staff structure of the Company of Young Canadians in late 1966 was an awesome one. The field was divided into regions, with each having its own staff member, main office, and secretarial staff. The regional offices were backed up by the head office in Ottawa, now located on 323 Chapel Street. The Company office in Ottawa was a mammoth, old, red brick mansion with 52 rooms. It had originally been built by one of Ottawa's lumber kings, but eventually passed over to the government and had been used as a barracks until the Company moved in.

The Ottawa staff was even larger than the regional staff. There was an executive and administrative branch headed by McWhinney and supplemented by such stalwarts as Stewart Goodings, Jacques Noel and Bob Olivero. There were also of course, the usual assortment of clerks and secretaries. The next branch was responsible for domestic and international programs, and information and volunteer liaison. Cam Mackie, Michael Valpy (who had jumped into the Company from the *Globe and Mail*), and Robert Lapointe held sway here. The most controversial, perhaps brilliant, and certainly most diverse branch was recruiting, training and internal education. These were the radicals, men like Rick Salter, Jim Kinzel, Dennis Gagne, Martin Beliveau and Rob Wood.

Taken together, the regional staff and the Ottawa staff far outnumbered the volunteers, and while the volunteers worked for pittances, the staff were all well paid. Salaries ranged from $3,000 to about $20,000, but most were in the $10,000 to $15,000 bracket.

Despite their numbers, the staff never seemed to be very effective. They enjoyed talking in philosophical terms, even about administration. Structure was an ugly word and any attempt at structuring the Ottawa office was quickly torpedoed. Memos flew haphazardly about. People came and went at a dizzying pace. Perhaps all of this disorganization could have been forgiven if the first training session and the first forays into the field had been successful, but the first reports were dismal and the staff started to look for fall guys. They may never have looked in the direction of Bill McWhinney, but, as it turned out, he had had enough after less than a year on the job and less than a month after the Antigonish period.

McWhinney had visited Antigonish for two days and had come away visibly shocked. The *Globe and Mail* carried reports then that he was thinking of resigning. He denied the reports emphatically, then less than two weeks later announced his intention to leave.

McWhinney had always been interim executive director but most people believed that he would enter the contest for the full-time position. If he did, it was difficult to see how he could be denied the post.

In 1961, McWhinney had been one of the first 15 volunteers sent out by CUSO. After nine months in Ceylon, he returned to Canada to organize the first CUSO group to go to Asia. In 1962, he was appointed national director of CUSO and remained in that position until he joined the CYC. His decision to leave ended five years of work with volunteer agencies.

Publicly, his reason for not contesting the executive directorship was "a strongly personal feeling that I'm not the best man to be executive director". The fact that McWhinney was not on the best of terms with many volunteers and staff members was no doubt a factor. When the committee chosen to select a new director met in September, this became apparent. Many of the committee members, Harvey Stevens reported, felt that McWhinney had not been effectively directing the staff. This was reflected, Stevens said, in the problems involving communications, money to volunteers, and regional staff difficulties over project development. There was another problem. McWhinney was generally regarded as a square, as establishment. Whether he was or not, this is how he was regarded by many volunteers.

A decision was then made to find a new director, as quickly as possible. This was the first opportunity for participatory democracy. A nine-man committee was formed to select the director and the council. The staff and the volunteers would each have three members on the committee. The volunteers were elected and Lynn Curtis, Peter Mussalem and Harvey Stevens came to Ottawa to experience their first disillusionment with the council. The staff elected Olivero, the CYC's financial administrator, George Martell, an Ontario regional staff member, and Wilf Pelletier, Indian liaison program staff. According to Stevens, more than three council members sat in on the meetings. He listed Marc Lalonde, Father Soucie, Doug Ward, Art Pape and Ed Lavallee as participants.

The committee met in the middle of September and allowed themselves 18 hours to come up with a director. There were four candidates to consider — Alan Clarke, a council member; Jacques Noel, a CYC staff member; and Walter Rudnicki and Arthur Stinson, both outsiders, but both well-versed in community development and human relations.

The meeting began with the three volunteers expressing concern at what they felt was too little time to make such an important decision. The council and staff members countered this with an explanation of why the director was needed so quickly. Stevens relented, but Curtis and Mussalem still held firm to their belief that more time should be taken.

The committee was looking for many things in an executive director. Their list of criteria included: awareness of the Canadian social scene; expertise in community development; rapport with young people; bilingual ability; administrative ability; and leadership — in other words, a superman. They eventually decided in favour of Alan Clarke. It was not a unanimous choice. The final committee vote was eight for, one undecided and two abstentions. Jacques Noel had been Clarke's closest contender and it was decided to give him an associate directorship in French-speaking Canada. Stewart Goodings was his English counterpart.

The choice was quickly relayed to the council and rubber-stamped. Clarke was in. However, the volunteers were unhappy.

Stevens was angry about two things. The first concerned the council meeting. He had wanted to attend as an observer, but was refused.

"I'm concerned about this attitude of council. While I agree fully that the council members alone must make the decisions for the Company, I cannot agree with their policy of excluding volunteers as observers. How in hell are any of us going to learn how a council operates, how Company decisions are made, in short, how to run the Company if we are never allowed in at the council level of operation," he wrote to other volunteers.

About participatory democracy he was even more harsh.

" . . . we were merely an effort to placate volunteers. We had no power and a decision was made despite our objection to it."

Mussalem, in his letter to the volunteers, struck out at the general condition of the Company.

"My opinion was that the locating of a new executive director was not the solution to the problem — *which is the Company administrative process* (Mussalem's emphasis). The present process is inadequate — the process which has left so many decisions to a dominant personality; the process that has passed an impossible burden upon the few and a confusion of principles upon the many," he wrote.

"It became apparent to me after a few hours that few of the council cared. It became obvious to me that the committee was going to choose an executive director by the four point criteria that had listed 'damn the torpedos and full speed ahead'.

"I can only say that this meeting indicates to me that volunteers in the field would do well to develop their own resources in the community because they can expect precious damn little volunteer support from council."

Lynn Curtis agreed with both Stevens and Mussalem.

"I must emphasize that the volunteers who attended the meeting had no power in the decision made. The decision was made by council. The meeting itself was a snow job.

" . . . If one can remember the strained relations between volunteers and staff at Crystal Cliffs — the mistrust and the fears — one can easily feel the problems presently involved in relationships between staff and council. The internal problems of the Company now are similar to the internal problems in each of the people who attended Crystal Cliffs . . . "

" . . . I think I must have asked 30 times in that (selection) meeting, 'what is the purpose of the Company?' I received no satisfactory reply."

It is important to remember that the Company of Young Canadians was only two months old in the field, at this time. The feelings of Curtis, Stevens and Mussalem were not original or isolated. Already, there was mistrust between staff and council and volunteers. The first experiment in the much heralded participatory democracy had failed. The volunteers were angry at being duped. This was only a warm-up, though, for bigger dupes, for greater mistrusts and more bitter feelings. The long struggle between staff, volunteers and council was only beginning. The selection of Clarke marked a turning-point in the Company's history. Until then, a good many volunteers believed they did have the power and would gain control of the Company. They didn't yet realize that their power would come too late for it to mean anything.

Like the problems of communication and administration, the problem of the volunteer role was quickly identified. The job of solving all of these problems was now turned over to Alan Clarke. At the time, many people including the volunteers thought he could be successful. Clarke had identified himself throughout the selection process as a man concerned with volunteers and field. It was an honest feeling on his part. And, although the volunteers protested against the selection process, against the administrative jungle of the Company, and against the council, at no time did they turn their wrath against Clarke. They believed that his concern was for them.

The man chosen to be the first full-time director of the CYC had an established agency background – the very kind of background that had so repulsed volunteers at Crystal Cliffs. Mingled in with the agencies, however, were some very different kinds of interests.

Thirty-seven-year-old Clarke was born in Stratford, Ontario, and spent the 1950s working with youth recreation, education and leadership programs with the Toronto YMCA. During those years he worked for and received his BA in philosophy and ethics from the U of T. He also became involved with Frontier College and worked for four years as an instructor and supervisor, working by day with railway gangs, and teaching them English at night. At the time of his appointment to the head of the CYC, Clarke was a director of the National Council of YMCAs, a deacon in the Baptist Church, and a director of the Ottawa Welfare Council. But these were only part-time affiliations. He was also executive director of the Canadian Citizenship Council and the Canadian Centenary Council.

Not quite so conspicuous in his biography was his membership in the Students Union for Peace Action.

He assumed direction of the CYC on November 1st and began to implement his style of leadership. Quiet, soft-spoken and sincere, Clarke had an amazing way with people. They inevitably liked him and many would grow close to him during his tenure. Some of these friendships would later turn to hatred, but never really of Clarke personally.

His form of leadership was non-directive and he explains it best himself: "My concept of administration is best expressed in the Indian saying 'the best chief is not the one who persuades most people to his point of view, but the one in whose presence men find it easiest to arrive at the truth.'

"I think I can operate that way. I see myself as providing an ultimate base for something that's honest to develop," he told Canadian Press.

These words would come back to choke him.

5

The Hip, Young Radical

Moncton and Orillia came and went, and the Company's problems increased.

Moncton was the second training session and Jacques Noel had no intention of letting it become another Antigonish. He succeeded to a point. There was much less stress and strain, due mainly to the lack of a pre-determined plan. The idea was to let things develop naturally. The content changed little, however, from Antigonish and its faults would be seen later when the volunteers, stuffed with sensitivity and community development theory, were shipped to the field and discovered how ill-equipped they really were to handle their situations.

The Antigonish graduates were already experiencing that feeling, and the staff, certain that the first training session had flopped, gathered them together in November for a week in Orillia, Ontario.

The volunteers had gone into the field brimming with idealism and anti-establishmentism. They limped into Orillia bruised and angry.

For six days, the volunteers screamed and made demands. They felt they were being manipulated by their staff, or at least, were not receiving the kind of support they needed. Their anger was justified, especially when one considers that the staff outnumbered the Antigonish volunteers, at this stage.

But the Orillia meeting did not accomplish much. It did allow the volunteers to publicize their hostility towards the staff and to vent their anger about the operation of the

Company. It resulted in more immediate participation by the volunteers in Company decision-making. However it left Orillia citizens upset about the morals of the volunteers.

Rumours began to spread through the little town that the CYC was engaging in giant sex orgies. The same kind of rumours had been circulating at Antigonish, but most were unfounded.

The result of the rumours was to call further attention to the meeting. It was revealed that the meeting had cost more than $8,000. Many felt that this was a waste of good tax money. The Company reacted with boredom. Finances were still of little concern, especially when the Company was deeply involved in high priority items such as programs and volunteer selection.

Indeed, the Company was lost. The debate around social action projects versus service projects had still not been resolved. The Aims and Principles had played their part, but many of the Company's projects could be called service-type projects and this bothered the radicals. Hand-in-hand with this problem was the one of volunteer selection. The radicals on staff and on council were not pleased with the breed of volunteers the Company was hiring. At this juncture, the power of the staff comes into focus. The battle for control of the Company was on and the staff would emerge as the winner

In the beginning, it had been envisioned that the staff were there to service the volunteers and to maintain some kind of continuity in the day-to-day workings of the Company. The council and the volunteers were to have the real power. They were to decide the policies of the Company and in effect, to run the Company. This never happened, and the staff quickly took over the direction of the Company. For example, in the first week of December, 1966, a working group meeting was held to discuss program, volunteer selection and other matters. This meeting would clarify some philosophies in the Company and the meeting would be effectively controlled by the staff on the working group.

The idea for such a group came from Alan Clarke, and it was a good one. Clarke wanted staff, volunteers and council members to work more closely together. He saw this as a lever for breaking down the obvious mistrust between the groups and, at the same time, as one way of arriving at policy recommendations in a democratic fashion.

The first working group consisted of the above three factions and it tackled many of the problems that should have been solved months before. No one thought it strange, though, that they should be attempting to organize the Company. The main discussion revolved around volunteer selection and when that discussion was over, the radicals had won an important victory, and effectively shut most young Canadians out of the CYC.

A transcript of the meeting clearly shows the trend that developed. The major cast members were Alan Clarke; Rick Salter and Cam Mackie, from staff; Lynn Curtis, David DePoe and Barb Hall, volunteers; and Art Pape and Wally Kubiski, council members. The staff, Mackie and Salter, were pushing their philosophy. The volunteers, Curtis and DePoe, tried to hold them back.

The discussion begins with Salter.

"Our major source of recruits have to be young people, not because of the terms of the legislation, but because something is happening to North American youth . . . they're developing new values. Given the kind of job to be done, we need strong, socially-conscious, hip, radical kids . . . . "

Pape: "The ideal volunteer that Rick described — strong, hip, radical — there aren't many of them."

Barb Hall: "What does radical mean?"

Salter: "Someone who gets to the root of the problem. I have sent the North Test off to a psychologist friend of mine for an analysis. I haven't seen the results of it yet. The instrument itself is ante-dated. That type of test had its hay day 25 years ago. It's the kind of thing IBM would use to hire workers. The kind of data it gives is middle class; it's a middle-class test. Stability is defined as how well integrated a person is to middle-class values."

Pape: "CYC hasn't provided any situations which are easy growth situations. If the Company is about to change then the Company must increase the quality of work and of the people we attract. When we have strong projects, then we can talk about sending volunteers into them to learn.

"But most of our projects aren't growth situations. We have to get people who are pretty strong, as Rick says. We've got to be hard about who we invite in to form this core. I come down against our ability to be helpful to people (referring to non-strong volunteers)."

Clarke: "The market worries me. There isn't a large market out there for these kind of people. Could there be an interim trainee set-up, I am wondering, of about three months or so."

DePoe: "We've already been trying to set up something like that in a half-assed sort of way (probationary volunteers). We've been projecting too far ahead and not looking at the reality of what we have now. I don't think we can look at these interim plans right now. We're overextending ourselves."

Salter: "At the moment we have no real organization on Canadian campuses. But what we have to keep in mind is that the Company is going to trump other organizations which are supposed to be doing this kind of thing. The kind of push CYC is going to make is going to push everyone. It's all a process of building a big constituency of social activists in and around the Company."

Curtis: "You see what Rick has done. He's just about wiped out everything the CYC has done."

Mackie: "There has been a change. You're right. There has been a narrowing. But opinion, the conglomerate of opinions is very strong: we can make change and to do this we have to take a pretty activist program of putting in people who can really effect these changes. This leads to the logical conclusion that CYC is becoming more hard and I say it's a good thing."

Kubiski: "Maybe we should just call ourselves the Company of Hip, Young, Radical, Turned-on Canadians. The criteria I'm looking for is an open mind, a minimal degree of personal problems and responsibility. I don't think we should just look for turned-on Canadians. I have trouble differentiating between service and community development. This is no reflection on the volunteers we have in the field at present, but let's just establish some simple, basic philosophy . . . .

"I don't think we'll last as an organization if we remain the Company of Hip, Young, Radical, Turned-on Canadians. There are a lot of people waiting in the provinces for us to step out of line. In some ways we have to please the establishment. We've got to have both kinds of projects."

Pape: "The mid-1950s was the end of the ideology . . . . the mid-1960s means the end of language. The kind of person you're describing is exactly what I have in mind for hip, socially conscious, strong and radical."

Curtis: "What we're really talking about is changing the whole Company and I can't take it for granted that's what we're going to do. The idea of having a core of radicals is quite a good idea so long as we have a lot of people around them. Maybe the Company's total commitment will be two volunteers and a lot of names."

This working group was to make policy recommendations to the council, and no one thought it likely that the council would reject any of the recommendations. This issue of service versus action was tackled from the side during the debate on volunteer selection. It turned out to be a clear victory for the radicals. The Company, in the future, would be after hip, radical, turned-on young people for volunteers. Lynn Curtis wrote about the dangers of this approach.

"This introduces a new concept to the Company. If we narrow down to this type only we will, indeed, be able to carry out much more real social action. However, what happens to the other young people who want to do something about the problems of our country? It appears the Company will become a hard core of activists who will be able to build a movement for social change in this country and that other people would be able to work as self-supporting, part-time volunteers. The Company would be much more difficult to join and demand much more from its members . . . . We should not reject people because they are just not 'young, hip and radical'. We must provide some kind of program to allow everyone a chance to work. At the meeting there was general acceptance of the hard-core organizer concept."

His advice was not taken.

Volunteer selection was not the only topic discussed at the meeting to these lengths, but it was about the only one with any real clarity. The issue of volunteer deselection, as an example, was badly garbled and it is doubtful if anyone really understood what was going on. If they did at the beginning of the meeting, they certainly didn't at the end.

On the first day of the meeting, Clarke said there was a possibility of discontinuing projects and deselecting volunteers. Cam Mackie, however, said there would be no deselection for some time and that deselection and project analysis would only be done with full volunteer participation. The next day, Clarke said there was a chance of volunteer deselection soon. The volunteers left the meeting confused.

At the next working group meeting in early January, 1967, two volunteers returned to the radical ideology and began to question it.

Their feeling was that the CYC was becoming too narrow, and that concern over largely theoretical long-term questions was inhibiting immediate day-to-day project activity. Ron Skippon referred to the great influence of SUPA on the organization. He suggested that this was one ideology, but that it should not become the single ideology of the Company.

Skippon, a volunteer, was a little late with his objections. SUPA did indeed have large influence on the CYC, not so much in terms of the SUPA organization, but in terms of the people the Company drafted from it. Art Pape was one prime example. Pape was generally described as being a genius. He was Jewish, highly-articulate and persuasive. His influence in the early days of the Company was immense. He was the radical on the council and made his opinion felt, he also had marked success at making his opinions become acceptable.

His counterpart on staff was Rick Salter. There was disagreement about whether Salter was an American or Canadian. There was no doubt about his philosophy, it was on the left. Jewish, like Pape, Salter was as articulate and bright. Salter claimed he was Canadian-born, but had been employed at the University of Buffalo and had been secretary of its Students for a Democratic Society cell. Rumour had it that he had been chased out of the United States by the CIA and couldn't go back. Salter neither denied nor confirmed the rumours.

Together, Salter and Pape had considerable influence. Any measure that the two of them pushed stood a better chance of being accepted. Salter would continue to rise in the Company until he became the equivalent of Clarke's right-hand man. Pape would resign from the council in 1967 to accept a fat consultant's contract from the Company.

Their influence was not too noticeable in late 1966. The Company was still hashing out its problems and neither Salter nor Pape had taken on any sinister appearances. It was true that a $4,000 grant was given to SUPA, but no one within the Company was greatly concerned about it.

The working group would meet several times during its short history. Besides trying to iron out role definitions, and setting a general philosophical pattern for the CYC, it attempted many other things but without much success.

"The working group was an instrument for talk," Clarke would say later. "It never really worked things out."

Whether it did or not is immaterial for what the working group managed to do was to implant in the Company a philosophy of change that would remain.

6

The Depoe - Curtis Incident

David DePoe. The name strikes up an immediate image —
long hair, gaucho hat, beard, moustache, sideburns, jeans.

At the time, it seemed a strange role for the Ottawa boy,
just 23 years old. DePoe had been a model high school
student and moved on naturally to university in Toronto.
He caught something there — an awareness about the
society around him, and a mistrust for the situation he was
in — and left. He left for an office job and quit six months
later. For another six months he read, played the guitar
and started to move in on Yorkville, the small, square-mile
area in downtown Toronto that was the nesting ground for
non-conformists. He tried cab driving and enjoyed it. He
probably would have stayed at that, but he went to the CYC
training session in Moncton and signed up. Three months
later he was fingered nationally by the press and the legend
of David DePoe began. So did the most indestructable
myth about the CYC.

There had been a SUPA meeting in Waterloo, Ontario, in
early January, 1967. It was considered a flop by many and,
to liven things up, it was decided to have a demonstration
against the War in Vietnam in front of the American Consulate on University Avenue in Toronto. About 150 delegates
to the meeting agreed to take part and off they went, with
placards, balloons and guitars. The demonstration lasted
three-quarters of an hour. It was an orderly, fun-type thing.
That Monday must have been a difficult day for news for
within 24 hours two names, David DePoe and Lynn Curtis,
had been plastered onto every front page in the country

and blasted from every radio and televison set.

It was reported that two CYC volunteers, paid by tax-payers, were demonstrating in front of an ally's consulate. The volunteers were described as long-hairs and much attention was paid to the fact that DePoe was the son of CBC newscaster Norman DePoe. DePoe and Curtis had instant celebrity status and the public began to hear their first news about the CYC.

The uproar over the demonstration came just after the Company had been nailed for printing obscene four-letter words in its internal newsletter. The press was ripe for controversy and it created all it could from the relatively minor incident.

"The Actions of CYC Pair: Disgrace," read one headline.

"Kooky Carryings-on Crumbling Company of Young Canadians," read another.

The entire episode was blown up entirely out of proportion. It was reported, for example, that DePoe and Curtis had organized and led the demonstration. DePoe, writing to volunteer Bill Poole, denied most of this.

"I had better explain that I didn't lead the damn thing in the first place, and that in front of the consulate, I fell into a leadership role simply because I had my guitar with me (we didn't elect any leaders)."

Besides DePoe and Curtis, a dozen CYC staff members had taken part in the demonstration but little was heard of this. DePoe and Curtis, the two hippies, were the targets the press chose.

Reaction in the Ottawa office and from the council was swift. Doug Ward decided that the Company needed some kind of policy to cover actions like those of DePoe and Curtis and got on the phone to council members. A policy was roughly hacked out. A synopsis read:

"Volunteers for the Company must take care not to involve CYC in political and religious protests which are not official CYC projects. There is nothing to stop a volunteer acting in such protests as a private citizen. But he does not have the right to suggest that the Company or any of its funds are in any way involved."

The demonstration took place on January 2nd. On January 4th, a press conference was held and Ward explained the policy. On January 6th, an executive committee meeting of council was held and it was decided to hold an emergency council meeting on the 7th and 8th. Council members were notified and started to head for Ottawa.

MPs were angry with the actions of the two volunteers and the Prime Minister sympathized with the MPs. The public was clamoring for some kind of punishment, or at least an explanation. The press had put the Company under a microscope and, in all parts of the country, volunteers were being checked for a shred of evidence that they were hippies.

Internally, the problem was no less serious. The council was having second thoughts about the policy it had so hastily approved. Fellow-volunteers were angry at DePoe and Curtis for forcing them into the spotlight. Alan Clarke was preparing to fight to defend DePoe and Curtis. The relatively minor incident was now a full scale crisis and it was threatening to destroy the Company — it almost did at the time, and it certainly played a large part in the Company's future troubles.

As the council began to gather on the morning of the 7th, a Saturday, Clarke received a phone call from Don Peacock, one of the Prime Minister's speech writers. Peacock had heard about the council meeting and informed Clarke that he was coming over. Clarke, angry at Peacock's manner, immediately called Derek Hodgson, Mr. Pearson's principal secretary and the designated link between the Prime Minister's office and the Company, to complain. Peacock, a junior official, was told to stay away from the meeting.

The council did not manage to meet until Saturday night and by then it was split. Some members wanted to reverse the policy, others wanted to retain it. Tim Reid led the fight in favor of keeping it. He saw the Company's independence at stake. Nothing was resolved that night.

When the council re-grouped Sunday morning, Clarke had a surprise for them. He presented his letter of resignation and said it would take effect at 1 p.m. on Monday unless the CYC's independence was reaffirmed by the Prime Minister. The council supported his stand.

On Sunday night, Clarke met with Hodgson and informed him of the decision. Hodgson was, understandably, upset by the proposal and refused to let Clarke see the Prime Minister.

On Monday morning, Clarke met once again with Hodgson and reiterated his stand — either the PM supported the Company or he would resign on principle. The principle was the independence of the Company.

Once again, Hodgson informed Clarke that it was hopeless and Clarke left the office. He went straight to a meeting that included such people as Jacques Noel, Stewart Goodings and Marc Lalonde. Lalonde had hurried up from Montreal for the crisis. His arrival was fortunate, for Lalonde intervened with the Prime Minister and an agreement was reached. The Company was independent and the Prime Minister would say so. Lalonde helped draft the Prime Minister's statement that would be read later in the House of Commons.

Canadian Press reported it briefly:

"The demonstration had 'nothing whatever to do with the CYC', the Prime Minister said . . . .

"He said the two CYC workers who took part in picketing at the consulate-general had acted privately and 'as citizens of a free country'.

"The CYC operates with a maximum degree of independence, the Prime Minister said. 'I do not think the government should interfere with the details of their operations.' "

On the surface, it appeared that the Company had won an important battle. In reality, it had alienated the Prime Minister and earned a measure of mistrust that would be visible in future government-Company dealings. There were other repercussions that were just as important.

"The DePoe incident polarized things internally and externally," Clarke said. "Externally, it was the first real content on the CYC that the media carried. The image was bad, and it was an image the Company couldn't get rid of.

"Internally, it showed the volunteers that the council and the staff would support them to the fullest."

It also angered some volunteers. Instead of being kind to DePoe and Curtis, some took offense at what they considered a badly handled affair. Eight of them sent an open letter to the entire Company in which they outlined the way they believed a volunteer should act.

"He (the volunteer) can have no strong personal image or it will undermine his work. He must, therefore, learn to keep his mouth shut on public occasions. This is even more important when the organizer belongs to an association of organizers, for, should he inadvertently establish a public image of himself it creates a public image of the association . . . .

"Both DePoe and Curtis took leadership roles in the demonstration, established strong, personal images, used the CYC to expand the public knowledge of these images, and did not think about the affect of this step on other organizers in the CYC. We don't quarrel with their right to demonstrate, but with the overtness of their role in the demonstration. Leadership and publicity can and must be avoided."

Others in the Company took a calmer approach to the whole subject. Art Pape, in the minutes of a working group meeting, said that the Company reacts defensively when labelled by the press as beatnik or radical because it accepts the conventional assumption that any of those things would be bad. If the Company is confident, he said, of what it is and what it is trying to do, then it needn't be defensive about labels but could explain itself in its own terms.

This naive approach to bad press and a bad public image would persist and lead to more problems.

The facts to be faced in early 1967 were dismal. Two volunteers had been involved in a minor event and their participation had been reported. During the next month the Company had made enemies of the government, become infamous with the public, marked by the press, and had been made singularly aware that the Company was not a string of isolated projects.

All four points were important, particularly the last. Volunteers had always presumed that they were separate from the rest of the Company. The DePoe-Curtis incident had drawn attention to the entire Company, and to them and their work. From now on, volunteers would tend not to isolate themselves. They would become more concerned with the Company as an entirety. As for the press, they had a field day with DePoe and Curtis and recognized the news value in the Company. With only a few exceptions, the news media would hound the Company incessantly for the next three years with a fixed image in their mind — irresponsible hippies — and would reconfirm this image over again.

This was the turning point in the history of the Company. It could no longer afford mistakes for mistakes would be national news. The fact that the first year was experimental meant nothing to the press and public. One attempt was made to salvage the Company's image later in 1967, but the long, downhill trend was beginning and it would continue.

7

The Continuing Story of Depoe and Curtis

There is a possibility that the furor over hippies in the CYC would have died if David DePoe and Lynn Curtis had stayed quiet after the demonstration in front of the consulate. But that wasn't in the nature of either of them, much to the distress of the council, they continued to reinforce the original image during all of 1967. DePoe even managed to add a new wrinkle by getting arrested.

Neither DePoe nor Curtis was a megalomaniac, although some volunteers and council members tended to think they were. Both of them were remarkably similar in their approach to life. Basically quiet, soft-spoken, non-pushy and kind, they often surprised strangers on a first meeting. Expecting wild men, people were always overcome by their mild demeanors and logical minds.

Both were dissatisfied with the standing order. They saw young people being torn apart by society and rejecting that society and tried to help them build alternatives— DePoe in Yorkville, Curtis on the west coast. In the process, they took on the appearance of the people they worked with. Perhaps this was a transition that would have taken place anyway, but in light of their work it was a totally necessary one.

In the spring and summer of 1967, Yorkville was inundated with a new breed of young people calling themselves hippies. Thousands of them poured into the area espousing a new philosophy — love. Along with the love went drugs, poverty and misery, for many of the young people were escaping from middle-class homes and middle-class values.

Alienated youth was a new phenomenon in 1967. There had always been a fringe, such as the beatniks in the 1950s, but never a group this large. Unfortunately, while the fringe could take care of themselves, many of the new generation were 16 and 17 years old, not yet out of high school and hardly equipped to manage on their own.

David DePoe was put into Yorkville to help them and to find out some of the causes of the alienation. Other agencies tried to do the same thing but, for the most part, they failed. The reason for DePoe's success is tied closely to the concept of the CYC.

Other agencies tried to help, but sent agency people in to do the helping. With their shirts and ties they hardly presented an image the young people could identify with. DePoe, though, was one of the young people. He thought and acted as they did. He didn't moralize or lecture. He simply went along and took things as they came.

DePoe gradually became an accepted part of Yorkville (he lived in the village and was always available). His acceptance led to his election as spokesman for the Village Council, an organization set up by the Diggers to run hippie affairs in the village. The role of spokesman would hardly keep him out of the limelight, but he did not refuse it.

The Diggers were DePoe's main ally in Yorkville. A loosely-knit group of older hippies, the Diggers took it upon themselves to see that every young person in the area was fed. This was one of DePoe's main accomplishments. During the summer of 1967 when everyone was wringing their hands about Yorkville, and doing very little, the Diggers were establishing feeding centres and health treatment clinics, and making contacts with a local hospital for emergency drug treatment. They were also, when asked, giving advice and trying to straighten-out some of the confused young people coming into the village.

This was a large accomplishment, but it received little notice. Most people were too concerned with the long hair and dirty faces and the stories about sex orgies and drugs to see that a very real social problem was being played out in front of them. They also refused to see the misery, the suffering and the destruction of many young people. The Diggers were one of the few groups to care and they did what they could. It is not enough to say that most young people survived Yorkville, but what else can one say? The Diggers did what they felt they had to do for no credit, while the smug middle-class drove through Yorkville at night to look at the freaks. Is it any wonder that young people were bitter towards a generation so blind and self-centred?

This then was DePoe's role, and he performed it well. The Company of Young Canadians need never have felt apologetic for the job he did in Yorkville but, towards the end of the summer, it did.

On the west coast, Lynn Curtis was performing a similar role with the hippies on Vancouver Island and the mainland. In many ways he was far ahead of his time. While others were scratching their heads wondering what hippies were, Curtis could see trouble and predicted that police intervention was highly likely. While the word underground still meant basement to most people and the Georgia Straight was yet unborn, Curtis was helping turn out an underground newspaper. He was also running a hippie commune and trying to keep the bodies and souls of people together.

Curtis amazed even those who knew him well. Once, on a cross-country trip, Clarke visited with local government officials at nearly every stop. Most volunteers didn't care about that, they wanted to know what was going on in the Ottawa office. In Victoria, Clarke had an appointment with the provincial secretary and told Curtis this upon his arrival.

Curtis said nothing until Clarke was ready to see the secretary.

"I'm going with you," he told the director.

Clarke took him to the legislative buildings and in to see the secretary. They talked for some time, but whenever the discussion revolved around what was going on in Victoria, Curtis talked and Clarke listened.

DePoe's trademark was his gaucho hat and his beard. Curtis had an even more magnificent beard and wild, long, unruly hair. He also had an overcoat several sizes too large which made him look like a 200-pounder, about 60 pounds above his actual weight.

It seemed unlikely that these two young men would become a symbol of hate to the middle-class, an immense problem for the Company, and a great news source for the media, but they managed it.

Both of them were often requested for public speaking engagements and, DePoe particularly, had a difficult time saying no. As a result, DePoe saw most of Canada during the year and was constantly in the news. This caused some resentment in the Company. One incident was widely reported.

DePoe was flying west and the Ottawa office called the Company project in Fort Qu'Appelle, Saskatchewan, about 40 miles west of Regina, to see if a visit from David would be appreciated. The staff member there had just come through a harrowing experience with townspeople up-in-arms about the Company's image and the response was, "I don't even want that guy to fly over Fort Qu'Appelle."

This attitude was understandable, especially if one remembers the open letter written by the volunteers about publicity. DePoe was breaking with their plea. He had a message and he intended to take it across the country.

Curtis was less mobile, but caused a bigger fuss in the Ottawa office. In February, 1967, he informed the office that he was going on Front Page Challenge in two days time. This was not the kind of news the office was anxious to hear. Already concerned about the hippie image it could scarcely think of anything worse than Curtis going on national television to reinforce it. Clarke decided to stop him.

The method was crude. Clarke called Curtis and told him that if he went on Front Page Challenge he would be deselected. The threat worked and the Canadian public missed an opportunity to see Lynn in action.

The publicity DePoe and Curtis received during the spring and early summer was only a warm-up. The main events were rolling around. Although anti-climatic after the consulate demonstration, they were strong additions to the list of sins being compiled against the CYC.

In late August, the *Montreal Gazette* carried a front page story accusing the Company of being infiltrated by radicals.

The newspaper said, "some of them are Marxist and others possibly Communist oriented."

The main evidence the newspaper used was an article in *Scan*, a Communist youth publication, that had been written by Lynn Curtis.

In the article, Curtis had written about a shift to the left in the Company, the acceptance of social change over social reform.

"The analysis accepts that many of the things thought to be problems are really only symptoms of a rotting middle class system and that this is what needs changing," he wrote, and then explained the hard-core volunteer concept that the Company had embraced in its working group meetings.

A beleaguered Alan Clarke held a press conference and denied the Communist charge. The simple truth was that the charge was childish and paranoid. Most young people in the 1960s regarded Communism as old-fashioned. They saw the flaws in it, as well as the flaws in their own system. The Company had a smattering of Marxists, but they probably constituted less than three per cent of the volunteer body. The majority of Company volunteers were very orthodox politically, most of them supporting the New Democratic Party.

The charge that the Company had its share of radicals, though, was accepted by Clarke, as it had to be.

The affair turned out to be entirely pointless, especially when *Scan* later repudiated the Company and urged its readers not to join. But what it did accomplish, was the planting of another suspicion in the minds of the public. Now, in addition to being hippies, sex fiends and peaceniks, the Company was also Communistic.

Silly as the Communist charge may have been, it took its toll, especially since it came hard on the heels of the eruption in Yorkville.

On the night of August 20th in Yorkville, the so-called hippie revolt took place. For months, the city of Toronto, its politicians and the public, had been seething about the "great unwashed" in the Village. Property owners began to complain and the area began to attract attention. The attention resulted in the public driving through the area at night, mainly on Yorkville Avenue, a short, one-way street. So many drove through to look at the hippies that a constant traffic jam was the result.

The hippies asked for the avenue to be closed to traffic. The property owners demanded it remain open. Controller Allen Lamport of Toronto asked for a meeting to resolve the issue. It turned into a circus, complete with TV cameras and lights, and Lamport made use of his time by asking the hippies why they wouldn't bathe and get jobs like decent people.

In anger, the hippies marched back to Yorkville and

conducted a sit-in. The police moved in. It was an ugly scene with snatches of punching, slapping and pulling. The police used three paddy-wagons to haul kids away. DePoe and others headed for the police station to protest. He got arrested. The charge — disturbing the peace.

The Company had just gone through a similar experience with another volunteer — Peter Mussalem in the Northwest Territories. Mussalem had been charged with supplying liquor to a minor. The council had adopted a supportive policy, the Volunteer and the Law, to cover that case and others. It paid off when Mussalem was acquitted.

The council was more hesitant about supporting DePoe, but the support finally came through, in the form of a Company-paid lawyer. He would also eventually be acquitted, but not until legal costs soared over $3,000.

The episode did not end there, however. DePoe then went before Toronto Board of Control to present a brief. He was treated badly. At first, the Board wouldn't hear him. When they returned from lunch they found their chairs occupied by hippies. The hippies agreed to leave if DePoe was heard. The Board acquiesced and another chapter in the legend was written.

And a legend it did become. DePoe and Curtis became the symbols for an entire movement and their presence in the CYC evoked all the emotions that the movement evoked — from young people, admiration; from the public and the press, hostility and fear.

Whatever the emotions, DePoe and Curtis became the CYC to the public. The fact that they, as long-hairs, represented a minority of volunteers was unimportant. The Company would suffer from being linked with them, but the Company would not have been the Company without them. They provided the fireworks, the excitement and the caring. And, they managed to accomplish something. They got to part of the lost generation and helped many young people through difficult times. The lives they saved could probably justify the cost of the CYC.

8

The Company in 1967

The problems in the CYC at the end of 1966 were difficult enough to analyze, and nearly impossible to solve. Basically, there was a lack of trust between volunteers and staff; between volunteers and council; between staff and council; and even between regional staff and Ottawa staff.

In 1967, these problems still existed and they became more complex as more volunteers entered the field.

The hostility of the volunteers was understandable. A good number of the Company's young people had been placed in isolated areas, such as northern Alberta. Upon their arrival, they usually discovered that their Antigonish training in no way reflected the problems they had to face. At Antigonish, the talk was of loving and trusting fellow men. In the field, the volunteers were stunned and hurt by the hostile reactions that greeted them. Some of them never recovered from these reactions. The project that was to be started in Newfoundland, for example, never got off the ground and was scrubbed within months of its start. The volunteers found the transportation facilities non-existent. Instead of plunging on, they quit.

The tactics the volunteers used were, in many cases, totally unsuitable. Walking into a small fishing community and acting like a saviour would be difficult enough for Christ in this Twentieth Century. When you are a young mainlander, you're credibility slides down even further. But this was the attitude many volunteers had. They acted as if they had all the answers, as if their life style was the only legitimate one. Long hair is one example. In 1967, long hair was hardly acceptable in Toronto. In smaller, rural Canadian communities it was completely unacceptable. Yet, volunteers insisted on keeping their beards and long hair when they went into such communities. The volunteers expected the communities to adjust to them. They rarely did.

Adding to the volunteers' woes was what they considered to be the ineptness of the staff. The Company ran on a regional set-up, this meant that if you were working in northern Alberta your regional office was in Winnipeg. This isolation was bad enough, but the volunteers aslo maintained that when the staff visited them they did nothing.

The volunteers had other beefs as well. Money was a sore point. The volunteers were trying to survive on less than $200 a month, and most of them were in areas where the cost of living was high. Yet volunteer pay cheques were inevitably late in arriving, causing unnecessary hardships. What further angered the volunteers was that the staff were being paid enormous sums of money, and being given fat expense accounts as well.

The interim advisory council also irked them. At Antigonish, Stewart Goodings, now an associate director, had promised them that the volunteers would control the Company. After a year or more in existence, the volunteers felt no closer to achieving this. And to make matters worse, the council seemed to have no real understanding of field work or volunteer problems.

The volunteer list of complaints did not end there. The Company hired a great many consultants and researchers during 1967, at immense cost. The thought of all that money being wasted drove many volunteers to distraction.

One volunteer, Torben Angelo of Toronto, wrote an article in the Company's internal newsletter that summed up all of these complaints. The seemingly wild examples of extravagance that Angelo uses are not so wild. Many of them had their roots in fact. Others were only rumours, unsubstantiated but accepted by the volunteers.

"I can recall with some measure of nostalgia the good old days when we were operating on naivity, inexperience and willingness. It is with much regret that I see these valuable work tools give way to professionalism. It is high time Parliament passed a law which would outlaw high priced consultants, research and things like that. It would be nice to get back to the old thing about people working with people and leaving the psychologists, trainers, housing experts and philosophers out of it . . . . , " he wrote.

" . . . I have the sure cure for all our ills. It is completely safe, it will not change anyone's work pattern, and it will enable the Company to realize a large financial saving over the next few years, which could be put into salaries and further misappropriations, i.e. research. The obvious solution is: Eliminate Volunteers . . . .

"All departments could continue to function as usual, the recruiting staff could give lectures and show movies. The training staff could sit in ski-resorts and drink beer and talk to girls from finishing schools . . . . The program development people could go up and shoot the guff with Eskimo and Indian people about things such as the power structure in Hoboken. The secretaries could continue their three-hour hair dresser and Vic Tanny deals during lunch. The research department could continue to measure the power structure in Hoboken . . . . I think international program also deserves a mention or two, whoever is in charge of the world-wide revolution could go to Moscow and spend a month at the Hilton Hotel there before leaving for the Havana Ritz with all the goodie credit cards.

"I am not too sure what the directorate would be doing, but I think it is only fair to put Alan Clarke to work teaching illiterate Eskimoes to read at 30,000 words per minute . . . . (a slap at Clarke's association with Evelyn Wood Reading Dynamics).

"If there are not enough history students around for Stewart Goodings, he could come to Toronto and write press releases for David DePoe.

"The regional directorate initially would present a bit of a problem, but they would be no means become dispensable. The fellows in Halifax could take trains to Vancouver and then fly back to take another train to Vancouver. The executives in Vancouver could constantly be on route to Halifax. Every month or so they could coordinate their schedules and meet in Winnipeg for a few kegs of beer.

"As a last major research expenditure I recommend that we hire 'Ian Martin and Associates' for $50,000 and have them do a two-month research study on the feasibility of eliminating volunteers in order to streamline and smooth the operation out."

Angelo's tirade hit directly home. The Company had an immense staff and most didn't know what any other staff person was doing, and didn't really seem to care. This is not to criticize all the staff. Some were doing fine work and the volunteers respected them — Geoff Cue and Peter Stein in British Columbia are two examples. Others earned the wrath of the volunteers. What can one say about this comment from a volunteer in New Brunswick:

"At first, we (the volunteers) were having some difficulties working together. In my opinion, the regional director could have helped us, but when I phoned him I was told he was too busy . . . "

Angelo's comments about the Ottawa office were also true. There was no organization to speak of and certainly no definable structure. Most people reported to work when they felt like it. Some came in at nine a.m. Others would saunter in at noon and work till late at night. No one seemed to be shirking, but no one seemed to be working with anyone else. Letters that arrived at the office were just as likely to be lost or misplaced as to find the desk they were intended for. Three hours for lunch was not unusual.

The recruiting team that Angelo mentioned became infamous, even within the Company. The team rented a Volkswagen bus and set off for a six-week tour of Canadian university campuses. When they arrived at the campus for the day, they set up a table and began to distribute literature. They also showed movies, talked about the Company and about social issues. The scheme could not be considered a wholesale success. A PR report, commissioned by the Company, later stated that "the student bodies were singularly unimpressed when recruiting teams visited their universities. This unfavorable reaction is attributed almost solely to the appearance of those representing the Company."

There were also rumours, unconfirmed, about the recruiting team smoking marijuana on the steps on one western university. This seems far-fetched.

The extravagance showed by the Company staff in other areas was as bad as Angelo claimed. Countless meetings were held across the country at enormous cost. Jacques Noel was sent to New Delhi, India, Paris and London on one tour of duty. Most CYC staff had Air Canada credit cards and made liberal use of them. The administration made the mistake of not getting the cards back when people left, and one result was a staff member, who had resigned from the CYC, flying to Paris on his card. The cards were soon discontinued.

Letter writing was passé in the Company — a dying form of communication. People phoned across the country without giving it a second thought and even to such exotic places as Hong Kong. Joan Cohen reported in the *Ottawa*

Citizen that the Company's long distance phone bill approached $40,000.

The Company's council was not blind to these faults and, in March, 1967, made a move it hoped would help eradicate them. Two firms of public relations consultants — Berger, Tisdal, Clarke and Lesly of Toronto, and Gilles Desroches et Associes of Montreal — were hired to do a comprehensive study of the Company's public relations. The firms did not content themselves with a superficial look at the media versus the Company. They explored volunteer-staff relationships, staff-staff problems and, in fact, the Company as a whole.

In August, 1967, their confidential report was turned in to the council. It should have been enough of a warning for anyone.

"The majority of volunteers are highly critical of Ottawa staff. This attitude is coupled with a degree of apprehension about the future of the Company, and a general feeling of insecurity . . . .

"There is a general feeling among volunteers that the provisional council is not in a position to make decisions that affect the volunteer's work in the community . . . .

"Ottawa staff is aware of the break-down in the relationships between themselves and volunteers, and for the most part is prepared to accept a reasonable share of the responsibility for this breakdown . . . .

"Most members of Ottawa staff feel they are competent. There are those, however, who feel that staff competence cannot be measured because staff has not had sufficient time to prove itself. There are, however, some members of Ottawa staff who place the entire blame for the volunteers' problems on Ottawa staff . . . .

"There is concern among regional staff as to the competence of some members of Ottawa staff. It is generally believed that Ottawa staff is long on ideas, but short on the abilities needed to put them into effect. There is also general distaste for a form of nepotism which permits friends of Ottawa staff to be hired to fill staff vacancies . . . .

"Lack of organization, clarification and definition is one of the major causes of the poor internal relations and has been largely responsible for the failure of the Company to get off the ground."

These were the general comments of the report. All of the comments were gone into in great detail and recommendations were made. A beginning in this direction was made, but never completed. The problems pointed out in the report continued to exist and no one was any happier. The warning had been given, accepted and acted on. But, like most things in the Company, the action died out and the reformation ended in a whimper.

Sitting at the top of this mess was Alan Clarke. His responsibilities were enormous and he needed all of the help he could get. Unfortunately, his help began to disappear. Bob Olivero resigned as financial administrator. Jacques Noel, an associate director, resigned.

Noel's reasons are indicative of the shape of the Company in July, 1967.

"It is more a question of mental, rather than physical health that has brought me to leave the Company," he said. He then explained that he required rational structures within which to work. He hadn't found them in the CYC. Many others would leave with the same sentiments.

The structure of the Company left Clarke with nearly total responsibility for everything. In just the area of finance, for example, no expenditure of more than $250 could be made without his approval. In the hiring of volunteers, Clarke's signature had to be affixed. There were many other items of less importance and taken together they all heaped a tremendous burden on him.

One of Clarke's first deeds as executive director was to form the committee structure. The working group was the first of these and when it died, Clarke replaced it with separate committees for program development, planning, public relations, and international program. These committees were made up of volunteers and council members with staff supplying the input. Clarke found himself taking part in preparations for these meetings and attending them. He also had the council meetings to contend with. Since there were several meetings a month, this took up a good deal of his time.

Apart from chores such as these, Clarke had to look after the field and the volunteers. This involved listening to volunteer complaints and visiting projects.

All in all, he often worked sixteen hours a day trying to get his work out of the way and rarely succeeded.

There was never any real delegation of authority in the Company. Field staff, regional directors, Ottawa staff — all of them made promises, but only Clarke held the power to make the promises come true. He never relinquished enough of that role.

Because his time was so thinly spread around, Clarke could never pay proper attention to things like finance and administration. They were left to go their own ways, with disastrous results. And in his dealings with volunteers, Clarke's personal philosophy generated resentment. Clarke believed that people should solve their own problems. He did not want to be the Great God or Father to the volunteers. When the volunteers, or staff, would come to him with problems he would listen and then say something like, "I'll see what can be done." Nothing, of course, would be done, but the volunteers were always expecting action. This led to some labelling Clarke the "fuzzy man".

The paradox is there as well, of course. Because he held so much power, Clarke could not be anything else than Father to the volunteers. In the long run, he was fighting a losing battle.

Clarke was not helped in his struggles by the council. The council had left administration and finances alone too long and were now rapidly trying to make up for the lost time. A firm of chartered accountants was called in to help unravel the Company's chaotic books. Meanwhile, Clarke was still trying to operate in a policy vacuum. Policy had a habit of emerging at times of crisis. When the crisis was over, council made no decisions.

After 1967, the scene was to become more chaotic and more complex and more devious. The first warning of the restlessness came at the end of Canada's Centennial Year. The government had been hearing reports, and undoubtedly reading newspaper stories about the situation of 323 Chapel Street. Money was being wasted, of that there was little doubt. So a warning was delivered in the form of a budget cut. In its first full year of operations the Company had been given a budget of $2.4 million. An increase was expected for 1968-69. The Government slashed all such expectations in December when it cut the Company's budget to $1.9 million for the coming year. The Company reacted with anger. Statements were issued about the government impairing the work of the Company. They pointed out that the international program would now have to be postponed. The real import of the message was missed: clean up your books". When the Company's annual report was issued, some six months later, it showed that the message had not been received.

9

The Field in 1967

While in Ottawa, the council and the staff were trying to bring order to chaos, the volunteers in the field were simply trying to get things done. It was difficult. Put into situations in which they had no experience, hampered by what they considered administrative incompetence, worried about participation in the Company-at-large, pestered by newsmen, some volunteers reacted by exploding, turning to navel-gazing, and resigning. Letters like the following were becoming routine:

"I am resigning because of a training program (Crystal Cliffs) which encouraged an unreal atmosphere of euphoria and graduated volunteers who had visions of organizing radical social action projects and absolutely no organizing skills.

"I am resigning because of the lack of support we received in Glace Bay. We knew what had to be done there but hadn't a clue about how to do it. And no one in the Company of Young Canadians knew or cared enough to give us practical, close to the ground directions and ideas.

"I am resigning because of a staff meeting where I saw Company people who were incapable of talking honestly to the person across the table, dreaming aloud of a project-based Company. Such a Company must rest on what is now happening in the field — not on far-out fantasies, e.g. an alliance between Cape Breton Miners and Alberta Indians.

"I am resigning because of the ruthless sabotaging tactics used by some members of the Company against co-workers."

There were now close to 200 volunteers and trainees in the field. The Company had changed its training program somewhat. There was still sensitivity and group dynamics, but there was also a period of time on-project. The regions were being sliced up at the same time. The regional set-up had not worked well enough. The Prairies and British Columbia seemed to be doing not too badly, but Ontario and the Maritimes were suffering. It was decided to put one staff member with each project; the staff member would report to an associate director. It was felt this would provide better support for the volunteers. Unfortunately, the system was not fully developed until the end of 1967.

During that year the volunteers worked valiantly trying to keep themselves and their projects together. Not all of them succeeded. One by one, projects began to disappear. In the Maritimes, the Newfoundland project, the Glace Bay project on Cape Breton Island, and the Halifax Welfare project had all gone by June. The other Maritime projects, Gerry Fatels in St. John, Joan Jones at Kwacha House in Halifax, Karen Embleton in Moncton and Bill Poole on the Eskasoni Indian Reserve hung on, but they were fighting for survival. None of them would last six months into 1968.

The problems they were facing were the never-ending ones of inexperience, lack of support and lack of trust.

Lack of support was more visible in the Maritimes than elsewhere. The first regional director there resigned after only a few months in the field. The second, Harold McKernin, resigned in August, 1967, claiming his move was spurred by "a completely unjustified refusal of co-operation" from Alan Clarke. Clarke, McKernin said, "Froze me in a position where I could make no further contribution to the work of the Company".

Ontario was much more stable, but was also beginning to rot at the seams. The West Central and Don Area projects in Toronto were verging on a point of disappearance. Lanark County and Deep River didn't have much life left. Problems were beginning to creep into the Toronto Youth Project of David DePoe.

The Prairies and the Northwest Territories lost Prince Albert, the Selkirk Mental Hospital and Inuvik as projects. Winnipeg was beginning to limp, but the others, Calgary, Great Slave Lake, South Saskatchewan, Oak River Reserve and Lesser Slave Lake, seemed strong. But two of them, South Saskatchewan and Oak River would soon die.

In British Columbia, the sun shone and the Company prospered. The province was not without its share of difficulties on projects like Victoria and Outreach, and the volunteers on Vancouver Youth would hardly talk to those on Vancouver Housing but, overall, the province was in strong shape. The credit for this was given to the staff, plus the fact that B.C. was isolated from Ottawa and managed its own affairs.

If this seems bleak then it is not the whole picture. Certainly, 45 volunteers resigned in that fiscal year, and more than five projects would die and another ten come close to death. But some work had been done that astounded the professionals. That work was also helping to save the Company. Whenever the Company came under attack, the Ottawa office would tell people to visit some projects and then recommend Calgary, Vancouver Housing, Everdale Place and Winnipeg.

These projects were the Company as it could have been. Along with a few others, they represented the dream of the CYC. The young people had worked miracles despite the cynics. They had accomplished, despite the efforts of some of their own people to hinder them. And they had guts, enough guts to take a shellacking and come back for more.

The Lesser Slave Lake project was one example, Winnipeg another.

Al Burger and Jeremy Ashton arrived in Faust, Alberta in August 1966. Faust is a backwoods community about 200 miles north of Edmonton. It has a population of about

800, of which a majority is Métis, and a weak economy consisting of fishing, logging and mink ranching. The economy was for the whites; most of the Métis were on welfare. The CYC was invited in to help organize recreation for Faust's teenagers, hardly a radical role, but Burger and Ashton soon turned it into a controversial one.

Through late 1966 and into 1967, they worked at the recreation job — starting a mens' basketball team, helping to start the Faust youth organization for teenagers, trying to start a Boy Scout troop. They also attempted to improve relations between whites and Métis. Trouble was not long in coming. In February, 1967, 45 townspeople met in the Faust community hall and debated running the two volunteers out of town. The discussion was heated and the complaints numerous.

One man charged that the volunteers were dirty, unkempt, lazy, rude and proponents of Communism. Others agreed.

"He's rude, doesn't wash often enough and wears muddy boots in other people's houses," said one woman about Burger.

The worst charge came from the man responsible for bringing the CYC into Faust.

"They have floundered around, without any clear-cut objective, just getting people mad," he said.

Not everyone was mad, though. The Métis community rallied to their support, as did several whites.

"Those fellows may not have accomplished much in a practical sense, but at least they got us thinking and talking and looking," one supporter said.

A Métis woman remarked, "They are interested in us, in our problems and our needs. For the first time in 40 years, I think the Métis problem is being recognized here and those boys are responsible."

Responsible they were and they paid for it. Burger was pulled out of Faust by the Company; the Company didn't have much choice. Ashton stayed for a while, but eventually left as well. It seemed that the whites had won their victory in Faust, but it didn't turn out quite that way. The Métis community circulated a petition asking them to come back and in July they responded. Not many people would have gone back. The white community tried for months to drive them out and when they succeeded in April, the project seemed doomed. Ashton and Burger showed a toughness that other volunteers lacked. They also cared enough to recognize their mistakes, admit them and try to correct them. The project would fluctuate from this time on, but no one could ever doubt the devotion of Burger and Ashton to the principles of the Company and to the métis community in Faust.

Harvey Stevens in Winnipeg was never faced with anything that dramatic. His challenges came in subtler, person-to-person duels. No boat-rocker, Stevens, 22, moved into the Logan Street area of the city and tried to establish contact with the teenagers. It was difficult. Deeply religious and thoughtful, Stevens was not out-going and had few of the social vices. This was resented by some of the kids in the area. They regarded his unwillingness to drink with them as a sign that he didn't want to be seen with them, and they reacted against him.

It was a lonely and trying experience, but he stuck it out doing what he could — organizing dances and a variety program, and working with individuals in an unspectacular way. In one case, he helped a woman get her cheque from a welfare department that was giving her the run-around. In another, he helped a man who had been in and out of jail for six years by simply getting him a place to stay and someone to talk to.

The work that Stevens did was never spectacular, and the Winnipeg project was never regarded as one of the Company's best. But Stevens had a particular kind of devotion that won him the respect of other volunteers. In the CYC that was enough to prove merit.

The Company's most publicly successful projects were west of Winnipeg. Some volunteers claimed this was because the projects were further away from Ottawa.

Bernie Muzeen was lucky when he moved into Calgary. A community organization was already in existence, and a strong staff person, Elaine Krause, was living in the city. Muzeen knew nothing about Calgary or its problems. He was an easterner and when told he would be working in Calgary's slum, he envisioned something like Toronto's Cabbagetown. The so-called slum was Victoria Park, an eight-by-ten block area in the middle of the city, next to the Calgary Stampede grounds. In reality, Victoria Park was a neat, well-kept community that was being threatened with destruction.

The Calgary Stampede had expansion plans and needed more land. The nearest available land was in Victoria Park. The Stampede and Exhibition Board of Directors is a large cross-section of the famous and the wealthy. It was a board with influence and its chances of obtaining the land seemed excellent.

When Muzeen entered the community, the issue was not really boiling. So he took his time becoming known. His techniques were simple. He rented an apartment in the area and began to walk around it. As he walked, he talked to children and to those adults who would pay him any attention. Within a few months, local residents were accustomed to the burly six-footer and he began to visit homes, and began to chat. Several problems were always discussed — the move to wipe out Victoria Park and problems with young people. Muzeen, with the help of Elaine Krause, began to work in both areas.

He began with young people by hanging around the community recreation centre and talking. Some of them were soon coming to him with their problems and his days as a natural resource to the community were beginning. The Stampede's expropriation drive was much more volatile. Muzeen helped arrange community meetings to discuss the problem. The residents made it clear that they wanted to fight. He provided them with some alternatives.

The first plan of action was aimed at city hall. Muzeen began to help gather data on the proposed expropriation and on the area. Once enough had been brought together, the residents wrote a brief and presented it to city council. They were rebuffed. City council stood firm with the Stampede board — Victoria Park had to go.

Instead of being discouraged, the community became angry and started to put into use some of its other alternatives. An intensive publicity campaign was used to bring the attention of the rest of the city to the plight of Victoria Park. And plight it was. Calgary in 1967 had a housing shortage as severe as any city in the country. Yet, the city government wanted to destroy the homes of thousands of people. The government promised to help them relocate, but couldn't answer the questions Victoria Park was asking. Namely, how do we buy new homes with the amount of money we'll be getting? Where will we find the homes?

There were many old people in the area and their fears were particularly well-founded. Many of them had been living in Victoria Park for 30 to 40 years and their homes represented their entire life savings. The city was going to tear down these houses and they would have to move elsewhere. They were all aware that they could never find comparable housing for the same money.

Through early 1967, publicity was the approach used. It seemed to have little effect as the city government once again refused to back down. Muzeen and the community group kept plugging away and were soon blessed with luck.

Expropriation is a three-way cost-sharing plan between civic, provincial and federal governments. The community had struck out at the city level so it turned to the next one — the province.

A provincial election was called for the summer of 1967 in Alberta. The Social Credit Party of Ernest C. Manning was expecting no large problems province-wide, but in the city of Calgary the Progressive Conservative Party was causing some concern. Some ridings were definitely up for grabs and one of them was the riding that included Victoria Park. A Socred cabinet minister was the incumbent in the riding and it was obvious he was having his troubles with his Tory opponent. The community saw its opportunity to practice real democracy.

A community delegation visited the Socred and presented him with an honest proposition. If he would fight against expropriation, the community of Victoria Park would vote for him as a bloc. If he supported expropriation, they would vote against him the same way. The cabinet minister said he would join them and a bargain was struck. The community looked good when he was re-elected in the riding by an extremely slim margin, several hundred votes. The minister looked good when the province announced that it would not take part in the expropriation of Victoria Park. The community had won a very large battle.

To understand the victory in Calgary and to realize its significance are two different matters. Democracy is supposed to function in a way that would have helped the community, but democracy is rarely any of the things its supposed to be. Victoria Park had been marked for extinction by the city's elite. That elite usually had its requests granted. When the community decided to fight, no one gave them much hope of winning. When the city government backed the Stampede, all seemed lost. But, by persisting and by using their strongest weapon, their numbers, against the Stampede's main weapon, its money, the community won. This was the first victory of its kind in Calgary. It would not be the last. Victoria Park awakened other parts of the city to their rights and the fighting is still going on. In Calgary, city hall can be fought and be beaten.

Bernie Muzeen's role in the victory shouldn't be over-played. He was not the leader in the fight, nor was he the originator of it. But, he was a resource available to the community 24 hours a day, and he was a resource that seldom let them down. When ideas were needed, Muzeen had them. When a leg-man was needed, he had the legs. When they needed someone to organize a meeting, he had the time and the skills. He was, indeed, the very person that Dr. Des Connor had described at Antigonish — the ideal volunteer. This is not to say that Muzeen had no problems and that he had a perfect relationship with the community. For the truth is that Muzeen's acceptance was only partial. He had enemies and they worked hard against him. One example has always remained clear in his mind.

Muzeen used to visit Ottawa periodically for Company meetings. His absences raised some questions, and one of his enemies was willing to provide the answers. Muzeen had left the community, people were told, and wouldn't be back. The reason given for his disappearance was that he had been molesting young children. When Muzeen arrived back in the city he found many friends reluctant to talk to him. He soon found out why and had to begin all over again at building trust. It was a long and arduous process, but just part of the job.

The lies and malicious gossip that Muzeen was subjected to in Calgary upset him greatly. The fact that he recovered is due partly to his own character and partly to the tenacity of the staff person there. Elaine Kraus was a Saskatchewan girl and a former agency worker. When she joined the CYC no one expected miracles to follow. A firm believer in efficiency in action, she insisted that nothing be done until it had been thoroughly planned and all the alternatives had been covered. Not that she held back action, far from it. She was a prime mover for action, perhaps the most consistent, devoted and skilled mover in Calgary. Her assistance to Muzeen was invaluable. When things looked bleak, she was there to prod and encourage him. When he was smug about a success, she was there to bring him back to earth. Not all volunteers were fortunate enough to have staff support like Elaine Kraus. She was a promoter of change, but at the same time she realized the importance of doing it efficiently.

Calgary best epitomizes the philosophy of the Company of Young Canadians. It is here one can see most graphically the role of the volunteer as a resource person, and the emergence of a community with the ability and the will to handle its own problems. The Company was trying to spread grass-roots democracy. It was trying to involve people in decisions that affected them. This is now an accepted belief in most Canadian communities, but in 1967 it was something new and rather frightening. The role of volunteer was a delicate one to perform. The necessary ingredients varied from individual to individual, but some characteristics always seemed present — a willingness to let communities plan their action; a desire to help; an ability to talk with, not talk down to; and a knack for integrating. Muzeen was not the only volunteer with these characteristics, nor was he the only one with excellent staff support.

For some reason, British Columbia was never beset with the same kinds of problems as other areas. The projects appeared stronger, beefs were less and successes were common. Ottawa didn't have much to do with B.C., perhaps because B.C. didn't want much to do with Ottawa.

It is impossible to review British Columbia in 1967 and

point to one or two projects as the best, for it appeared at the time that all of them were progressing well.

Dal Brodhead was now firmly established in Alert Bay and continuing his service-type role. The probation system had been changed and he was given much of the credit for that. Young people had somewhere to go and things to do. Alert Bay was very happy with their volunteer.

There was a new kind of school in Vancouver that was exciting people at the same time. It was called Knowplace and the Company was its main sponsor. Knowplace was established as an alternative to an existing school structure that seemed to reject many bright, young non-conformists. The parents of these children went looking for something better and Knowplace emerged from the think-in. It was to be an unstructured school — designed to inspire learning. Students would be able to study the subjects of their choice at any time of night or day. The school was set up in an old house and the students would be responsible for paying the rent and maintaining the building. The Company was supplying the teachers in the form of volunteers. Teacher is not the proper word; resource person fits once again. The volunteers could not sit down and teach higher calculus, but they could tell the students where they could learn it.

Knowplace was an experiment and the immediate dividends surprised many educators. Students spent their time drawing, talking and reading. Some of them proved amazingly adept at this self-learning process and ventured back into the regular school system with their proof. One 15-year old boy stunned Simon Fraser University with his knowledge of physics. A girl successfully condensed three years of high school into one. It was all very exciting and flashy, a totally different kind of project than the one Maeve Hancy was pursuing on the other side of the city.

In Vancouver, as in most other cities, people on welfare are not appreciated. Thus, when the time comes for building public housing for these people, city governments have a habit of building on the outer limits of the city. This, the thinking goes, keeps the unwelcome at a place where they can't be observed daily. It is difficult to observe them at all for most don't have cars and bus fares are a luxury for them.

This isolation causes many problems, and in the Orchard Park-Skeena Terrace part of Vancouver, the problems were severe.

Most of the adults in the public housing development were female, and most of the families were single-parent families. The area had few recreation facilities and this, combined with the isolation and the lack of fathers, was causing havoc with many of the children. Drugs, booze, homosexuality, crime, all of these things were beginning to develop among the children. The city's welfare policy, instead of helping, added to the intensity of the troubles.

Most of the women in Orchard Park-Skeena Terrace were on welfare. Some could have found work, but why should they bother? If they got a job the money they earned would be subtracted from their welfare cheque and, since most would not be earning high wages, their income would not increase. Their incomes, in fact, would have been smaller since bus fares and lunches and work clothes would be new costs.

Maeve Hancey moved into this area and began to help the mothers organize. She found them eager to become involved. They had two primary targets — welfare policy and recreation. The latter was solved first. The mothers had an impact on the housing development managers and recreation facilities were promised. Now, they concentrated on welfare and went after the provincial and city governments. Briefs were written and presented. They picketed and marched. Someone listened and found their arguments logical. They wanted to work, but were held back by welfare policies. Changes were made in the policies. The mothers of Orchard Park-Skeena Terrace had proven that they were as capable of handling their own lives as anyone else. The stigma of welfare had been attacked and partly licked in Vancouver.

With successes like these in the field, one wonders why the CYC was in such trouble in 1967. The fact is that hardly anyone knew about the successes. Most volunteers were leery about the press. They felt that their role was to be a catalyst, not a leader. When a project became involved in controversy, the volunteers preferred to let the community leaders speak — this was all part of the development process. Then too, these volunteers were for the most part middle-class. The press was paying more attention to hippies and the apparent chaos in the Ottawa office of the Company.

Actually, the Ottawa office was more concerned with the hippies and radicals as well. The middle-class volunteers in CYC, people like Hancey, Muzeen, Stevens and Brodhead were never really taken seriously by some staff members. Fixed in their minds was the image of the hip, young radical and these four volunteers would never fit that mold. It seems strange that the Company was searching for the ideal volunteer and ignoring the examples in its own organization. The successes at this stage, were, with few exceptions, coming from the so-called squares.

10

The Selection Weekend

The problem of selection and training of volunteers never seemed to be resolved in the CYC. It seemed that every training program after Antigonish was different. Sometimes as in the cases of Moncton and Val David it differed only slightly, but generally the Company was dissatisfied with its past performance and was trying something new. In late 1967, the Company decided to allow more of the training to take place in the field. This pleased many, but just as many regarded it as a half-way measure. They wanted the complete responsibility of selecting which volunteers were to serve on which projects.

Eventually, selection and training changed until the monstrosity known as the selection weekend was born. There were actually two selection weekends. The first took place when the Company invited applicants to gather in one particular city for a weekend of discussion. Any applicants who impressed the staff during that time were allowed to move on to trainee status. After six weeks of training, nearly all of it on the project that the trainee would serve on after completing his training program, another selection session was held — this one to determine if the trainee was ready to become a volunteer.

This sounds pretty good in theory, but it was a system that never worked efficiently. Like all things in the Company, the system had to stand up to personal problems, feuds and incompetence. It was impossible for it to survive, and it didn't. But while it was in operation the selection weekend was a miniature replica of the Company as a whole, and all the problems of the Company could be seen in the way the weekends were carried out. There are two examples.

The first was in Winnipeg, in November of 1967, and the information comes from a memo written by Gerry Gambill, then associate director to Alan Clarke, in charge of English programs. The second was held in Toronto in early 1968.

The Winnipeg session was held to decide whether a group of trainees, just finished their training program in the city, would become volunteers. Gambill arrived in Winnipeg on November 17th to be part of the process and was met at the airport by Harold Harper, a staff member. They went to the motel where the selection was to take place and then to the regional office to meet everyone concerned with the selection — volunteers, trainees, staff and consultants. Harper made numerous phone calls in an attempt to get everyone together. By 3 p.m. the trainees had gathered, but Jackie Briskow, the main trainer, hadn't been reached. Without her presence, Gambill considered it impossible to do anything concrete and chit-chatted with the trainees about their experiences in Winnipeg.

At 4 p.m., Briskow called to say she had not been informed about the meeting, and did not believe that attempts had been made to get hold of her earlier. She added that she was not willing to go down to the office for a meeting. Upset, Gambill arranged to meet her at 6 p.m. at the University dining hall. Murray Smith, a staff member, was asked to go with Gambill.

The trainees were, at this point, becoming afraid that their selection could not proceed. Gambill praised them for their desire to get something done, and said that the responsibility for things being upset was the Company's.

He added that they shared the responsibility by not sitting down and getting things straightened out.

"I went through the bit about the Company being operated by the volunteers, and about them assuming full responsibilities on the project as equal partners with staff," Gambill writes in his memo.

Gambill was at the dining hall at 6 p.m., but Briskow was not to be seen. He ran back to his motel, about a mile away, to see if she had gone there. She hadn't, so he left a message and ran back to the university, again without finding her. Returning to the motel once again, he found Smith waiting for him. They waited there for Briskow, but never found her.

Shortly after this, Gambil received a phone call from Wally Kubiski, a council member. Gambill thought that Briskow was Kubiski's girl friend. Kubiski and Gambill talked for a while and Gambill reports that the conversation was not based on trust. When he tried to set up another meeting with Briskow, Kubiski told him that she wasn't available.

The following day, the trainees gathered at the motel. Gambill told them that he was unable to do a selection as he was not able to get a recommendation from a staff person regarding their status. Smith, who was present, agreed to assume the responsibility for the training program, and to give Gambill his recommendations as soon as possible.

"My own analysis of the situation is that it never should have happened in the first place," writes Gambill. "Trainees should not have gone to Winnipeg until there was a staff person present to carry out the training, to take responsibility for it, and to be responsible for the selection of the trainees for volunteer status. Jackie's position was untenable in that the trainees did not know what was going on in the tangle of staff and consultant relationships. While

I can appreciate the confusion, my main concern was that there was very little understanding of the feelings of the trainees in the situation by most of the people involved."

It is difficult for a layman to understand that such confusion could take place in a multi-million dollar organization, but it did — repeatedly. The Winnipeg affair was even more complicated than Gambill suggests. He concentrated only on the weekend, but there had been trouble before and there would be even more trouble after. To be fair, Jackie Briskow was not the major villain. She was hired as a consultant to conduct a training program and she tried to do that. The trainees, however, weren't so enthusiastic. Appointments would be made for them to visit hospitals and the like, and none of them would show up. This was disconcerting for the hospitals, bad public relations and an unfair reflection on the capabilities of Briskow. It is logical to assume by the end of the period she was just fed up with the entire thing and wanted nothing more to do with the Company.

As it turned out, Briskow was probably the most aware of all. The selection process was finally carried out and the projects started. They folded within six months.

The Winnipeg selection was an example of non-organization. The Toronto selection pinpointed the Company's ideological snobbery, and the inability of staff members to get along.

About 25 young people were invited to Toronto for the weekend. They were all, supposedly, interested in joining the Company and this was to be their first step. If they impressed the selectors, they would be brought in as trainees.

The weekend was held at a downtown hotel and the staff gathered first to discuss their strategy. Present were Stewart Goodings, participating in his first selection; Ron Krupp, staff member for the Toronto Don Area project; Jim Kinzel, staff member for the Toronto Youth Project; Jim Littleton, a national program staff member; and Ed Smee, Company director of selection and training.

The trainees were to be chosen for the projects of Kinzel and Krupp, but all of the staff members present were to have a say in who was chosen.

The weekend began Saturday morning with meetings in several rooms. Staff members conducted the meetings and were intended to bring the applicants into the open. In one room, political and economic ideology were discussed. Some applicants were well-versed in Marxism and knew how to smatter their speeches with anti-establishment clichés and curses. There were some middle-class squares present. They protested, feebly, that, for example, all agencies weren't all bad. They were shouted down by other applicants. In the other room, Smee was conducting a role-playing session concerning the job of a volunteer. The applicants took part in this enthusiastically. The staff did not appear to like it.

At the lunch break, this came into the open. Kinzel and Krupp wanted Smee to leave. They did not want him ruining a selection weekend. They wanted to choose their trainees in their own way. Goodings protested and supported Smee. It was of little use. Smee left and a few days later, resigned from the Company.

It is important to note that Ed Smee was regarded at the time as one of the finest trainers in Canada. A sensitivity expert, he had worked for the YMCA for many years and had conducted one large training session for the CYC as a consultant. The people at the session had been pleased with him, and he was hired to work full-time with the CYC. Smee had been popular with many volunteers and his departure was not easy for some of them to bear. His absence from the Toronto selection weekend, though, was welcomed.

The weekend continued on a predictable pattern. Films were shown and discussions followed. Then there was a question and answer period, with the applicants asking the questions. When it was all over, about eight applicants were asked to become trainees. The applicants were for the most part those who knew the new left rhetoric and the right swear words. Many of those who weren't chosen left with bitter tastes in their mouths; one young man was particularly hurt. He had been in a state of excitement throughout the weekend. He had read the book *Summerhill* and this was his main topic of discussion. He seemed bright, aware and concerned, but was obviously naive, and without rhetoric. The awareness and concern counted for little. He wasn't selected. Perhaps he should have been thankful for that. The two Toronto projects that chose trainees had difficult times ahead for them. One would fold by the summer of 1968. The other would hobble through until 1969.

11

The Beginning in Quebec

For the first year of its operations, the Company of Young Canadians ignored the province of Quebec. In January, 1967, the Company had four volunteers in the province. In August of the same year, it had only twelve. They were spread out and not very effective.

Robert Landreville was a Company staff member in Quebec almost from the first day the CYC went into the field. In February, 1967, he was appointed regional director. The job was taken away from him four months later and put up for grabs. The Company was looking for a man who could build up an organization in Quebec.

Two applicants initially came forward, Pierre Lecours, a staff member and acting regional director, and Claude Piche, a CBC reporter. Piche soon dropped out; the Company's Director of Training, Martin Beliveau entered his name.

The candidates were put through a grueling routine. They were interviewed by volunteers, Quebec staff and Ottawa staff. The final decision was made by Alan Clarke. Clarke drew up a list of criteria — a lengthy one of 26 points, more involved, in fact, than the list which had been used to select an executive director. On August 9th, Martin Beliveau, 29, was appointed to the position of regional director, a position that would soon be changed to that of associate director for Quebec.

Beliveau wanted to improve the Company's position in Quebec. No one realized how good a job he would do.

At the time of Beliveau's appointment, both he and Clarke issued short statements that were reported in the

Company internal newsletter. Looking back, the statements sound like bad jokes.

"First of all . . . . Martin's appointment in no way gives my approval to the new direction he wished in the region. He will have to function within the existing structures," said Clarke.

Beliveau responded in kind: "I shall work with everyone in the Company and in the Quebec region in particular in accordance with the action and policies undertaken during the last few months."

Those statements aside, it did not take long for people to realize that Martin Beliveau had his own ideas about how the CYC should function in Quebec. He also had remarkable success in having his ideas accepted.

One of his first aims was recruitment of both staff and volunteers. He acted quickly, perhaps too quickly. From the twelve volunteers it had in August, the Company in Quebec mushroomed by December, 1967, to more than 50 volunteers and trainees. In another three months the total was 92 volunteers and trainees. The staffing was just as heavy. The rest of the Company was now operating on a project-based principle. The regional offices had effectively vanished and the staff on projects were doing both program and administration. Not so in Quebec. By December, Beliveau had 18 staff at work in Quebec. The staff included a financial administrator, an information officer, researchers, recruiters and program staff. This staff occupied several offices in the Montreal area.

What kind of power did he have? In a document presented to the council of the Company, Beliveau stated:

"Personnel will henceforth be retained by and responsible to Quebec. Previously the person charged with recruiting was hired by recruiting service in Ottawa, and responsible to the Director of Recruitment there. In future, all personnel, whether engaged in recruiting, selection, training, research, documentation, information etc., will be engaged in Quebec and responsible to the regional director . . . . "

From this point, Beliveau ventured forth to set up a separate training program for the province, and a separate selection program. Candidates would be subjected to interviews and if they seemed suitable for a project, they would be sent to that project. There was no further training envisioned, outside of that which the volunteer would receive on the project. There was an explanation of what the Company was in Quebec, but little or no reference to the federal ties.

In addition to selection and training, Quebec set out to establish its own working structure. Beliveau was a believer in participation and said repeatedly that the volunteers must establish and run their own program. The staff would be there to support, but not to lead. Towards this end, volunteer assemblies were set up. The assemblies gave the volunteers a chance to work out broad policy recommendations and to question their staff, and the council members from the province. It was this organization, inspired by Beliveau, that would later take over Quebec and virtually control the staff, the money and the power in that province.

Beyond the structural differences between Quebec and the rest of the Company, there was an ideological split. The split could be attributed to the cultural difference between Quebec and the rest of the country. For some reason, the Quebecois in the Company were always more organized, more efficient and more dedicated than their English counterparts. The volunteer assemblies are one example. The Quebec volunteers were for the most part united. The English-speaking volunteers never had an effective equivalent. Perhaps one of the reasons was that the Quebec volunteers had a hand in drafting their ideology; The English-speaking volunteers were presented with theirs.

The Company's Aims and Principles were meaningless in

Quebec. That province's guidelines were its own and Beliveau, in a letter to applicants in Quebec, outlined them briefly.

"The Company of Young Canadians in Quebec is a social action movement with a clearly defined goal: democratic participation.

"We believe that by educating the masses we will succeed one day in establishing true democracy here in Quebec. We believe that in order for democracy to take root, it is essential that the entire population, regardless of race or class, be aware of the collective problems inherent in the society in which we live . . . . "

This amazing manifesto has the ring of Marxist philosophy. It is a call to revolution — to ignite the masses. The tool which would bring about the revolution was *animation sociale,* a French-developed technique. Beliveau listed several of the main working points of the process.

Some basic assumptions of *animation sociale* are:

A. The success of the policies adopted depends on the conscious, co-ordinated participation of the masses.

B. The masses must be able to hold meetings, discuss, make suggestions, receive instructions.

C. The dynamic drive needed by the policy-makers to achieve any undertaking of size must spring from the base.

D. It is therefore essential that this base have a solid framework capable of directing the opinions and forces born within it towards the summit.

E. Experience has in fact proved that the masses can have a complete understanding of the most complex problems.

F. An isolated individual may reveal himself slow to understand a problem, but a group will grasp surprisingly quickly.

G. Everything can be explained to the masses, provided that one really wants them to understand.

So, complete with its own tool, its own method of operating, its own ways of recruiting, training and managing, its own view of participation, and its own philosophy, the Company in Quebec stood at the beginning of 1968 in an envious position in the Company, thanks to the drive of Martin Beliveau. Beliveau had created a separate Company and intended it to function that way. Ottawa staff and the council both went along with him. It is easy to see why. Beliveau was remarkably organized. When the Quebec branch came to a council meeting it came en masse, and well prepared. It never presented a shoddy project report. It never appeared to leave any information out. When it asked for something, the reasons were clearly outlined. Compared to the chaos throughout the rest of the Company, Quebec came across like Paradise Gained and its requests were granted, almost without question.

Alan Clarke and the council trusted Beliveau. They had no reason not to. He had been with the Company for some time and had always functioned well. His performance in Quebec, compared to what had gone on before, was inspiring. So he was left alone to plan his own structure and in effect, his own Company.

Beliveau's Company in late 1967 and early 1968 consisted of four large projects. These projects, using the figures of March 31st, 1968, had between 19 and 28 volunteers on them, two to three times larger than any English project.

The largest project was ACET — *Association co-operative d'economie familiale* — a joint venture between the CYC and the Confederation of National Trade Unions. The ACEF objective was far reaching, but started from a small base. Its purpose was to help people manage their own money. The volunteers could see this leading to democratic participation through mass education. Starting with consumer education, ACEF would start venturing into other areas with a compact, well-established base. The base would be in Montreal.

Centre-Est was more diversified than ACEF. It was situated in the middle of Montreal and included areas like Saint-Jacques, Saint-Jean Baptiste and Mile End. Its objectives were the same long-term objectives as all other Quebec projects — participation by the masses — and the issues were housing, welfare and recreation. The volunteers began by integrating themselves into existing citizen's committees. From here, they hoped to pick out leaders for taking over these groups or forming new ones.

In south-west Montreal, the volunteers on the Petite Bourgogne project were primarily concerned with urban renewal and expropriation. The city of Montreal wanted to tear down many homes in the area, but various factions in the city organized themselves to help the citizens fight the move. One faction was the CYC. There was an awareness, though, that the citizens would not become concerned until the threat from the city became imminent, so another plan was established to create communication links with other citizens in the area. The volunteers were sent to do surveys in industrial plants and to make contacts with union leaders. From this, it was felt that action committees and worker committees could be established.

The Lanauidiere project was the only one outside of Montreal, about 50 miles north-east of the city. The objectives were rather blurred at the beginning. The Company decided to become involved with all aspects of life in the area, but set about first compiling facts and asking questions which would lead "us to forms of intervention we are as yet unable to define".

To the Company's council and to the Ottawa staff, the projects in Quebec seemed sound enough. Their objectives sounded no more radical than the objectives of various projects in English-speaking Canada. But, there was one essential difference — political motivation.

If there had been someone on Ottawa staff well versed with Quebec and the subtle structures in that province in late 1967, early 1968, he might have been alarmed at the people being hired as volunteers and staff. The name Louis-Phillipe Aubert meant nothing to English-speaking staff, but even in 1967, it was a name known in the inner-circles of Quebec. Just as well known was Bernard Mataigne. Both Aubert and Mataigne had formerly been affiliated with the FLQ or the FLP, hard-core separatist organizations. There were other people being hired too whose pasts were suspect, but who weren't quite so well-known. The logical question could have been, why is Beliveau hiring these people? Beliveau must have been aware of their beliefs. As a man who knew and understood Quebec, this leads one to question Beliveau's own political stance.

No one did until it was too late, until indeed the Company in Quebec was firmly set on a course that would lead to a parliamentary inquiry almost two years later. The villains that Mayor Jean Drapeau and Lucien Saulnier, executive committee chairman of the city of Montreal, pointed to as subversive elements in the CYC, were, nearly without exception, people hired by Beliveau.

But, the Company in late 1968 was pleased with its choice of an associate director. Quebec was booming and Beliveau got the credit and the praise. The praise was unanimous until January 17th, 1968. It was on that day that the reality of what Beliveau had done began to emerge, and the Beliveau image began to crack.

At a Company press conference in Montreal, called obstensibly to show that the CYC was still alive and growing in Quebec, Beliveau stressed the independence of the Company in Quebec from the federal government. He went as far as to ask that the Company in Quebec be called "The Company of Young Quebecois".

His reason for the name change was that "this is an accomplished fact.

"The Quebec organization is now different and original in that it now has its own methods of recruiting, selecting and training volunteers, as well as its projects, internal structures, aims and methods.

"We constitute an independent organization of Quebec volunteers, independent of the federal government, independent of the provincial government. We now want this fact officially recognized."

For an employee of the Crown to make this statement was amazing enough, but the fact that it was made without the approval of Alan Clarke or the council of the Company served to magnify Beliveau's belief that the Company in Quebec was independent of the federal government and, consequently, of the Company of Young Canadians.

Alan Clarke had to respond.

"We don't see it as a declaration of independence," Clarke said. And added that Beliveau might have been misinterpreted. Unfortunately, most newspapers that covered the press conference carried Beliveau's viewpoints in some detail. Those viewpoints were explicit and misinterpretation was not a strong argument.

At its next meeting, the council reacted more strongly. It stated that the Company in Quebec was not independent. No one in Quebec really listened, and the receptionist in the Montreal office continued to answer the telephone with — "Bonjour, La Compagnie des Jeunes Quebecois".

Quebec was independent. Beliveau had given words to the obvious. No number of statements from Clarke or the council could change that fact — they had trusted too much and waited too long. Getting rid of Beliveau was not going to change the shape of things to come.

12
Problems with the Council

As the Company was breaking apart in English-speaking Canada and breaking away in Quebec, the governing body of the CYC continued to exhibit an amazing inability to solve problems.

The council membership had changed since the early days in 1966, but not enough to result in a substantial improvement in council's efficiency.

By the spring of 1968, Normand Asselin, Alan Clarke, Duncan Edmonds, Jacques Gerin, Claude Lebon, Art Pape, Gordon Selman, Lloyd Shaw, Richard Thompson and Maurice Strong had all resigned for one reason or another. Some of them weren't missed as they either contributed little at council meetings or didn't attend many. Others were difficult to replace. Shaw and Edmonds were two who had contributed a good deal of time and energy to the Company. Edmonds had left, presumably, because of the Company's veer to the left.

The most interesting departure was that of Art Pape. Early in 1967, the council became involved in a heated debate centering on remuneration for council members. The discussion took place on a Sunday afternoon and attendance at the meeting was poor. The issue was whether or not council members should be allowed to work as consultants on contract to the Company. Those in favor of contracts won, due in part to Alan Clarke's quoting of a government authority on the subject. The ceiling for the contracts was set at $100 a day, and it was fully expect-

ed that Art Pape would receive a contract to do research
work for the Company.

At the next council meeting there was a reversal. More
council members were in attendance and this, undoubtedly,
had an effect. It was decided that council members should
not accept contracts and remain on the council. Shortly
thereafter, Pape resigned from council and accepted a
contract at $75 a day.

The story of Art Pape doesn't end there. When his first
consultant's contract came up for renewal, council decided
that it should not be renewed. The decision was never
properly recorded in the council minutes and Pape got a few
more months of work with the Company. If this added
expense was not enough to rile council, an all-expense paid
trip to California and New Orleans by Pape on the Company's behalf finished them off.

The vacancies on council were filled by a series of
strong appointments. Some of these were: Leo Dorais,
director of permanent education at the University of
Montreal; Roger Tessier, professor of social psychology at
the same institution; Joseph Kanuka, a lawyer from Regina;
and Bevan Patterson, dean of Women at the University
of Calgary.

Through 1967 and into 1968, the council struggled
inefficiently with the Company.

Agendas were drawn up for meetings, but rarely completed. Discussions were long and disjointed, with little emphasis on the nitty-gritties. Administration, as an example,
was still being placed at the end of agendas and not receiving the kind of attention it so desperately needed. The
council, admittedly, was faced with many crisis situations.
There was the DePoe incident in Yorkville, Musallem being
charged in the Northwest Territories, DePoe again in Yorkville and Curtis on the west coast. The Company just never

seemed quiet enough to allow time for reflection and fore-sight. As a result, planning ahead was a dream the council never realized.

If all of the factions in the Company had been working together at this juncture on the many problems facing the organization, the outlook might not have been so drab. The truth is that a severe rift developed between the staff and the council, and the lack of trust between the council and the field remained constant.

The staff-council feud boiled down to a lack of faith in Alan Clarke on the part of some council members. They were becoming worried about the state of the Company's administration and, indeed, about the entire fabric of the CYC. When these concerns were brought to Clarke, one council member recalls, he would admit that administrative problems were evident and would say a re-organization was coming.

"The re-organizations became a bad joke. There were so many of them," the council member said.

Another area of doubt for council members was Clarke's method for implementing policy decisions. When he disliked a decision, implementation seemed to be either slow or non-existent. On the other hand, when council tried to slow down some moves, Clarke might proceed full steam ahead. This at any rate was the view of many of the council members.

At one point, some council members started to write questions before council meetings to ensure that the information they wanted would be forthcoming. The staff regarded this practice as a form of harassment, and it did nothing to help co-operation.

Clarke, for his part, was not entirely satisfied with the council. It was slow, undisciplined and did not develop some of the policies that he felt were needed. As a result of this lack of policy, Clarke was often forced to improvise. Some council members regarded this as Clarke's method of making his own policies and bypassing them. But two future executive directors were forced to follow the same course which seems to justify Clarke's position.

The field didn't pay much attention to the staff-council fight. The volunteers often had no particular liking for either of the parties and didn't really care who won. Their dissatisfaction with council was growing though.

Their main complaint was that the council was out of touch with the field and thus couldn't make proper policy decisions. A second complaint was an old one — volunteers should be controlling the Company, not appointed members. The volunteers were anxious to take over.

No one could question the validity of the volunteers' second complaint. The council in early 1968 was still wholly appointed and the legislation that formed the Company, and promised volunteer control, was becoming a farce. The volunteers agitated for representation on council for months. The staff and council, to lesser extents, began to make pleas to the government towards the same end. It was obvious that unless representation did come through the volunteers would rebel.

The government finally moved in early 1968 and announced that five council members would be elected by the volunteers. A half-way measure to be sure, but better than nothing. The Company election process swung into action, a process that had been set up months before, and came up with a pleasant surprise. Many council members and staff had been afraid that the volunteers would elect all radicals. Instead, they elected four moderate volunteers and one outsider.

The four volunteers were Dal Brodhead, Bob Davis from Everdale Place School, just outside of Toronto, Maurice Cloutier from ACEF in Montreal, and Paul-Andre Baril from the Joliette project in Quebec. The outsider was Stan Daniels of Edmonton, president of the Alberta Métis League.

The elected members were absorbed immediately into the council. Many outsiders expected an explosion to take place when the appointed and elected members met head-on. This was under-rating both groups. The elected members quietly inserted the field problems into meetings, but at the same time added their support to council's stand on administration. The appointed members began to become more aware of the field. Within a few meetings, appointed and elected members had come together so far that it was nearly impossible to tell them apart. The results should have calmed some of the government's fears about volunteers being too irresponsible and immature to run the Company. It didn't. There were too many other things worrying the government about the Company.

13
The Jerry Gambill Affair

As the Company of Young Canadians headed into Year Three, the staff-volunteer relationship looked worse all the time.

Volunteers felt that they were being manipulated by power-hungry staff members.

The staff voiced support of Alan Clarke's goal of decentralization in the field. They would talk about the committees of council, including the important program committee, where volunteers had representatives.

"It's tokenism. The staff still have control," the volunteers insisted.

Jerry Gambill and Rick Salter were their chief targets.

The staff were indeed powerful. Most of their power was not written into their job descriptions. It existed all the same, much to the discomfort of the volunteers. The staff in the Company decided virtually which volunteers should be hired and fired. The staff worked out budgets and allocated funds. The staff decided what kind of work was acceptable on a project. The staff decided who could travel and who couldn't.

At its peak, there were more than 40 Ottawa staff. When decentralization came in, this number was chopped to about 25 and field staff then numbered about 55. Despite their advantage in numbers, the field staff were no match for the Ottawa group, especially in the program area.

In the field, staff control was not so noticeable. Many staff members earnestly attempted to spread responsibility around to volunteers. Others did not. But the success of the field staff in handling their projects, in either case, was linked to their relations with the Ottawa staff. If the field staff had a friend in Ottawa he had security. Only two areas in the country managed to keep out of the favors list — Quebec and British Columbia. Quebec because Martin Beliveau had sole jurisdiction; British Columbia because the field staff were more competent there and would not tolerate the antics of Gambill and Salter.

For a while the two feudal lords, Gambill and Salter, prospered. They were making fat salaries, had good expense accounts, lots of responsibilities and part of the ear of their overseer — Alan Clarke. But inevitably, the lords became angry with each other. At stake was the balance of power in the Company. The two men, backed by their respective knights, began to make passes at each other. The resulting clash started the Company's time for plots and assassinations.

It also marked the beginning of the end for Alan Clarke.

Gambill joined the Company in the summer of 1967 as a consultant on the Lanark County project. He had been picked up by the CYC immediately after Indian Affairs had fired him from his job on the St. Regis Indian Reserve on Cornwall Island. Gambill had not left quietly and the affair had been particularly messy. Once with the Company, Gambill rose very quickly. Towards the end of the summer of 1967, he was appointed regional director for Ontario. And when the Company decentralized, he was appointed associate director in charge of English programs.

The reasons for this appointment are somewhat mysterious. One could assume that Gambill had done an outstanding job in Ontario as director. But, at the time, there were certainly stronger projects elsewhere. He had an amazing talent for helping Indian projects get off the ground, that no one denied. He also exuded a quiet charisma and was quite likeable. His knowledge of community development seemed sound enough, though hardly outstanding, and he was not without administrative talents. On the other hand, Gambill's previous work record was spotty. He had held many jobs for short intervals of time. It could be said that the Company offered a man with his talents, integrity and unstructured ways the perfect opportunity. No one seemed to think that Indian Affairs might have had good reason for getting rid of him.

In any event, Gambill was hired. It was the highest position he had ever held and the salary was about $14,000 a year.

Rick Salter was even more of a mystery. Salter was a Company veteran and the Company's radical of radicals. So radical was he that when the Company considered putting a project in an iron curtain country and was conducting talks with that country's embassy, the embassy called to ask secretly if someone other than Mr. Salter could come to talk to them — he was too left wing. Whether this is part of the Salter legend, or a true event, it was a favorite story.

Salter was a man who drew extreme reactions from people. Some in the Company worshipped him for his intellect, his community development knowledge, his ability to turn-on projects, and his love of people. His detractors accused him of being sneaky, of bleeding the Company, and of playing great job-giver. They pointed to the fact that despite his love of people and volunteers he still drew a large salary, in the $14,000 a year range. His wife was also on contract to the Company as a consultant. And, it appeared that many of his American friends were employed by the Company, in fact, given preference over Canadians.

Gambill's job turned out to be the main contention between the two men. The job carried enormous responsibilities. Gambill had to oversee the activities of more than 20 projects spread from British Columbia to the Maritimes. For several months, Gambill criss-crossed Canada by airplane. He travelled for more than 20 days a month, living out of a valise. At each stop he would run through his assorted tasks, offer advice if any was needed and then head for the next project. It was a grueling pace and the work accumulated rapidly. He tried to cut down on it by phoning instructions to Ottawa as he travelled. But many of his instructions were not properly carried out. By the time Gambill returned to Ottawa, he would have to face the regular paperwork that someone in his position always has, plus try to solve the problems that had been raised in the field. As it would turn out, he just didn't have time to handle everything before he was off again.

The things that weren't done, the promises that weren't kept, began to cause bad feelings on some projects. Some understood Gambill's predicament and still stood by him. Others felt he was deliberately trying to destroy their projects. Many of Salter's friends believed the latter.

For as Gambill travelled, so did Salter. He too had many responsibilities, some of them over-lapping with Gambill's. Salter gave advice on such things as techniques of community development and the way to be the ideal volunteer. He developed a hard-core of supporters.

Jerry Gambill, over-extended as he was, kept making enemies in the first two months of 1968. If his enemies had been volunteers only, he might have survived. Volunteer dissatisfaction alone was never enough to cause a staff person to be fired. But he aggravated some staff members whose real power now became visible.

The lever that was used against him was the southern Saskatchewan project. The complaint was that he was playing favorites with projects — giving favors to those that he liked; damaging those he didn't like. His enemies claimed that he had a share in the responsibility for the collapse of the Saskatchewan project.

The project had started in fall of 1967 as an experiment

in adult education. The man behind it was John Ferguson of Fort Qu'Appelle, a former Indian Affairs man who had bucked the bureaucracy much like Gambill. It wasn't enough to bring them together.

The Company gave Ferguson 13 trainees to teach the skills of adult education. The training would take months, but once completed, the young people would be turned loose on Indian Reserves and small towns as educators to prove Ferguson's belief that adult education was the key to solving many of the Native peoples' problems. His CYC project would never back up this belief.

Things started to go wrong almost as soon as the trainees arrived in Fort Qu'Appelle, a dusty, rural town with strict notions about right and wrong.

The trainees had been a motley bunch. Some of them more concerned with rhetoric than work, others more with sex than rhetoric. Ferguson found this group singularly disinterested in adult education, and bored with the idea of training. On the other hand, many trainees blamed their attitudes on Ferguson. He had made them promises when they were selected and some of the promises were never kept, they said. They also disliked his authoritarian attitude.

By February, 1968, Bob Luker was the only original trainee left. A sincere young man, but not one without problems, Luker headed into the field in early 1968 and soon became convinced that his biggest problem was John Ferguson. He was convinced that Ferguson was misusing Company equipment and funds. He was convinced that Ferguson was lying to him. He started talking to Jerry Gambill.

Ferguson, meanwhile, was also talking to Gambill. Luker's volunteer contract should have arrived in Fort Qu'Appelle by February. Luker was convinced that Ferguson had never asked for it. Ferguson kept saying that Gambill wouldn't send it. The truth has never come out.

The situation became so bad that Luker arrived in Ottawa

in February with his complaints against Ferguson. A meeting was held in Clarke's office. The upshoot of it all was that Ferguson was asked to resign. The bad blood between Gambill and Ferguson was visible. Gambill thought that Ferguson was withholding support from the volunteer, and considered him to be not suitable CYC material. Clarke evidently agreed with Gambill's evaluation.

After the axe had fallen, Gambill was afraid that Ferguson might raise a stink in Saskatchewan and ordered his information officer to go to Regina to avert a possible disaster. He was met in Winnipeg by Wally Kubiski, a council member, who was going to Saskatchewan to clean up administrative matters.

Both men went with Gambill's warnings ringing in their ears. He told them that Ferguson had probably been misusing Company funds and was perhaps guilty of misleading volunteers.

When the two men finally met with Ferguson in Fort Qu'Appelle. Jerry Gambill's assessment was slightly undermined. Kubiski found that all Company equipment was intact and all Company purchase orders were in order. Ferguson also talked at length about his battle with Gambill. He swore that Gambill had been trying to destroy his project. One example of harassing tactics used was the apparent presence of Marty Sawma in Regina. Sawma, an American, had been listed several weeks earlier on a staff list as a program consultant attached to Gambill's directorate. Ferguson said that Sawma had been in Regina a week before and had called him. The American, apparently on Gambill's orders, had wanted Ferguson to turn over the Company purchase orders to him.

At this point, the subject of Ferguson's resignation was raised. Was he going to go quietly or raise a stink? He said that that depended on the outcome of a meeting being held in Ottawa that weekend.

At the Parkway Motel on Rideau Street, about a dozen

staff gathered on the second weekend in February. The main adversaries were Gambill and Salter, but Salter was backed by most of the staff present. There were Ron Christiansen from Northwestern Ontario, Jim Kinzel from Toronto, Judi Bernstein from Toronto, and Jim Littleton, destination Ottawa, among others in attendance. Clarke did not take part in the proceedings.

Gambill was out-numbered and was forced to retreat. It is significant, however, that the incident that sparked the rebellion, the Ferguson resignation, was not reversed.

Gambill called a small staff meeting, himself and three others, and outlined his position. On a board he listed the duties of Martin Beliveau, Rick Salter and himself. According to Gambill, his responsibilities had been pared away to almost nothing. Rick Salter, however, stood shoulder to shoulder with Martin Beliveau.

The outcome of the meeting was completely clear. Salter was now an unofficial associate director.

What should Gambill do? Protest, he was told.

At the end of March, Rick Salter appeared in Clarke's office and quietly dropped a bomb.

Jerry Gambill had had an alleged homosexual affair with a volunteer!

What an extraordinary thing for a new leftist to use against anyone! The people's Company, the organization that represented the new enlightened spirit in Canada was lowered to this level.

Alan Clarke regarded Salter's information as a political ploy designed to get rid of Gambill. He told Salter this, but reacted predictably.

He went to Gambill, told him of the disclosure and asked him to leave.

The CYC had hit an all time low, even considering its short history.

Clarke's role in this turgid little drama is confusing. He

claimed that he never knew of Gamibll's loss of power to Salter. Since nearly everyone else in the Company was aware of it, this appears unlikely.

The reasons for Clarke's actions are well known.

Clarke maintained that Gambill's supposed homosexuality was not a factor in his decision. The important point was that Gambill's actions had jeopardized the working relationship between the associate director and a subordinate, the volunteer. If Gambill had an affair with a female volunteer, Clarke said, his decision would be the same.

Gambill's letter of resignation was polite and restrained, and hinted a little at the deep pain he must have felt. He had not been an evil man; the number of people in the Company who loved him proved that. He had just been a staff member with power who offended another staff member with power. The structure of the Company was perhaps as much at fault as Gambill.

"I regret, but without apology, that my position as associate director has been considered as untenable. I have assured you that I would do nothing inconsistent with the effort I have made to build a strong Company and this I will be leaving," he wrote.

The reason for Gambill's resignation was not kept a secret within the Company. Clarke told one staff member while he was in Toronto to give a speech. He also told some volunteers. The protests began.

The volunteers, as idealistic and straightforward as ever, knew that the staff controlled the Company. They had remarked on that often enough. A fight between two staff members should not have shocked them, for after all two enemies fighting was not an uncomfortable situation. That the fight should be resolved in such a manner, though, revolted them. They wrote letters to Alan Clarke and to the Company-at-large to express their disgust.

Lynn Curtis was particularly abrasive. He stated that

Gambill should have been fired for incompetence, but never because of his sexual relations.

If there is any event in the Company's history that marks the turning point, this was it.

Up until the Gambill affair, the Company seemed to be an instrument for potential good. It was an instrument that sputtered, ran into problems, and never lived up to many expectations, but at least the ends were decent, as were most of the means. When the Company destroyed Jerry Gambill, though, a lot of the decency left. And instead of being an inexperienced organization making the mistakes of youth, the CYC became as sordid and ugly as any of the institutions and structures it was fighting.

Alan Clarke lost some respect. He had had a difficult decision to make, of that there is no doubt. The most moral volunteers, though, felt he had made a poor choice.

Rick Salter did not, in the long run, gain the foothold he was seeking. He still seemed close to Clarke, but left Montreal shortly after the Gambill fiasco. He would never again be a major factor in the Company.

Overall, the Gambill affair helped no one in the Company and, in fact, did the organization a good deal of harm. The Company and Alan Clarke had been able to weather all criticisms thus far, but its morality was now tainted and the Company would never regain it. Quebec lay ahead and would continue the self-destruction that the Company had chosen.

14

Enter Phil Girard

At about the same time that Jerry Gambill was being toppled from power, the Company's first full fiscal year of operations was ending. The financial picture did nothing to brighten the months of April and May for Alan Clarke.

Phrased simply, the Company's administration hadn't functioned properly. More elaborately, it had created the worst kind of financial mess imaginable.

The council had guessed this might happen at the end of the fiscal year and months before had hired Touche, Ross, Bailey and Smart, an accounting firm, to help clean the situation up. The firm placed one of its men, Glen Brown, in the Company full-time in January, 1968. Two months later Brown became the Company's financial administrator. Both he and the firm tried valiantly to help, but there was only so much they could do.

They discovered a multitude of expenditures without proper authorization; when they found some with authorization, receipts would be missing. Travelling was another sore point. Company policy demanded that there be explanations for trips that staff took. There were hundreds of trips without such explanations. The entire batch were turned over to Clarke and memos sent to staff members asking why they took such and such a trip two, four or eight months before. It was, at the least, an unsatisfactory way of keeping books for a $2.4 million dollar organization.

The auditors threw up their hands in disgust and it was rumoured that they almost walked off the job. The government decided to step in.

Early in the spring, Doug Ward was asked to come to

the Prime Minister's office. He went and was informed that the government wanted to put a comptroller in the Company. Ward took the proposal to Clarke and the council. Clarke was furious. He regarded the government's plan as a personal insult and as an infringement on the freedom of the Company. He found some council members agreed with him. Ward returned to the government and a compromise was reached. He outlined the plan in a memo to the Company.

Some weeks ago, the Prime Minister's Office expressed concern to me about aspects of our personnel and financial administration during this past period of rapid growth within the Company.

The Provisional Council discussed this and the proposal that a government comptroller be assigned to our staff. Council decided that such an assignment would not be helpful for the independence of the Company. At the same time, we recognized that we could make good use of someone with skills in the above areas for a given period of time. We also realized that having a government person working in cooperation with our staff, under conditions agreeable to us, would have a long-range positive effect upon relations with the government. This latter consideration is extremely important in light of the support — financial and otherwise — that we will need from the government for the expansion of our programme.

As a result, Mr. P.F. (Phil) Girard is presently working with the Company in personnel and financial matters, with the title "Administrative Counsellor". He has both the work of a consultant for systems development, and involvement in current business — with whatever exceptions the Council considers advisable. Any reports he makes to the Council first go through Alan Clarke, and reports to the Government will first go to the Council. Under this arrangement, which we have agreed should last until the end of August, the Council feels that the internal lines of authority within the Company are not interrupted, and that our relations with government stand to be improved without loss of independence. Phil has already done an excellent report for us on personnel administration. Most of his recommendations were approved at the recent meeting of the Provisional Council. He will continue to work on this, and on financial administration with Glen Brown — who merits the praise of all of us for the impressive innovations he has implemented in this area since coming to the Company in January.

Council members regret the great amount of time that they have spent on administrative matters, when this is but "housekeeping". There is certainly a confident feeling on Council now that the work of the staff in these areas is going to free us for policy and programme discussions, which we know is the most important thing for you, and the most interesting for us.

Even the compromise did not please Clarke much. He suspected that some council members were out to get him and that Phil Girard was nothing more than a spy. He knew that Girard had worked with R.A.J.Phillips for some time and linked the two of them together.

Girard was aware of Clarke's suspicions when he arrived in the Company office, but didn't let that deter him. He started doing job descriptions and did some preliminary work on an organizational chart. The work was forwarded to council and nearly all of it met with its approval. Then a freeze began and Girard's work began to slow down. Clarke had absolutely no time for him and made it clear he would only be happy when Girard was gone. Girard did not make things easier for himself. An extremely efficient man, he was appalled by many of the things he saw going on in the Company. His efficiency was coupled with an honesty that moved him into face-to-face confrontations with Clarke, hardly the thing for an administrative counsellor to win at. And, Girard didn't win.

His consolation prize was very little work to do and lots of time for golf.

In the meantime, the auditors were compiling the year's financial report. It wasn't good.

In the year 1967-68, the Company managed to spend $90,000 more than it had been granted. It had spent money in some strange areas.

Staff salaries accounted for $623,604; Transportation and communications for $427,401; Professional and special services, $489,019. The volunteers received $526,904, or less than 25 per cent of the Company's funds.

The auditors capped off the figures by providing a lukewarm letter to accompany them to the minister responsible for the Company at that time, Jean Marchand.

The letter read in part:

"Throughout the year we worked with the Company's staff to introduce controls to overcome various weaknesses that became apparent as the year progressed. Finally, we found it necessary to perform a detailed review and analysis of the transactions for the year . . . .

"In our opinion and according to the best of our information and the explanations given to us and as shown by the books of the Company, these financial statements are properly drawn up as to give a true view of the state of affairs of the Company."

In the lexicon of the auditors' world, this was a disapproving statement. Alan Clarke was in trouble and Martin Beliveau was waiting in the wings to help finish him off.

15

Clarke and Beliveau Resign

The spring of 1968 was a time for plots.

In English-speaking Canada, the plotters met in each others' homes and in restaurants. They were council members, staff members and people not directly connected to the Company. The Jerry Gambill affair was discussed. The Company's financial picture was analyzed. Everything was done indirectly at first. No one said that the time for action had come, but they felt it all the same.

In Quebec the meetings were perhaps not quite so secret. This was an all-Company plot. They talked about the problems of Quebec and like those in English Canada decided the time for action had come.

The Company of Young Canadians was wobbling. The financial picture was jumbled; the staff situation apparently out of control; projects were suffering from the internal strife so noticeable in Ottawa. Something had to be done to get the CYC back on the road towards its destiny. The Company could not be allowed to drift towards destruction. But, how could one get the Company moving in the right direction again?

"Get rid of Martin Beliveau," was Quebec's answer.

"Get rid of Alan Clarke," said some of the English.

Quebec moved first.

In March, Alan Clarke received a letter from Andre Bonin, the CYC staff member on the Montreal ACEF project. The letter was signed by other staff members as well, but Bonin was the main man to deal with.

The letter demanded that Martin Beliveau be fired. If he wasn't, the staff would hold a demonstration on Parliament Hill in May.

There were two major items in the letter. One concerned the recent suspension of Bonin by Beliveau; the other was a hint at the separatist leanings of the Quebec associate director.

Since Beliveau had taken over Quebec, the Company there had grown quickly under his sure, effective hand. The position of strength and unity, however, was an illusion. Beliveau had built too quickly and not supplied enough of a base. In English-speaking Canada there was at least the concept of social change and volunteerism to keep things together. In Quebec, nearly every concept was subjected to the pressures and strain from two issues — project sovereignty and political ideology.

The fight originally sprung from the budget cut that Prime Minister Pearson inflicted on the Company the previous December. The government pared away half-a-million dollars from the Company's budget, a cut of about 20 per cent. The Company decided that the regions would have to operate on budgets cut by a similar percentage. This was unpalatable to Beliveau.

Beliveau came up with two ideas that would ease the financial pinch. He suggested that staff become volunteers. This would result in the saving of thousands of dollars in salary — money that could be channelled into the project. He also suggested that some projects become supporters of other projects. This integration would help most projects grow without really adding to total volunteer numbers.

The reactions to his methods of saving money were predictable. Some staff did not want to lose their salaries and had no intention of letting Beliveau institute such a move without opposition. And the project that would have become the main supporting project, ACEF, did not want to be virtually disbanded. It decided, along with the staff, to oppose Beliveau.

The ACEF project was a jointly-financed venture between the CYC and the Confederation of National Trade Unions. It was not radical in its work — consumer budgeting — and could be called a service project. Beliveau was not an admirer of service work. He wanted change. The project assumed this was the underlying reason for his supportive role suggestion.

The opposing sides began to skirmish in February. By March, the battle lines were firmly drawn and project work almost stopped completely. The war was beginning and everyone seemed ready to take part.

On one side stood the staff opposed to Beliveau. With them were the ACEF volunteers, determined to hang onto their project and their independence. On another side stood Beliveau with the staff and volunteers who supported him. By themselves were the rest of the volunteers, those who owed no allegiance to anyone in the Company. They were, however, just as willing to get involved to advance their own beliefs.

In a document released in Quebec, the Beliveau side of the dispute was expressed.

The document slapped at the service-type project:

" . . . many members, volunteers and staff, no longer have confidence in the aim of participation of the population through '*animation sociale*' and openly challenge it. Here is the first element of division and conflict."

It accused the opposing staff of manipulating and leading volunteers.

"The day that project staff broke with the directorate (Beliveau) to make common cause with the volunteers, many Company members ceased to respect their particular status . . . . Some of the staff made use of their status, their authority and their information to consciously lead the volunteers astray and provoke their aggressivity against the directorate. Here is the second element of division and conflict!"

It charged that the Company in Quebec had no respect for the leadership of the directorate.

"Many have turned against the directorate and challenged it openly. Hence the third element . . . . "

Familiar patterns emerge — patterns that would repeat themselves more quickly as the Company aged.

As for the volunteers? They saw themselves as the only people who should have political power in the Company. They saw the staff as careerists and despised them for their high salaries. Against the staff, the volunteers had unity.

This unity was broken when volunteers faced each other in conflicting ideology. It was the radicals against the non-radicals, proving that the CYC was not a place to find the tolerance that the volunteers demanded government have towards minority groups and opinions.

The Quebec battle was, in fact, fought at this level of intolerance. No side wanted to give an inch — it would be all or nothing.

If this was not obvious in February when the sides were developing, it certainly became clear in early March. Beliveau set up a committee consisting of himself and the four project co-ordinators in an attempt to find better methods of co-ordination. The committee could not even co-ordinate itself. On March 11th, after barely a week in operation, the committee erupted; the co-ordinators walked out. They spent the next week organizing volunteers against Beliveau.

Andre Bonin was the prime organizer and Beliveau moved against him. He first tried to fire him, but eventually had to settle for a suspension.

Bonin reacted to the suspension by sending the letter to Alan Clarke.

It is interesting to note that the problems in Quebec were exceedingly complex and not really personality oriented. The moment the issue left Quebec, however, it boiled down to Bonin versus Beliveau and the important issues were forgotten.

Clarke did not respond to the threat the letter contained. The Company's council had been aware that all was not well in Quebec and had authorized council vice-chairman Roger Tessier to do a study in the province. Clarke called Tessier and told him about the most recent development. It was agreed that Tessier would handle the situation.

After some consideration, Tessier made his recommendation to Clarke. The status quo should be maintained, he said.

His reasoning was sound. Both the Bonin and the Beliveau camps were ready to fight. If Clarke came down on the side of either of the men, then the fighting would break out. The big loser would be the Company in Quebec.

If the situation would hold for a month until Tessier's report to council was completed then the affair might be more rationally handled. It was a gamble, but one that Clarke agreed had to be made.

Clarke was given the task of breaking the news to both parties. He went to Montreal and did his job. It was a futile attempt. Things had gone too far for such a long delay. Clarke had not been able to resolve the problem, Bonin's forces decided. The time had come to switch the battle to a higher level.

The Company had a new cabinet minister responsible for its activities to Parliament. He was Gerard Pelletier, the Secretary of State, and a man well acquainted with the climate of his home province.

According to the legislation, the Company was independent of the government. Pelletier had no actual power in exchange for his responsibility to Parliament. The Bonin forces decided to give this a test.

A dossier was sent to Pelletier from Quebec. It contained material designed to show that Martin Beliveau was a separatist. It included, among other things, a statement that said that the purpose of the CYC in Quebec was to get enough federal funds to build a strong nationalist movement in the province.

The statement was attributed to Beliveau.

The dossier found its way into the hands of Marc Lalonde, the principal assistant to Prime Minister Trudeau and a CYC council member. Lalonde called Clarke and asked for an explanation. Clarke called Beliveau and asked for the same. Beliveau denied the allegations and wrote a letter outlining his allegiance to the Company.

The government made no move towards the Company because of the dossier. But, this was only Bonin's first attempt. The seed had been planted, now it needed to be cultivated.

Separatism was the ideal issue. The Liberal party was becoming involved in an election and any hint of separatism in a federal agency would not have helped. The dossier had carried no threats with it, though. No promises of demonstrations. It could therefore be assumed that the government saw no need for interfering with the Company at that point. If everything was kept quiet then no harm would be done.

The dossier was not Pelletier's first clue that the Company in Quebec was becoming a separatist organization. He had had his first hint in a more personal way and, true to form, the Company in its disregard for Parliament and political processes provided the Secretary of State with that hint.

Pelletier's son had tried to join the Company in Quebec earlier in the year. He was interviewed by all four projects and then rejected. There was a rumour that he had been kept out by Beliveau's staff because he was not enough of a separatist. There seems to be some truth in the rumour.

Whether Beliveau ordered young Pelletier kept out or not is another matter. Beliveau was on shaky ground and his authority was being questioned. It is unlikely that he had that kind of power. In fact, his political ideology was not clearly known, and guessing what it really was became a sort of game.

On one hand, he pledged his allegiance to the Company in Quebec. On the other, he pressed for an independent Company in Quebec, hired well-known separatists and refused to commit himself to federalism.

Phil Girard, the man the government forced on the Company, went to Montreal to meet Beliveau on one occasion. Always frank, Girard asked Beliveau about his political leanings. Beliveau answered that he hadn't made his mind up yet. Given Beliveau's sophisticated commitment to *animation sociale* and other structures, Girard found this impossible to believe and came away convinced that the associate director was indeed a separatist.

Others were as sure. Andre Saindon, Quebec's main information officer, resigned in the spring. He told his Ottawa counterpart that he was frightened by the direction Beliveau was taking. He was certain that Beliveau would stop at little to aid the separatist cause.

Clarke believed that Beliveau was being misrepresented.

The government, as noted before, did not react to such personal opinions or to the dossier. It appeared genuinely determined to give the Company its independence. This changed rapidly.

In May a telegram arrived at Pelletier's office. It was from the Quebec staff who opposed Beliveau.

It stated that unless Beliveau was fired, they and the volunteers would demonstrate on Parliament Hill. They would claim that the Company in Quebec was being controlled by separatists.

This was the threat that had been missing from the dossier. It presented a political danger to a government that was moving into an election campaign within days.

The government reacted predictably and politically.

Pelletier called in Roger Tessier for a meeting. Tessier, the council's vice-chairman, was a Liberal and it can be assumed that he wanted no harm to come to the Liberal party.

The next day, Alan Clarke was called to Montreal for a meeting with Tessier, the minister, and Andre Ouellette, Pelletier's executive assistant. The men talked for several hours, but there was no compromise. The message was succinct.

Beliveau had to go.

This government intervention in Company affairs cannot be denied. It was a clear break from the Company's legislation. The question on everyone's mind was why did the government interfere.

Some argue that Martin Beliveau was a dangerous separatist and that the government interfered to save the Company. Attached to this is the presumption that Alan Clarke was incapable of solving the problem and, in fact, incapable of running the Company. So by forcing the Beliveau issue, the government could get rid of Beliveau and Clarke at the same time.

Others maintain that the government's action was solely political. The Liberal party was beginning an election campaign and Martin Beliveau was a threat to the smoothness of that campaign. The party could kill Beliveau without any major repercussions since he was relatively unknown in the province.

If it didn't kill him, Andre Bonin would demonstrate and unpleasant publicity would be the least of the problems. Bonin was backed by the CNTU, the organization that had spawned Jean Marchand, among others. It has a broad political base in the province and is not a body to be ignored.

No matter which direction one takes, it is obvious that

Beliveau would be the loser — and so would Clarke.

Clarke could have ignored the demands of Tessier and the Liberals. He could have refused to fire Beliveau — his right as executive director. But what would that lead to? It could mean the end of the Company, something Clarke did not want. It would certainly lead to a fight with the Company's governing council — a scrap Clarke was sure he would lose.

After the meeting, Clarke returned to Ottawa to make up his mind — fight or resign with Beliveau. It was a difficult decision. If the Beliveau issue was all that was at stake, Clarke might have stood a chance. It wasn't however. It is at this point that one must leave Quebec for a moment and look briefly at the other plot.

This plot in English-speaking Canada is important because it severely undermined Alan Clarke's credibility. It took away anything that he could stand on to fight, and undoubtedly helped the government decide to move against Beliveau.

It was not as well-organized as the one against Beliveau in Quebec, but it was much more secret.

The plotters worked separately, each doing his best to get at Alan Clarke. They avoided organizing in the Company, regarding that as too volatile. Their aim was to bring as much outside pressure as possible on Clarke, hoping that he would resign.

The first step was the press. Stories were leaked about the Company's administrative confusion, and about the unhappiness in the Company. The blame was layed squarely at Clarke's feet.

Editorials were asked for and delivered — editorials that were harsh on the present condition of the Company. The *Globe and Mail* was particularly helpful in this regard. Michael Valpy of that paper had been an information officer with the Company. He had returned to the *Globe* after his stint with the CYC with a bitter taste in his mouth. He disliked Clarke and Rick Salter and was not opposed to skewering either of them.

The next move was writing letters and sending telegrams to the government – all deploring the present situation in the Company and demanding the removal of Alan Clarke. The most explicit came from the Company's public relations consultants – Berger, Tisdall, Clarke and Lesly of Toronto.

The firm had been concerned about the Company for some time, but wasn't sure what could be done about it. In normal circumstances, a firm in this position would stop working with its client. BTCL took a different stance. It reasoned that everyone had been dropping out of the Company and letting the mess continue. Someone had to stick in and fight. They decided not to drop out.

A two-page letter outlining graphically the faults of Clarke and the Company was sent to the minister's office. Clarke also received a copy. It had an effect.

For awhile Clarke was deciding whether to fight or resign he was also concocting a strategy. If he fought, he would use government interference as his rallying cry. Informants within the Ottawa office told the English plotters about Clarke's plans. Soon after a newspaper story appeared in the *Ottawa Citizen*. It recounted the misadventures of the Company and said it was about time that the government did step in.

Clarke gave up. Whether the story was a reason or not, or whether the letter from BTCL was a factor, isn't clear, but it is obvious that they took away most of the fighting ground that Clarke had.

Clarke met with Martin Beliveau in Ottawa and asked him to resign. In Clarke's mind, it was either the Company or Beliveau. Beliveau left without giving an answer. His resignation arrived a few days later. Doug Ward, the council chairman, was notified of its arrival. He was told at the same time that Alan Clarke would also be resigning. Under the circumstances there was not much else that the executive director could do.

Clarke's intentions were expressed to Ward in person. The chairman said a council meeting would be held in two weeks at which time the letter could be presented. It turned out to be a hectic two weeks.

Some people in English-speaking Canada found it difficult to believe that Clarke was really going to resign. Some of them even met once to go over the entire situation. Present at that meeting were R.A.J. Phillips, a council member; Phil Girard; David Gamble, representing the Toronto public relations consulting firm; and Andre Ouellette, the minister's assistant.

The phones in Company offices across the country were in constant use during this time. Clarke's right-hand man, Jim Littleton, called every project in the Company to tell them not to organize on behalf of Clarke. It isn't known if they would have anyway. Others were also calling the projects with the same message, but for a different reason — they wanted Clarke to have no encouragement.

At this time, people were also trying to push various Company members into the interim directorship. They believed that Clarke was going to resign, and the thought did not make them that unhappy. The chance was there to put one of their own in command. Dal Brodhead, the Company's first volunteer and an elected council member, was touted. Some Ottawa staff, the Company members in British Columbia and the public relations consultant all thought Brodhead would be ideal. He was young, intelligent, middle-class, a volunteer and had a spotless record. Council members were called and given this opinion. But the members had other plans in mind.

On June 15th the phoning stopped. Alan Clarke presented his letter of resignation to the council.

He was resigning, he said, to underline the threat to the

Company from inappropriate intervention by the government.

There is no doubt that there was intervention and that it wasn't proper under the legislation. The larger question was whether the condition of the Company warranted such a move.

The council tried to present this argument in a memorandum to the staff and volunteers. In the memo, Doug Ward took the fault from the government's shoulders and placed it on the Company itself — finally answering the question that the press had been asking.

"The specific action of the government which precipitated Alan's resignation was the involvement of the minister in the discussions which led to Martin Beliveau's resignation," Ward wrote. "The personnel committee of the council looked into that situation very carefully and recommended to council that . . . . 'there were no grounds for refusing Mr. Beliveau's resignation . . . . ' This decision of committee was reached on the basis of a careful study of the staff situation in Quebec and not on the basis of irregular pressure from any source. It was noted by the committee that some mysterious documents had been compiled for use against Martin. The committee went on record by rejecting these documents as having had any influence on the decision of the committee.

"As the weekend meeting progressed, it became clear to us that the problem underlying the present was not government interference as much as it was strife internal to the Company. In brief, one group of people was able to involve the minister in an internal problem in an unfair and improper way. This is not to say that the government has not interfered with the affairs of the Company . . . .

"Alan's resignation was accepted with regret and with great gratitude for his long, patient and most valuable service to the Company. His often sacrificial contribution to the Company now demands a like contribution and commitment from the rest of us if we are to survive independently and go ahead, as we must . . . . " Ward concluded.

With that last flowery paragraph, Alan Clarke was officially gone from the Company. Ended were his two hectic, crisis-filled years.

The council was more than glad to see him go. The fact that his resignation would not mean fewer problems for the Company in future months and years didn't occur to them at the time. They were too happy at Clarke's departure, so sure that he had been mainly responsible for the Company's woes, to realize that the troubles he left behind would magnify themselves, not disappear.

What were the problems?

Quebec stood high above the rest. The incidents in Quebec seemed to show that the province was out of control. No one knew how accurate the insinuations of separatist domination were. No one know if Martin Beliveau was a separatist leader and had built a separatist-based organization. No one could be sure how strong the projects in Quebec really were.

There were other questions as well. How strong were the volunteers? Could the council and the Ottawa office exert authority in Quebec?

Finally, council members and staff asked each other: Had the Company been involved in recent bombings in Montreal? How much did the RCMP know?

These last questions were the result of rumours and hints that had been circulating in the Company. There had been bombings in Montreal and the separatist charges tended to link, indirectly, the Company with those bombings. If the rumours were true, no one could blame Pelletier for interfering with the Company.

The English-speaking projects were causing some concern as well. So much time had been spent trying to iron out Quebec, applying administrative bandages, and watching internal staff bloodletting, that these projects had been virtually ignored. The quality and stability of the English-speaking projects was in question, and it was generally assumed that they were deteriorating.

Administratively, the doubts were just as severe. The Company had wasted untold thousands of dollars. Staff had been living and travelling in luxury. Consultants came and went at a dizzying pace. The books were garbled.

All of these worries, Quebec, administration and English-speaking projects, had been translated eventually into government and public dissatisfaction with the Company. This worked its way into council displeasure with Alan Clarke. The problems, all of them, were attributed to him.

As executive director, Clarke was the man who was responsible for the day-to-day activities of the Company. He hired and fired staff. He saw to it that projects functioned smoothly. He was responsible for the efficient administering of the Company's funds.

Clarke's personal philosophy did not lend itself to these responsibilities.

"I am not a leader," he said on more than one occasion.

His analogy of the Indian keeper of the fire was another favorite. He would not build the fire or determine how well it would burn, he would simply make sure that it never went out.

Clarke believed in the concept of the Company. He saw it as a unstructured body that was different from anything yet created by any government or business, and refused to bring into it the philosophies of business or government.

Administratively he was not a worrier. The Company badly overspent during his last year and obvious policies, such as a travel policy, were missing, or not implemented. He believed that administration could be humane, but had difficulty seeing how efficiency could be added without destroying the humaneness. He kept several people in administration, for example, whose competence was in doubt. Shortly after he left, they were fired.

Firing people was another taboo with Clarke. He considered that procedure to be authoritarian, a control-mechanism, and could not see its relationship to the Company. Firing was fine for the establishment — business and government — but not for the CYC. The result was that the Company kept many incompetents on its payroll for months. This was a waste of money and damaging to the rest of the Company.

People did leave during Clarke's reign and the procedure that was used was perhaps more painful than plain firing. Business and government may be authoritarian in their attitudes, but at least they are quick and sudden. The Company's way was ostracization. People who earned the displeasure of senior staff would be effectively shut out of the Company's decision-making process. They would no longer be consulted about anything, and when they asked questions would be given no answers. They would eventually assume they had done something wrong, but when they asked would most likely be informed that their work was satisfactory. The subject of the torture would believe that for a few days, but the ostracization would begin to have its effect again. He would begin to worry. His work would become worse. The worrying would increase. Finally, totally frustrated, alienated, and sometimes bitter, the person would resign.

For some unfathomable reason, the Company regarded this as humane treatment of its employees.

Clarke was regarded as a kind, committed man. His trust of people was well-known. He saw the good side of most and forgave, quite easily, the bad. Unfortunately, not enough people returned the trust that Clarke put in them and, his judgement when hiring was suspect.

Clarke hired Martin Beliveau and Jerry Gambill. He gave them huge responsibilities and trusted them to carry them out. When they got in trouble and nearly tore the Company apart, their failures were a reflection on Clarke. If he had had a closer check on them, if he had not trusted them so totally, he might have been the one to initiate their demise in the Company. Or he might have been able to defend them more adequately when they were subjected to attacks from sources other than their immediate superior — Clarke. Instead, he did trust them and when they got tarred and feathered he was spattered.

One could assume that Clarke had an overwhelming desire to see the Company grow and survive. One could believe that he had faith in the Company and its future. Most people affiliated with Clarke in the Company accepted this as so, but it raises questions.

If he wanted the Company to be something special why did he leave it open to attack on issues like administrative incompetence? Clarke personally could have ignored a good many parts of administration if he had hired competent people to run things properly and to clear out the dead wood. Not until Glen Brown arrived as financial administrator did this house-cleaning really begin. By then it was too late.

The program area was Clarke's strongest, but even here he was at fault? Many projects folded during his tenure and the reasons given were usually lack of support from field staff, lack of project definition, and lack of Ottawa support. Clarke hired the field staff. He was supposed to be spearheading the Ottawa support.

All of these problems facing the CYC and Clarke's contribution to them undoubtedly turned the majority of council against him. The Beliveau affair was a lever and not much more. If that hadn't worked, another excuse would have been found. Alan Clarke had exhausted the council's patience and he had to go. That action seemed to place the blame for the Company's misfortunes solely on his shoulders, an unfair act.

The provisional council was the Company's supreme body. It had the policy-making and fiscal powers. It could and did involve itself in nearly every area of Company activity. Yet, when the government-prompted axe fell it landed on Alan Clarke. The council, and its chairman, Doug Ward, emerged publicly unscathed.

The council during Clarke's tenure was guilty of many things. It spent too many hours in dialogue and not enough time creating policies to give Clarke the help he so desperately needed. The council could see the chaos. Even if policy recommendations in areas like administration weren't coming from Clarke, the council should have had the foresight to initiate and implement its own. Some councillors, indeed, tried to do this. They were blocked by others.

The council, when it did create policy, was ambivalent in many cases, and found it difficult to reach a happy central ground. Some policies were too lax, others too severe. And there was little follow-through when policies were created to find out how workable they were.

This is not to attack all councillors. Some like Pere Roland Soucie, Ed Lavallee, R.A.J. Phillips, and Joe Kanuka, faithfully attended council meetings and gave their all to the Company. Others, however, regarded council meetings as monotonous, lengthy discomforts. They always found something else to do with their weekends, placing an inappropriate burden on those who were dedicated.

The council knew it was not doing a good job. Ward would even later refer to it as a "lame-duck body". Lame-duck though it was, it did not suffer with Alan Clarke.

Surely it should have been forced to accept its part of the blame.

There were at least two alternatives for the council. It

could have accepted Clarke's resignation and then resigned with him as a signal that the blame was not entirely his. Or, it could have refused his resignation and decided to stand by him against the government. Since Ward himself pointed to internal strife, and not government interference, as the main problem, then the first alternative would have been the most likely.

Ward's action was especially suspect. He had stood by Clarke for some time. When other councillors were crying for his scalp, Ward refused to join their chorus. Why then did he act when the government became involved? Did he feel his own reputation and career as a CBC-Radio producer was at stake? Did he feel genuinely that Alan Clarke had made mistakes and had to be replaced? Did he feel that it would serve no purpose for him to resign with Clarke, that the Company needed to retain some continuity?

The actions of Gerard Pelletier can be considered in several lights, some of which have been discussed before. There are more, though, which should be mentioned.

The government knew the Company was having a difficult time with administration. According to the legislation, the government could do nothing to either help or hurt the Company directly. Yet, Pelletier clearly broke with the legislation when he stepped in on Clarke. Why, if he was so concerned about the Company, did the minister not take his complaints to the Company's supreme body — the council? Why did he choose to step in over a Quebec issue, and not over administration and other matters?

Once again we have Alan Clarke being made the sole victim. Pelletier chose to hassle with him, not the council.

Finally, where was the rest of the Company while Clarke was being axed?

They were hiding.

If Alan Clarke had his faults, so did others in the Company. He, though, had to take the blame for their faults too, and not one of them was strong enough to come forward and share the blame with Clarke.

Some talked of resigning in sympathy with Clarke's position, but none of them did.

Clarke did contribute some positive things to the Company. These things were forgotten during his hasty exit, but were revived by subsequent directors.

He was the man who constantly fought for the Company's independence and the man most responsible for transferring that feeling into the field.

He was the man who believed in participation in the Company. His application of that belief may not have worked as well as he had hoped, but he tried to involve the volunteers and to a large extent made the democratic points of the legislation more real to them.

Finally, he was a man who believed that the Company of Young Canadians could be something special and tried to make it so. He imparted this faith to many volunteers and staff and they benefitted from their contact with him.

That Alan Clarke failed to make the Company what it could have been is not so much a measure of his own talents, as it is a reflection of the Company-at-large. No one man could have solved the dilemmas that Clarke faced daily. Some would have done better, and others worse, but none would have been perfect when forced to deal with the forces at work in the Company at the time.

Certainly Clarke helped to create those forces. The Company, though, was supposed to be an experiment and who could see where these new ideas might lead.

16

The Stewart Goodings Era

The same day that the council of the Company of Young Canadians accepted the resignation of Alan Clarke, it chose his successor. The successor was to have a limited life, the council decided. He would be an acting executive director until the country had been scoured and the perfect director found. The search would take months so the acting director was given full powers.

During this interlude, the Company found happiness within itself. This was the time it took its first calm breath since Antigonish, nearly two years before. This was the time that the Company united behind its objectives and all levels worked at making them become real. This was the stewardship of Stewart Goodings.

In June, 1968, the Company looked like the creation of a mad scientist, out of control and plunging headlong towards its own destruction. It would take a superman, the experts said, to stop the trend. Goodings was a strange superman.

He looked like a choirboy and a good few years younger than his 26 years. He was about the same size as a jockey, although a good bit chubbier, and his small frame was topped off with a shock of red hair. Unimposing as he was physically, Goodings had amazing success at winning people over and gaining trust. His rise to the top of student politics is one example. While attending Queens, where he got his B.A. in history, and the University of Toronto for his Masters, Goodings became president of the Canadian Union of Students.

Since the beginning of the Company in 1966, Goodings

had been devoted to it and the concept of volunteerism. He was rewarded for his devotion in late 1966 by being appointed the CYC's assistant director – the position he held at the time of his boost to the top. To Goodings, volunteerism and the Company were two powerful forces, forces that could change the shape of the country. As assistant director he got plenty of opportunity to take this message to the people and did, with unfailing success.

His job with the Company as Clarke's second-in-command was nebulous. He had an imposing title, but not much power. He would pinch-hit for Clarke on occasion and do some chores that Clarke preferred not to touch. His main role was that of public relations man. With his conservative, middle-class, innocent appearance Goodings was not the kind of person who would turn off an audience. Coupled with his appearance was the ability to speak logically and articulately. He was a difficult man to beat in a debate.

The relationship between Clarke and Goodings was a strange one. Reticent by nature, Goodings rarely talked about it, but conveyed the impression of being loyal to Clarke. Indeed, no one ever doubted that this loyalty existed. There is reason to believe, though, that Goodings was going to leave the Company in the summer of 1968 and that only the raise in position kept him there. In May he and his wife left for a two month European holiday. Goodings left his replacement a taped message and concluded it with a hint that he wasn't coming back. When Clarke was boxed in over Quebec he called Goodings in London, England and asked him to return. Kathy Goodings tried to talk her husband out of it, but a week later he flew back and took over the Company.

No one knew quite what to expect from Goodings when he took over as director.

Two matters swung the staff over. The first was the resignation of Rick Salter. No one knows if it was forced or voluntary, and no one really cared. Salter was gone and many people felt more secure. The second was a re-distribution of power in the Ottawa office and in the field. Goodings set up a committee of department heads. This committee met with him once a week to review problems and give opinions. Clarke had never done anything on this scale. The difference in attitude was quickly noticeable. The staff felt they were part of the Company and took the responsibility seriously. They also began to like Goodings. He gave them the power to set their own budgets, their own programs and their own timetables. All of these things had to be cleared through him, but he usually agreed. When he disagreed it was done politely and first-hand.

The result was a happy headquarters staff — concentrating on its work and not on internal feuding.

The field took a quick liking to him as well. With the unofficial delegation of power in the Ottawa office he had time to deal with their problems. He did so in an efficient manner. He also was saying yes and no, and making decisions, something that Clarke used to avoid. The field was finally getting to know where it stood and appreciated it.

As his tenure of six months progressed it remained pleasant for the English-speaking projects and the headquarters staff, and most of them discovered that their fears about Goodings were gone. He was trusted, respected and liked. He returned that trust.

This is not to suggest that the six months were entirely free of problems for the Company. There are two incidents that stand out. Goodings was the clear victor in one, and a sad loser in the other.

In the fall the Company had to appear before a Parliamentary committee for the first time. The appearance was routine — Goodings was to explain what work the Company had done and justify the money it was receiving. He expected a rough time from the members of the committee and

prepared himself in advance for it. The main issues —
DePoe, Communism, fiscal irresponsibility — were all
covered in detail. Goodings elected to face the committee
himself, and its just as well that he did for he gave a
virtuoso performance.

The questioning was not difficult at first and the issues
were the ones that Goodings was prepared for. He answered
the queries smoothly. Then Ray Perrault, the Liberal
member from Burnaby, threw a wrench into things. The
former provincial leader of the B.C. Liberal Party hauled
out a consultants' report that had been done for the
Company's proposed international programs. He then
delivered a short speech, quoting from the document, and
implied that the Company was going to subvert governments in other countries.

It was a ludicrous charge. The Company had hired a
consultant, Gerry Hunnius, an internationally recognized
community development expert, to do some preliminary
planning in 1967 for an international program. His report
was accepted in principle by the Company, but his specific
recommendations never were. In fact, when the Company's
budget was cut in late 1967, the international program was
shelved and forgotten.

Perrault's claims of subversion came from parts of the
report that talked about conditions in potential countries
for CYC entry. Hunnius had spoken frankly about the
exploitation of peasants and the miserable living conditions
some of them had to bear. He later remarked that volunteers would find it difficult to accept these things. The
remark came as much as a warning as anything.

What gave credence to Perrault's claim were the countries
that had invited the CYC to their borders — Cuba, Yugo-
slavia, Mexico, and the United States, among others. It is
an impressive list and one the Company should have been

proud of. No other international bodies were allowed into some of these countries.

Goodings answered Perrault's charges by stating that the CYC had scrapped its international program and said the Liberal was arguing a moot point. Perrault kept storming ahead. The news media were in attendance at the meeting and grabbed Perrault afterwards for comments. Goodings was furious. The rest of the meeting had gone well. The Company had stood up and explained itself in a non-apologetic, concise manner. For the only details coming out of the meeting to be Perrault's charges was unfair. Goodings met with some of his staff back at 323 Chapel and decided to counter-attack. Newspapermen were called and arrived late in the afternoon. Goodings let them read the consultant's report and made some harsh comments about the motives behind Perrault's remarks. He, in effect, called Perrault a publicity-hound and questioned his honesty.

The Company had to make a second appearance a few weeks later before the same committee. Perrault wasted little time before lashing into Goodings. He demanded that Goodings retract his press statement. Goodings refused. At this point, the chairman intervened and the matter was settled. The impressive thing about the encounter was that Perrault lost his temper during the initial exchange of the day, while Goodings remained cool and never raised his voice. It was a performance that many MPs commented on. Goodings had challenged an MP and come away a clear winner. He had also brought the Company through its first committee hearing with considerable aplomb. He didn't act like a 26-year old rookie.

While Goodings was scoring in Ottawa and with English-speaking Canada, Quebec was nearing the explosion point.

After Clarke's resignation the council attempted to change the structure in the province with the hope that it would calm things. It was a futile gesture. The four large projects were broken up to form 17 smaller units. Some staff members were fired and the large central unit virtually disbanded. The responsibility for running the CYC's program there was given to Peter Katadotis on a consultant basis. Katadotis at the same time was working with other groups in Montreal and could give only a couple of days a week to the Company. Katadotis supervised the setting up of the smaller units and helped mold the remaining staff into a mobile team or flying squad — the idea being that this team would tackle problems together, but each member would have distinct project responsibilities.

Katadotis was a brilliant people man. He worked with many disadvantaged groups in Montreal and was a firm believer in grass-roots democracy — this extended to the CYC. Katadotis thought the volunteers should have more say than they had. His attitude was that the Company had to give it to them, or the volunteers would take it. To avoid serious conflict, this power was given, bit by bit. Later, Katadotis recognized the volunteer assembly as a legitimate representative body — Ottawa never recognized it as such and would only speak with Katadotis. The assembly set up committees to handle budgeting, program planning and other aspects of operations. The volunteers in Quebec became strong through actions like this — strong enough to beat off staff attempts to fire volunteers.

From May, 1968, the Company had become increasingly concerned about the actions of some of its volunteers in Quebec. Rumours began to circulate that the Company had been involved in several bombings in the Montreal area. It was common knowledge that CYC cars in the city were marked by the police and their whereabouts recorded. Some cars had been spotted near bomb sites. There was also the matter of demonstrations. The city of Montreal had hundreds of them in 1968 and the CYC was usually involved. Among the Quebec volunteers were some known FLQ-

FLP members. The most prominent, most sophisticated and most militant were Francois (Mario) Bachand, Bernard Mataigne and Louis-Phillipe Aubert. Having them listed as CYC volunteers was not healthy for the Company, which was becoming an almost totally separatist-dominated body in Quebec. Goodings and Katadotis decided to get rid of them, plus four others, not necessarily for the same reasons.

On November 22nd, 1968, Katadotis made his recommendation that the seven volunteers should be deselected. Goodings accepted the recommendation and sent telegrams to the seven to that effect. The result was disastrous.

The volunteers of the St. Marie and St. Henri projects in Montreal met and agreed that only two of the seven volunteers (their projects contained all seven) should be deselected — Mataigne and Bachand. The volunteers sent a telegram to Katadotis informing him of their decision. Katadotis did not respond to their telegram in the way they wanted and they planned more drastic action.

On December 11th, 1968, about 20 volunteers and trainees occupied the Company's office on Rue St. Antoine. The staff in the office at the time were thrown out and the doors locked. The volunteers were determined to stay until Goodings' decision was taken back. To accentuate their stand, a press conference was held and their position outlined. It was not a pretty story — CYC volunteers occupying their own Quebec headquarters to ensure that justice prevailed.

The Ottawa office was in a flap. It couldn't decide whether to involve the police or keep it inside the Company. It decided to let Katadotis work out a solution. He called a three-day conference of Quebec volunteers. On December 12th, 13th, and 14th, the volunteers hashed out their problems and made their demands. It boiled down to a simple fact — either the volunteers controlled the Company in Quebec or they would blow the Company apart. Katadotis' recommendation that the seven volunteers be deselected was "out-voted". He decided to withdraw that recommendation. Goodings complied with his decision and the deselection process was curtailed.

Katadotis' reasoning behind his decision not to force an immediate showdown seemed sound. He believed that most of the volunteers in Quebec were responsible, concerned, work-oriented people. He thought that if they were given the freedom, they, themselves, would deselect people who weren't pulling their weight. He advised Ottawa to have patience. He advised Ottawa to give the volunteers a chance to sort themselves out.

The conflict between the volunteers and staff in Quebec in late 1968 was the turning point for the Company in that province. The decision to keep the seven volunteers would haunt the Company until the inquiry; and the decision to give the volunteers a chance at running things would never be reversed. From this initial victory, the volunteers in Quebec would advance to virtually total control. Ottawa would have very little power and almost no opportunity to reverse the trend. The volunteers were in control from December on, and the fact was acknowledged, either directly or indirectly, by all.

Goodings' decision regarding Quebec was almost the last he made in the position of executive director. He held the post for six short months and did an amazing job during that time. The kind of work he did cannot be documented or measured statistically — it was more human than that. Goodings rallied the Company together and started the first real upward momentum in the Company's history. People in the Company stopped bitching and started working. They stopped worrying about headquarters and started looking at their projects. They felt Goodings was a man they could trust and left him alone to do his job.

17

The Betrayal of Stewart Goodings

Throughout the late summer months of 1968 staff people carried messages of hope to the field. Stewart Goodings would be the full-time executive director, they told the volunteers. To the staff, it seemed like the sensible thing to say. Goodings was popular with all segments of the Company and on the surface appeared to be doing a very competent job. The volunteers tended to agree and a consensus was reached — both volunteers and staff wanted Goodings for their boss. No intensive lobbying was done, as no one could help but give him the job.

When council accepted Alan Clarke's resignation in June, it had decided to take its time finding a new director. The Winnipeg council member Wally Kubiski was put in charge of the selection process and immediately went to work.

A management consulting firm was hired to run the initial national advertising campaign and do the first screening of applicants. The Company's name was not mentioned in the ad and more than 100 persons applied for the position. The applicants were interviewed, re-interviewed and put through numerous tests, including a pyschiatric examination. The number was winnowed down and the council then stepped in. A special council committee interviewed the remaining applicants and cut the list to three names. The council had a meeting scheduled for October 26th and 27th and the new director would be chosen at the meeting.

The entire selection process had been carried out with utmost secrecy. No volunteers or staff were involved in choosing the new director, and any questions they had were not answered. Obviously council wanted interference from no one. The principle of participation by this time meant nothing. No great furor arose, though, in volunteer or staff ranks; everyone was so sure that Goodings would be chosen.

A few days before the council meeting confidence began to waver. Some staff had a feeling something was going on, but there was nothing to substantiate the feeling.

An attempt was made to find out who the other two competitors for the job were. Only one name was uncovered, that of P.C. (Cam) Mackie.

Mackie was a Company veteran. He had been in almost as long as Goodings and a friendship had developed between the two men and their wives. In the fall of 1967, Mackie had left for the London School of Economics to continue his education, with the Company footing part of the bill. He returned in the summer of 1968, but for some strange reason decided against taking back the position he had held when he left — director of domestic programs.

An agreeable person, Mackie seldom scrapped with anyone. He could agree, it seemed at times, with two opposite opinions. This apparent lack of personal opinion made him hard to characterize, and even more difficult to understand. He was regarded by some as a relatively harmless talker and no one attached any special significance to his reluctance to be placed in a formal staff position.

Goodings didn't push Mackie upon the latter's return. He let Mackie feel his way back into an organization that had grown and changed during the previous year. There was a closeness and a trust between the two men that allowed this kind of arrangement to take place. The trust was broken when Mackie applied for the executive directorship.

In the first place, Goodings had serious reservations about applying for the job. But the pressure from fellow staff members and the field, plus his own ambition, finally convinced him to shoot for it. He thought he was moving from a position of strength. There were no other persons in the Company with his kind of knowledge and experience. His months as acting director had gone well and it seemed appropriate that he should be rewarded. It was generally considered inconceivable that the council would go outside the Company for a new director. The Company was too complex historically, and the structures too strange, for an outsider to master the intricate art of running the organization in any decent length of time.

There was, it was true, one other Company member that the council would have looked favorably upon — Mackie. But, Mackie had telegrammed Goodings early in the summer and given assurances that he had no intention of applying for the job. He urged Goodings to go for it.

When Goodings discovered a few days before the fatal council meeting that Mackie had applied for the directorship, and was one of the three men being considered, his reaction was strong. He was hurt, bitterly hurt. He felt that Mackie had lied to him and betrayed their friendship.

The reason for Mackie's application is not clear, and at the time no one especially cared what motivation he had. Everyone was still confident that Goodings would be the new director, despite his friend's intervention.

The council meeting began on the morning of Oct. 26th and there was nearly full attendance. Few staff were permitted into the meeting room, but that was of no concern. The choosing of the executive director was late on the agenda and the first part of the meeting was taken up with reports on administration and information. The staff that presented the reports invariably smiled encouragingly at Goodings on their way in and out. He seemed tense and unsure.

On Oct. 27th, the council got down to the job of selecting its director. The discussion was long and at first involved with two names. Gradually a consensus was reached and the decision made.

The staff and volunteers waiting for the word did not expect to hear anything but good news. The news that council member Stan Daniels relayed to some of them was a shock.

The staff and volunteers waiting for the word did not expect to hear anything but good news. The news that council member Stan Daniels relayed to some of them was a shock.

Goodings had not been selected! In fact, according to Daniels, Goodings was not even considered. All the talk had been about the other two candidates. This message infuriated volunteers and staff. Their fury was not lessened when they found out who had actually been selected. His name was Claude Vidal and he was an outsider — the one kind of person volunteers and staff had been sure the council would not select.

Phones rang across the country with the news. Vidal. It was even a strange name and Daniels did not know if it was correct. He also didn't know if Claude was his first name. Volunteers and staff were disgusted. Vidal was the director of the Ecole des Beaux Arts in Montreal. What, Company people asked each other, did he know about the Company or social change?

Nevertheless, the council's choice was relayed on October 28th to the Privy Council office for final approval. On November 8th, the entire Company was officially informed that the new director was Claude Vidal.

There were no cheers.

Vidal's qualifications were hardly cause for cheering. Instead of acquiring a social change/community development expert, the Company apparently had been saddled with an educator. He was French-Canadian on top of that. The Company was not bigoted against Quebecois, but the trend in government had been to appoint French-Canadians to nearly every recently vacated post. Apparently the CYC council was following suit.

A graduate of the University of Montreal, Vidal, 38, acquired his B.A. and M.A. He later completed his classwork at an American university for his Ph.D. in linguistics. He spoke three languages, English, French and German. His entire work experience was in education. Before going to the Ecole des Beaux Arts, he had labored for the Montreal Catholic School board as director of its language teaching bureau, and then as its director of adult education. He seemed to have no experience in the field of social change.

But, council hadn't hired him for his ability in the field of social change. Vidal had a reputation as a tough administrator. That, council decided, was what the Company of Young Canadians needed. He also had remarkable success at ending a strike at the Ecole des Beaux Arts in 1966. The strike had involved students and faculty. Vidal had reorganized the school, in consultation with all parties, and built up a system of elaborate communications channels.

During his stint at the school in Montreal, Vidal would later recall, he had been subjected to severe forms of pressure, particularly from the Union Nationale government. The government wanted building contracts, as an example, to go to its backers. Vidal inevitably found the contracts exorbitant and refused to pay some. He then had to sit back and wait out the government's dissatisfaction. He was a good waiter and won most of his battles.

Vidal's ability to wait, and to endure pressure, was not known when he was appointed director of the Company. His biography was the only information that Company people had, and his biography was not that impressive. His first appearance in public as the Company's new leader was even less impressive.

It was decided to hold a press conference in early November to introduce Vidal to the public. Vidal was telephoned and informed of this, and his immediate reaction was panic. He had not been officially notified that his appointment had been okayed by the Privy Council and the phone call was his first news to that effect. The problem was that he hadn't resigned from the Ecole des Beaux Arts and he did not want a press conference until that was done. It was done quickly and arrangements for the conference moved ahead.

The night before the conference, Vidal journeyed from Montreal to Ottawa. He spent that night in his motel room with Goodings and council chairman Doug Ward. They briefed him on all aspects of Company operations and what he could expect from the press. A similar performance was repeated the next morning — to no avail. The conference was atrocious.

To begin with, Vidal knew absolutely nothing about the Company, with the exception of the Company's Act — which he had read. The information he had been fed the night before was a jumble in his mind, as one would expect, and he decided not to make use of it.

Added to this large problem was his language handicap. Vidal may have been a linguist, but he hadn't spoken English in some time. Both his comprehension of the language, and his use of it, needed vast improvement.

The final straw was Vidal's tendency to talk too long.

The combination of these three things made the two-hour conference a fiasco. No more than ten questions were asked. Of the ten, Vidal answered about eight. Of the eight he probably understood about four. This, however, did not stop him from answering all eight in detail. Since he knew nothing about the Company his detail mainly concerned the Ecole des Beaux Arts and the education system in Quebec. He went on to such great lengths about this that some reporters were driven to rudeness. They obviously felt Vidal was playing games with them, which was not the case.

The press conference attracted its share of non-participating observers — Company staff and volunteers. They watched in total puzzlement as Vidal bumbled from one topic to another. Their reaction was the same as that of the press. Was Vidal for real?

When the conference ended, Doug Ward called the director of information into an office and asked him for his opinion of Vidal and the conference.

It was true that Vidal had botched the conference. It was equally true that he appeared to be singularly unimpressive. What the staff and volunteers did not know was that Vidal was a careful man, one who avoided commitments. He had no intention of talking about the CYC at the conference for one reason — he refused to discuss anything he had not discovered first-hand. His poor performance besides the content side was attributable to several other factors. He, for one thing, was not used to dealing with the press. He also was a below average communicator when speaking with large groups. At his best in face-to-face discussions, Vidal was uncomfortable with a group of strangers. Finally, he had been pushed into attending the conference. His initial reaction had been no, but Doug Ward had talked him into coming. He was therefore a reluctant showpiece.

All of this was unknown to the staff and volunteers or, if it was known, it was discounted. They were angry that Goodings had been passed over, and when they saw the person who had been judged better, their anger was translated into action against Vidal and the council.

A staff meeting had been arranged for Montreal in late November. Goodings had thought of it originally as a chance for staff to exchange information and learn new techniques. He had assumed he would be director. After the press conference, a group of staff decided that volunteers and council members should also be invited for a multi-level discussion on the last day of the November meeting. The council members were told that the meeting was an attempt to improve communications in the Company.

The meeting was held in the Laurentian Hotel. The staff arrived first and for the first day-and-a-half stuck to the agenda. When the discussion swung around to the role of staff in the Company things began to percolate in different directions.

Four program staff members began to push an idea that was eventually called the National Staff Co-ordinating Committee. The four, Jim Littleton of the Ottawa office, Bert Deveux of the Cape Breton Project, Ron Christiansen and Buddy Sault from Northwestern Ontario, argued that the staff should play a larger role in the matters of budget, planning, program priorities, and evaluation and hiring of staff. They asked that a staff committee be established. This committee would represent the field in Ottawa and make recommendations to the executive director in the above areas.

It was obvious why the staff wanted the committee. Vidal's performance at the press conference had shaken them. They did not want him to have the freedom of other directors. The committee would be their way of ensuring that things would be run properly.

The idea was accepted by a clear majority of the staff present and the National Staff Co-ordinating Committee was born. Its mandate was to advise the executive director on the aforementioned matters.

Stewart Goodings was asked to chair the five-member committee. He declined. Peter Katadotis was the next choice. He, too, declined. An election was held and Christiansen, Deveux, and Littleton were chosen to represent the English-speaking projects and the Ottawa program staff. Hubert Beaudry and Michel Maletto were to be the

Quebec members of the NSCC.

While the staff was concocting the NSCC to handle Vidal, volunteers from across the country arrived in Montreal. They wasted little time sight-seeing. There was a more important subject at hand — volunteer control of the Company.

During Goodings' reign, the volunteers in English-speaking Canada had been unusually docile. The usual screams for volunteer control had diminished and in some cases disappeared. They trusted Goodings and were willing to let him deal with the council. When the council chose Vidal over Goodings, their anger equalled that of the staff. They were now convinced that the council cared nothing for the field and should not be the supreme body in the Company. The time had come for the provisional council to disappear and the long-promised permanent council to come into being.

The Quebec volunteers, on the other hand, had remained as determined as ever, during Goodings' tenure, to obtain volunteer control. The fact that the English-speaking volunteers had different reasons for that aim was immaterial. The two groups could work together to reach a common objective. In this case, destroying the provisional council to make way for a new council.

Into the middle of this staff-volunteer beehive in Montreal wandered the unsuspecting council members and Claude Vidal.

For Vidal it was a get-acquainted accasion — a chance for him to meet the staff and volunteers with whom he would be working. A reception was held for him one evening and it turned into a massive display of rudeness. Stewart Goodings was the host and found it difficult to be civil, although he managed it. Others did not try so hard. Crude jokes were made behind Vidal's back. People chatted with him in a mocking manner. He was generally treated like a fool, but he pretended not to notice. Perhaps he thought the Company was this way all of the time.

The council members were not subjected to a reception, but some of them sensed something was going on when they arrived at the Laurentian. Staff people who were normally friendly shied away from associating with them. Volunteers lurked in corners whispering to each other. The councillors had no idea of what had gone on during the week-long meeting. As far as they were concerned, they were in Montreal to discuss Company problems.

The day after the councillors arrived, a staff-volunteer-council congregation was organized in a hotel meeting room. A rather lonely looking Claude Vidal joined them. Doug Ward started things off by reviewing why the council members were present. He didn't get far. The volunteers were anxious to get their work finished and cut him off. One of their number then read the volunteer manifesto. "The volunteers of the Company of Young Canadians." he intoned, "hereby express an overwhelming lack of confidence in their council."

They ask that the council resign immediately. That the government be notified so that a permanent council could be elected.

That during the change-over time, the provisional council make no decisions.

The council members were stunned. They knew there were problems in the Company — that was why the meeting had been called. But they had expected discussion, not unilateral demands. Volunteers had been hostile before; problems had been apparent before, but never had the Company resorted to blaming any one particular body, or presented such a harsh denunciation.

One by one, the council members trooped to a microphone to present their opinions. The age-gap was apparent. The volunteers had claimed that the council members could not understand the field or volunteers. This may have been so, but the councillors understood many other things. The volunteers had tried to degrade them; had accused them of manifold incompetence; had been harsh and spiteful. The councillors were wise enough not to respond in the same angry manner.

They all spoke with dignity. The hostility of the volunteers only served to bring them closer together. Bob Phillips, the civil servant councillor, summed up what they all had to say.

He was willing to resign because he agreed that a permanent council was needed. He could accept that the provisional council had its weaknesses. He would not, however, give up his decision-making responsibilities. The Company, he said, could not function without a council. Until the permanent body was established he would continue to serve, however distasteful that would be to anyone. He then remarked that vindictiveness and narrowness were not usual traits of the CYC. He hoped they would never be.

The debacle was over in a matter of a few hours. The volunteers got nearly everything that they wanted. The council members had insisted that their decision-making responsibilities could not be carelessly discarded and a compromise was reached. Until the permanent council was established, the provisional council would not make any major policy decisions.

The rest of the meeting was anti-climactic. The problems that had been on the original agenda were discussed half-heartedly. A start was made towards drawing up election procedures. The meeting was then adjourned.

As volunteers, staff, and council members headed for home their feelings were decidedly mixed.

The volunteers were jubilant. Their plan had worked

better than they had ever imagined and they would soon have control. There was little regret about the way the old council had been treated. The staff were also pleased. They had devised a plan to circumvent the powers of the executive director. After meeting Vidal they were sure it would work. The councillors left in varied moods. Some were angry that they should be treated so badly after giving hours and days of their time to the Company. Others were relieved that they would soon be out of the hot seat.

But what of the two men who indirectly caused the massive action in Montreal?

On December 2nd, Stewart Goodings forwarded his letter of resignation to Doug Ward. He gave six weeks notice. During that time he would tackle Quebec and help Claude Vidal enter the Company. His letter said in part:

" . . . Now that the Company has a new executive director, it is both possible and appropriate for me to resign. I have decided to leave January 15th.

"By that time, I will have been with the Company for almost four years. They have been four fascinating, valuable and challenging years. It has been a very satisfying experience to help establish a new social institution, and I have no regrets whatsoever about spending four years working under the kind of tension and frustration apparently endemic to the CYC. But it is long enough."

There is no hint of the disappointment that Stewart Goodings must have felt. This would have been unlike him.

He was such a popular person that it is difficult to predict whether or not Goodings would have been able to turn the Company in the right direction if given a chance. During his short stint as acting director he did more to bring the Company together than any two full-time directors. The council felt more than that was needed though. They opted for an administrator and left Goodings in the cold. He wasn't there for long. Shortly after leaving the

Company he would join CUSO as its Kenya director. Goodings could not get voluntary service out of his mind — he saw it as a power to change society.

The difference between Goodings and others in the CYC in this regard, was that he was willing to give the volunteers a chance. The rest mainly used volunteer-control as rhetoric and kept the Company under their thumbs. The volunteers knew this and missed Goodings.

As for the new director, he must have had mixed feelings about the Company after Montreal. He had applied for a job and been accepted, only to discover that those who hired him were being roasted for their choice. Where did that put him? Claude Vidal sat through parts of the Montreal meeting and, unless he was totally ignorant about the ways of people, could not have missed that he was in a difficult position. His main support, the council, had promised to resign. The people with whom he was to work, the staff and volunteers, had been rude and abrasive with him. He hadn't even started to work and already the "pressures that are endemic" to the CYC were beginning to appear.

He appeared to pretend that the pressures didn't exist at the Montreal meeting. He went about smiling and talking with staff and volunteers. When they tried to brush Vidal off or insult him, he smiled in return.

The year 1969 had not yet begun, but already the forces that would tear the Company apart were visible. Vidal had seen them in Montreal. He would not be able to handle them without help and within the Company this help seemed non-existent.

18
The Field in 1968

1968 was a bumper year for those who had time to spare watching the antics of the Company of Young Canadians. There were innumerable controversial stories to be uncovered as well as the intricate internal position jockeying to be charted. It was not an easy job, though it did pay dividends in the form of a constant stream of hot news stories.

Internally, the Company's staff had been decimated. Only four of the most senior staff that started the year, ended it. Of those, only one would stay for a year with Claude Vidal. The situation was as bad in the field, as at least seven project staff members resigned or were fired.

Many of those who left did so with a bang.

If a newsman wasn't noting the departure of some CYC staff person, he could as easily be writing about an internal feud. There were lots of them in 1968. If that wasn't enough, attention could then be turned to the Company's financial position or the longhairs who became volunteers.

The Company-watchers in 1968 were very thorough. All the incidents mentioned above, and many others just as unfavorable, were widely reported. Unfortunately, the Company-watchers missed the best action of the year. It was taking place in the field, at the very heart of the CYC.

Hectic and confusing as the year was for the Company, some volunteers managed to stay out of the mess. They did so by isolating themselves in their communities and working for something that Ottawa headquarters tended to forget — social change. The advances on projects weren't noticeable during the last months of Alan Clarke, but during the peaceful atmosphere of the Goodings era it became apparent to some that the CYC wasn't all that bad.

The volunteers and staff were improving their techniques and gaining confidence. The Company was now solidly project-based and projects were left on their own to develop programs and strategies. They did so with much success, and this caused some to ask what the Company might have been like if the volunteers had been trusted from the beginning.

Despite the success, though, the emergence of the Company as a potent provocateur of social change was ignored. The national accent was on the strife in the CYC. The issues that the Company was tackling were decidedly secondary concerns in the CYC of the media. It is unfortunate that this happened for many volunteers and field staff did not deserve to be tarred along with the general Company.

The Indians of Northwestern Ontario in 1968, for example, were coming alive and the CYC was mainly responsible. The initial organizing was done in Armstrong, a CNR town of 350 year-round residents.

Armstrong, like many small northern towns, was divided into two distinct sections — white and non-white. The whites had the services, the stores and the comforts. The Indians had no electricity, no running water; indeed all they had for their small community was a picturesque name — Happy Valley.

The 23 families that lived in Happy Valley had been there since 1945, when they were moved from the White Sands Reserve at the southern end of Lake Nipigon to help construct a radar base in that area. During their years there, the conditions in which they lived deteriorated. Drunkeness, unemployment, child neglect and extreme poverty were common, but accepted in silence. The silence ended when the CYC arrived.

The Company placed two staff members and about 12

volunteers into the Lakehead area. They immediately began to agitate and organize. The prime mover was Harold (Buddy) Sault, the Indian staff member. Sault was an intense, angry, committed person. He felt that he and his people had suffered long enough under the white man. The time had come to strike back. His attitude was militant and many of his methods crude, but Sault had a fierce charisma that made people listen to him, and respect him. The fact that he wore buckskins, wore his hair shaven except for a centre strip, and talked of Red Power added to his appeal among young Indians.

The first signs of the unrest that had been unleashed in Northwestern Ontario came in September, 1968, at the Ontario Indian-Eskimo Association Conference in London, Ontario. Mrs. Yvonne McRae blasted the federal and provincial authorities for their neglect of native Canadians. She cited the situation in Armstrong as an example, and made particular reference to the issue that the Armstrong people had chosen to focus on — the school situation.

The Indian people of Happy Valley were not allowed to send their children to the school in Armstrong, because the Indians paid no school taxes. The white community felt that the presence of Indian children "might lower the level of the school". This bigotry forced Indian children to travel between 300 and 1500 miles to school, and to be away from home for 10 months of the year.

Mrs. McRae's charges did not raise enough of a ruckus, so the newly-formed Armstrong Indian Association decided to use more drastic measures. At the end of September, the Indian-Eskimo Association of Canada held its annual conference at the Lord Simcoe Hotel in Toronto. The conference went smoothly until the annual banquet was held. Robert Andras, then a Minister without Portfolio attached to Indian Affairs, was to be guest speaker, but before Andras got his chance, the doors of the banquet room swung open and in marched Buddy Sault; Ron

Christiansen, the other NWO staff person; Dale Martin, a volunteer on the project; Jim Littleton, a CYC national staff member; and Hector King, a resident of Happy Valley and president of the Armstrong Indian Association.

Attempts had been made prior to this move to get time on the banquet's agenda for King to speak. They had been refused. Evidently unconcerned by this — the five men went up to the podium and demanded that King be heard. It was impossible to say no, although a weak attempt was made.

King addressed the delegates on behalf of his people. He called for Northern Indians to take charge of their own destiny, and added that if governments were going to help Indian people in Armstrong, then the people must be part of the planning. He made a decided impact.

After Toronto, the NWO crew flew to Ottawa and met Indian Affairs Minister Jean Chrétien, with the hope of having the Armstrong Indian Association recognized as the legitimate bargaining agent for the people of Happy Valley. That recognition never came, but the main issue was resolved when the government announced plans to build an addition to the Armstrong school for the Indian children of the area. A clear victory, and an important one for people who had been taking it on the chin for so many years.

And developments in Northwestern Ontario did not end with a promise for a new school. The victory served as an example for others and soon Indian associations began to crop up in places like Red Lake, Kenora and Timmins. An Indian newspaper was started and initial plans for community radio were drawn up. Northwestern Ontario in late 1968 was moving, and the CYC has to be given part of the credit.

On Canada's west coast, a smaller, but just as dramatic and colorful project was unfolding to the amazement of all.

The project was Dave Berner's. He thought of it, planned it, started it and ran it. He did it single-mindedly, not really caring about the CYC, and only acknowledging it as the provider of his salary. He technically was a CYC staff member, the volunteers (never very many) who worked with him were technically volunteers, and the project, the Indian Post-Release Centre, was technically a CYC project. In actuality, the Company was only a vehicle by which Berner's dream could be implemented. And once that dream got going — the Company would be expendable.

The advantages of this attitude are obvious. Berner did not become involved in CYC power-plays. He fought for his project and nothing else. The results imply that everyone else in the Company should have had the same approach.

The post-release centre was set up as a self-governing educational environment. It was to be run by and for Indians who had served sentences in Canadian prisons. Prior to the establishment of the centre, most Indians upon leaving prison would return immediately to the streets with all the problems that put them in prison in the first place. Berner envisioned the centre as being a half-way ground between prison and street. There, the Indians would learn to help each other and themselves.

"We are children whose task is to grow up in an adult world. We are a family," Berner wrote.

The centre was a house in a populated area and was run without the so-called professionals. Each house member took part in the domestic and business matters involved with running the operation. In addition, they were required to participate in twice-weekly group therapy sessions, and in house meetings which could be called for any reason by any house member at any time of night or day.

"We are our own house parents, gardeners, cooks, cleaners, advisors and therapists. We demand from one another a depth of personal involvement that is rare in families, tribes or institutions," Berner wrote. "Our program of activities runs the gamut from floor scrubbing to conversations about the meaning of conversation. Our techniques and approaches range from the tender and gentle support we offer a man who is suffering the pain of discovery and re-birth to the often brutally harsh 'facing-up' encountered in attack therapy."

Through most of 1967 and all of 1968, Berner and his group of ex-cons consoled, destroyed and re-built. The centre of the action was the "hair-cutting session". Here, one man would sit in a chair and face the others. They would talk frankly about his deficiencies and attributes. It was a technique that required strong men to survive it. Most of the ex-cons began to aquire that strength.

By late 1968, the post-release centre was incorporated as a society. It owned property valued at $60,000 and was looking for more. Approaches were made to a Canadian oil company by the society for ownership of a service station. The oil company was wildly enthusiastic about the idea, and the service station became service stations. On the academic side, Simon Fraser University asked society members to lecture and conduct seminars. Then, two prisons invited them to initiate programs within the walls.

What did all of this add up to? Berner says it best:

"The board members of the society are ex-convicts. They have been thieves, thugs, dope-fiends, alcoholics, homosexuals, maniacs and creeps. Most of them have wasted their young adulthood in prisons. They are now learning to be upward-moving executives.

"This has come one-and-a-half years from the time that three men put their money on the line to rent a small bungalow, . . . and some four years from the time that Indian inmates in the B.C. Penitentiary began to look around and see that they had a problem. Significant here is the fact that it has come the only way possible: The Hard Way.

"Governments may build counter- and sub-institutions and call them half-way houses, pre-release centres or whatever. They may stock these places with qualified shrinkers, gardeners and cooks. They may cull the best ideas and programs of Synanon, The Seventh Step and Sigmund Freud. But they cannot succeed. Only losers who had decided to win can show the way."

The ex-convicts were all losers. The system had failed them, and they the system. Berner with his methods helped them. But, what it really came down to was that the Indians learned to help themselves — the rather simple aim of the CYC, which was applicable to so many parts of Canadian life. When applied properly, as in Northwestern Ontario and in the post-release centre, that aim could change lives.

Northwestern Ontario and the post-release centre were only two of the Company's outstanding projects in 1968. There was at least one other in every other region.

In the Maritimes, the Cape Breton Island project, working out of Sydney, had started at the beginning of the year and by the end of Goodings' tenure had developed a solid program aimed at housing, pollution and alienation of youth.

Quebec, which had started the year as the most promising region for the Company, was at the end of 1968 the most dismal. It was obvious that some projects were working well, ACEF the prime example. The entire picture, though, was so clouded by political paranoia and lack of information that no one dared make a large scale, objective assessment of operations there.

The Ontario projects of Kingston and Everdale Place School joined Northwestern Ontario in the success column.

Everdale Place's development was no surprise. As a free school, it attracted lots of publicity. The people running it were fully aware that business and education had to mix — which is not to say that business took precedence. They simply accepted that the school could not operate as effectively without funds, and so ran it as efficiently as possible. Kingston, on the other hand, was the Company's sleeper. The project that no one expected great things of began to deliver. Almost without staff support, the Kingston project was run by volunteer Dennis Crossfield. Crossfield was a member of a well-known motorcycle gang, wore his hair long, and was given to cursing several times in a sentence. He was also a kind, dedicated man. He split his work into two main sections — youth and housing. He helped organize a club for young people in the city, despite the overwhelming lack of support from Kingston's city council. And then became involved with a citizens' group, Action Tenants Association Kingston (ATAK). The group made housing Kingston's main issue and began to radically change a long-standing power structure. Crossfield was there when help was needed to arrange a meeting, or run off copies of a newsletter.

The Prairies and the Northwest Territories lost some of their drive in 1968. The Calgary and Yellowknife projects continued to excite by finding new issues almost weekly. Bernie Muzeen had left Calgary to join the national staff, but Elaine Husband, formerly Elaine Krause, had recruited a batch of suitable replacements to keep Calgary's city council on the hop over such things as expropriation, day-care centres for children, and welfare. The accent in Yellowknife was, naturally, on Native problems. Volunteer Laura Dexter was helping the Indian Village outside of Yellowknife organize to get a school. Other volunteers were working to form a Native Association for the Territories.

The sun still shone in British Columbia at the end of the year. In addition to Berner, staff Geoff Cue and Peter

Stein had projects in Penticton, Alert Bay, and Vancouver to be proud of.

The successes of the Company's projects across the country should have made 1968 the year of acceptance for the CYC. It didn't. The reasons for the oversight are numerous and most have been touched on. There is one other that has been missed — the failures of many other projects.

These failures took place mainly in the first half of 1968 and attracted a good deal of publicity.

The Maritimes lost the last of its seven original pilot projects. The Cape Breton project that remained had been a new addition. The project deterioration in the Maritimes began in 1967 and the disappearance of the remaining original projects the following year came as no surprise to the Company. The same cannot be said for the Maritimes. The Company was roasted for pulling out, especially since some volunteers like Gerry Fatels in St. John, N.B., were extremely popular. The reasons for the disbanding of the projects were common — lack of staff support, little community support, and lack of experience.

As if pulling out of the Maritimes wasn't bad enough, the Company at the same time came under ridicule in the Atlantic provinces for seemingly wasting thousands of taxpayers' dollars. When the Atlantic region had been established, the Company had rented expensive office space in a Halifax hotel. A five-year lease had been signed and the office owner wouldn't let the Company pull out of the arrangement. So although the Company was down to one project on Cape Breton Island, it was still paying a couple of hundred dollars a month rent on an office it wasn't using.

Ontario lost as many projects as the Maritimes. Endeavours in Deep River, Keelerville, Lanark County and two in Toronto were all scrubbed. Lanark and the two Toronto projects went out with a noise.

On the Toronto West Central project, there was a deep division between the staff member, American Judi Bernstein, and the volunteers. She accused some of them of being racists because they didn't want to work with Toronto's Italian population. They, in turn, accused her of being manipulative and authoritarian. It was an unhealthy situation and not one that could easily be healed. To compound the problems, the internal bickering was taking time away from the objectives of the project and not enough work was being done.

Similar staff-volunteer split, for different reasons, took place on the Toronto Don Area project with the same results.

The western provinces suffered fewer losses than those in the east, but in some cases the losses were more painful.

South Saskatchewan was obliterated at the beginning of the year, only to be immediately replaced by a project in the northwestern part of the province. There were no replacements for the abandonment of a proposed project in the Territories, or for the death of the last two Company projects in Manitoba.

The Company's move to insert a new project in the Territories was thwarted at the last moment by the council. The decision to stop the project before it got going was a wise one. The Company intended to place two men and two women in the community of Baker Lake in the eastern Arctic, where they would work with the Eskimos on such things as education. The entire thing was carefully prepared, approved and then supplies were purchased. It was soon discovered, though, that none of the four Arctic-bound people had ever been in Baker Lake for any length of time. This raised some questions.

Where did the four intend to stay? Either in a government house or in a tent, was the reply. Neither was satisfactory. If they stayed in a house that meant there was one less house for an Eskimo family — hardly an unselfish way of entering a community. If they stayed in a tent, God knew how they would have survived the weather.

Were they going to live together? Yes, was the answer.

However innocent their intentions were, this was still an awkward situation. In the north, holding hands in public can still be frowned upon. Two men and two women living together would not meet with approval.

The council's feeling was that no one really knew what they were doing as far as Baker Lake was concerned. They ordered the project halted.

There was also a decision to put an end to the project in Winnipeg.

By early 1968, such stalwarts as Harvey Stevens and Doreen Jarvis had already left Winnipeg, disenchanted with the Company's empty promises of volunteer participation and token staff support. Remaining was a group of about eight volunteers, half white, half Indian. The whites were running a hippie type house in the inner-city for alienated youth. The Indians were working in conjunction with the Indian and Métis Friendship Centre, helping new arrivals adjust to the ways of Winnipeg.

The project split wide-open during the first months of the year. The Natives didn't like the work the whites were doing, and vice-versa. The two staff members, Harold Harper, an Indian, and Murray Smith, a white, could not seem to resolve the differences of opinion. A genuine hatred began to develop between the two groups and it took on racial overtones. Ottawa headquarters began to fear that the affair would boil over into the open, and not enchanted anyway with the work being done, decided to ask council to scrap the projects.

At the same time the man who rented the house to the white volunteers went to the press with complaints that the volunteers had ruined his building. The floors were filthy, windows were broken, the furnace didn't work properly, garbage lay all over. It did nothing to help the Company's image.

By the time it all ended, the Company had ruined whatever credibility it had had in Winnipeg and crawled out of the city.

The real tragedy in the spring of 1968 in Manitoba was not, however, Winnipeg. At the same time as it withdrew from Toronto and Winnipeg, the Company decided to close down the Oak River project.

The project was a one-girl show. The girl was 20-year Eleanor Hyodo from Brantford, Ontario. She was sent to the Oak River Indian Reserve early in 1967. Indian reserves are notoriously tough places for anyone to enter and be accepted, let alone a shy girl of Japanese descent. Yet, she did it.

A year after her initial experience on the reserve, Eleanor had managed to start a nursery school, become a sounding board for complaints from young and old alike, and become trusted.

"We really like her. She is welcomed in every place she goes. We have had nothing like this before," Chief John Sioux said of her.

In view of the popularity of Eleanor it was difficult to understand why the Company was closing her project. Alan Clarke said there was no staff support for her in the province and the Company could not leave her in such a vulnerable position. The community protested. Letters were written to Clarke asking that Eleanor be allowed to stay. There was nothing he could do. The decision had already been made.

Eleanor Hyodo was pulled out of the community against her own and the community's wishes. That was a new experience for the Company. Usually the disappearance of a project was greeted with joy. It would be nice to say that Eleanor went on to better things on the project she was sent to from Oak River, but unfortunately she never duplicated her original success. The Company failed her and the community.

The Company's projects in 1968 had either grown stronger or died. It was not a time for standing still. This would be the last year of such development.

19

Enter Claude Vidal

By the end of January, 1969, Claude Vidal was the centre
of an elaborate plot to get rid of him. He had been executive
director of the CYC for only a little more than one month.

When he joined the Company, Vidal hoped to have a
few months to become accustomed to the organization.
Its history was complex; its structure complicated; its
policies difficult to interpret; its employees hard to understand. He wanted to get to know all of these things in a
rational way.

There were, for example, more than 30 projects. He
wanted to know first-hand what the projects were doing;
what the volunteers were like; and what the responsibilities of the staff were. He was finding this area impossible
to analyze. Discovering even who was in charge of programs was hard enough. Stewart Goodings, Vidal had
assumed, was in charge when he arrived. After Goodings
left, both Cam Mackie and Jim Littleton presented themselves as heirs apparent. Vidal knew neither of them.

The time that Vidal wanted and needed was never given
to him. Within weeks of arriving he was being advised to
scrap Quebec; he was being threatened by a staff group that
he didn't understand; he was told to fire his administrator;
and he was being counselled on all sides by strangers. It
must have been very confusing and irritating. If it was, he
never showed any signs of being lost.

The advisory group, now the executive group, was meeting regularly. Vidal was getting most of his information from
these people, and supplying them with the first good look

at his personality and character. The executive group was a battle-toughened quartet. Most of the members had been with the Company for some time and were used to its rather extreme ways. They were all opinionated people and did not hesitate to give Vidal their opinions. He seemed to appreciate the frankness, and began to lean heavily upon the group. He really had nowhere else to turn.

The executive group, Glen Brown, Bernie Muzeen, Vidal's executive assistant Manon Vennat, and the Company's director of information, found Vidal a difficult man to analyze. He had come from Quebec and a Quebec bureaucratic background. He was a firm believer in efficiency, structure and effectiveness. His key phrase, though, was enlightened managerial philosophy. The Company, he said, had to be managed by objectives. In other words, the management practices had to fit the Company, not the other way around.

The only problems were that the objectives of the Company were not clear, administrative policy was, in some cases non-existent and the role of the executive director could be interpreted in many ways.

Vidal began to map out his philosophy.

He was the manager of the Company. It was his job to make sure the Company worked effectively. In the past, he said, the executive director had been the centre of attention. No longer would this be the case. He decentralized administrative responsibilities. The director of information would be responsible for information. Vidal would not talk to the press, and neither would anyone else in the Company without clearing it first with the information boss.

The job of administration, he said, was to handle the present. His role, as executive director, was to plan the future. There were policies missing and the gaps would have to be filled. Most of the staff lacked proper job descriptions. Without those how could they function and how could he measure their performances? The activities on projects were too secretive. He wanted to know what the objectives and plans were for all projects. He wanted to know how well the projects did at achieving their stated objectives. The financial situation in the Company was not clear. He wanted regular financial reporting and he wanted reports sent to the field. In this way, projects could compare budgets and measure results for themselves. And on and on he went.

The reaction from parts of the field towards this business-like attitude was immediate, and closely paralleled the attitude of the NSCC.

A typical letter of protest at the time was one from volunteer Wayne Choma of the Cape Breton Island project:

"The Company was to become a continually evolving and searching institution, instead it has become reactionary. The Company in its Aims and Principles has seen the immense growth of bureaucracies as one of the dehumanizing elements which is alienating and destroying the human process in our society. This force has now taken over the Ottawa office.

"The Company which started as a dualistic partnership has evolved into a reactionary Ottawa hierarchy which has failed to keep in touch with the outside forces that are changing the face of society." he wrote.

Choma was not alone in his dislike. Others, too, felt the Company was becoming too administratively-orientated. But what he and the rest failed to realize was that the pendulum had swung for a reason. The Clarke and Goodings regimes were aimed at people. Administrative concerns generally ran a poor second. Over this period of time, the Company's administrative shape took on a seemingly permanently saggy appearance. Vidal was hired to manage the Company back into fiscal and operating respectability.

Vidal emphasized his cold, pragmatic approach over and over again to the executive group. They were finally beginning to understand him. There were, in reality, two Claude Vidals. Outside of the office he was friendly, humerous and good company. Inside, he was all work. They also began to see his ways of operating. He refused to be pushed on anything. When people insisted on pushing, he stopped listening, or would say, "I don't understand" and dismiss them with a wave of his hand.

This ability of his to ignore pressure, to never even acknowledge its presence, would be valuable to him in coming months for trouble was brewing on all fronts.

The National Staff Co-ordinating Committee, established by Goodings to advise the director, had approached Vidal soon after he took over and asked him to recognize them as a legitimate body. They were annoyed when Vidal said he saw no need for special recognition and angry when, instead of allowing them to travel to Vancouver to evaluate the projects there, he suggested they go to Montreal and study the situation in Quebec.

The NSCC refused and presented Vidal with a manifesto demanding that the NSCC mandate be accepted and that Glen Brown, the Company's administrator, be fired.

Vidal rejected the group's demands completely. It was a humiliating defeat.

Members of the committee began to speak critically about Vidal to the volunteers. They claimed that he was a bureaucratic dictator trying to run the Company by himself. They said the volunteers would not be consulted on any matter. The volunteers responded by trying to establish a volunteer association in February, 1969.

The volunteer association was, of course, supported by the NSCC. The volunteers were being screwed by Vidal, the NSCC said, and had to retaliate. What the NSCC hoped to gain from it was never stated, but having been clobbered by Vidal it was obvious that they needed help. A unified front of volunteers and staff, they reasoned, would be more difficult for Vidal to beat.

The Quebec volunteers, of course, wanted nothing to do with it. They did not have much regard for the English-speaking volunteers, and some considered the English association as a front for Jim Littleton and his cohorts. In addition, they were setting up their own organization in Quebec and trying to get recognition from Vidal. They were hoping for success as their methods were a good deal more sophisticated than those of the English-speaking volunteers.

On February 8th and 9th, 14 volunteers representing nine English-speaking projects met in the Ottawa office. The volunteers had come from all over the country to re-assert their belief in participatory democracy. A Cape Breton volunteer, Sheila Gardner, started the conference by outlining the harassment she had been subjected to by the Ottawa staff.

She had come to Ottawa early to organize the meeting, and approached Vidal to explain what it was about and to get official authorization for it. He gave her no immediate answer, but later said the meeting would be unauthorized. This hurt the volunteers. A lack of authorization meant that all the costs of travel, accommodation and food would have to be paid for by themselves or their projects. But could they have expected Vidal to pay for a meeting that was organized to oppose him?

After Gardner had finished with her story, the projects in turn outlined their present circumstances and complaints. They were varied, to say the least.

Cape Breton was concerned about a car the project couldn't buy. They had enough money in their budget, and the car purchase had been approved months before. Glen Brown, they claimed, was blocking them. They felt he was controlling money badly.

Graham Deline of Ottawa was upset because his project

(a co-operative book store) was being considered unaccept-able for the Company. He claimed he was being discrimin-ated against by the person who told him his project was being phased out.

The Toronto Development project was very badly caught up with the staff co-ordinating committee. The project lacked a staff person and had been under the impression that the NSCC would hire someone for them (a subtle hint at the power the committee had envisioned it would have). This it had never done and Vidal had placed Cam Mackie with the project on an interim basis. They didn't want Mackie and wrote to Vidal asking him to recognize the volunteers as a decision-making body. He refused their request.

The complaints from the other projects centred on the old standbys — lack of information, lack of support from Ottawa, lack of participation.

It was then agreed that a self-perpetuating power struc-ture was in existence in Ottawa. To meet it, the volunteers saw a need for creating an opposing force of numbers. They decided to form a union.

The union would form a loose alliance with the Quebec volunteer body, and perhaps have a working relationship with the NSCC. A union executive was chosen and another meeting arranged for later in the month. The time would soon come to approach Vidal regarding the union's legit-imacy, and to ask for financing.

With Quebec, the NSCC and now the English-speaking volunteers organizing and asking for recognition, Vidal must have felt quite alone. In just over a month, most of the Company had lined up against him. He was left with only the executive group as his ally. His sin had been trying to make the Company efficient, and refusing to grant manifest powers to an organization that hadn't properly explained its terms of reference to him.

20

The Reaction against Vidal

Claude Vidal must have been perplexed by the activity going on around him. He preferred to believe that nothing was going wrong, and often told other staff members not to be upset when they commented on the rising tide of discontent in the field. But, it is difficult to understand how he could not have been affected by all these events. Perhaps he really thought that there were no problems.

The NSCC was still trying for recognition. Memos, increasingly abusive, were sent to Vidal demanding that he give in to the group's demands. Jim Littleton, who was still a program staff member and directly responsible to Vidal, treated him rudely in the Ottawa office and was hesitant about doing assignments given him by Vidal. Littleton much preferred to visit projects where he was well received — such as Northwestern Ontario and Cape Breton Island — and where his attitude towards Vidal was endorsed.

Vidal, for his part, had crossed the NSCC out of his mind.

This was the end of the NSCC. It passed into oblivion less than three months after its formation. But its demise did not make things any easier for Claude Vidal. He still had to contend with the volunteers in English-speaking Canada, the Quebec group, and discontented staff members.

The Quebec volunteers were at work building a strong structure in their province. They were not asking for the support of Ottawa, or for the support of anyone else in the Company. Their plan was to get Comcord functioning well, to organize committees, and to eventually take over unofficial control of Quebec. They were sure that once the volunteer-elected council was in power they would be granted virtual autonomy.

Vidal sensed the direction the province was taking and began to cover up. He insisted that his staff in Quebec follow his directives, no matter how disagreeable they were to the volunteers. More often than not, his directives were ignored and he would send follow-up memos. He demanded project reports and project evaluations. He wanted budget figures and proposed growth plans. His incessant demands and questions began to irritate the Quebec staff. They were in an impossible position. They could not move in hard against the volunteers. Yet, they could not pretend that Vidal didn't exist. So they compromised — obeying some orders, forgetting others.

In the early months of 1969, Vidal was invited to Quebec for a meeting with a part of Comcord. He insisted the invitation come directly from Peter Katadotis. If it had come from Comcord he would not have gone, not willing to give even that much recognition to the volunteer body. Two other staff members accompanied him and sat silently as a mini-drama unfolded. The volunteers, unlike their English-speaking counterparts, made no threats and no outright demands. They simply talked about what they were doing and made token requests. Vidal returned their politeness with his own brand. He rarely disagreed with them, but never agreed either. When he left, nothing had changed.

The English-speaking volunteers were not as well organized or sophisticated. Their attempt at constituting a volunteer association was more a personal reaction against Vidal, rather than a deep-rooted conviction that this type of structure was necessary, no matter who the director was.

The differences between the two volunteer groups was noticeable when their constitutions were compared. The Quebecois set up committees to evaluate projects; to deselect volunteers; and to establish project budgets. Staff were not welcomed into the inner circle. The English-speaking volunteers met in Port Arthur in late February and established as their main objective the implementing of structures to deal fairly with legitimate volunteer griev-ances, and to expedite the solutions of volunteer problems. They also listed as priorities the need to co-operate with the Quebec group, and expressed a wish to form an English field association with staff as members. To the Quebecois, this last desire was stupid. The staff were the prostitutes, those who lacked dedication. The volunteers were the soul of the Company and the soul should not be corrupted needlessly by too much contact with staff.

The two organizations differed in another way. The Que-bec volunteers avoided contact with Vidal at all costs. The English volunteers seemed to go out of their way to scrap with him. After scrapping, they then had the nerve to ask him for money to finance the association (the meetings across the country were proving costly). He told them that as a union they would have to pay the whole shot.

"If I finance the volunteer union, I'll control it. They don't seem to realize that money has that much power," he told one staff member.

Indeed, the volunteers didn't, but they needed money badly. Another association meeting was held in Calgary in March and the solidarity that had been displayed at the previous two get-togethers began to vanish. Some volun-teers railed at the suggestion that staff should be allowed into the union. The dissenters were frankly suspicious of Jim Littleton. Drew McDonald from Lesser Slave Lake accused Littleton of using the volunteers to further his own ends. The association finally decided it would be unwise to include staff in their current plans. They would proceed alone for the moment.

In late November, 1968, the volunteers had gained what they considered to be effective control of the Company. The provisional council had agreed to resign and the permanent council could not, in their mind, be far away. Once the volunteer body was elected the Company would finally have fulfilled the legislation and the volunteers would run the Company their way.

But the months dragged by and no further signs of advancement came. The provisional council did not meet, committees of council were virtually scrapped. In the volunteers' eyes, one man was running the Company — Claude Vidal. Vidal was making, single-handedly, all of the decisions and was answerable to no one.

This frustration led to an ignoring of project work in many cases, and a concentration on Ottawa. They complained that Vidal had no feeling for people. That he ruled by policy, and gave no consideration to the quality of the policy, or how harmful it could be in individual situations. They claimed that he was controlling and manipulating volunteers and projects. They argued that he was a dictator and should be tossed out of the Company. Many volunteers swore that as soon as the council was elected, Vidal would be fired.

Many of their complaints had their substance in fact, if not in Vidal's intent.

He was simply trying to run the Company efficiently.

His refusal to enter into the arena of hand-to-hand combat angered the volunteers and staff even more. His aloofness and apparent lack of concern for their problems was seen as a deliberate slight. Instead it was simply his way of doing things in all situations. Why couldn't people be professionals? was his attitude. Why couldn't they work for the Company instead of pursuing personal feuds?

The answer was that this was the Company of Young Canadians. This is the way it had worked. This was the atmosphere everyone was accustomed to. He was the stranger, the interloper, and he was trying to bring in new rules. They weren't being accepted. What it came down to was, the volunteers would break Vidal or he would break them. There was very little middle ground.

Vidal did attempt to find some early in 1969. The cries for participation were things he had heard at his last job at Ecole des Beaux Arts. He said he believed in participation. The Ottawa staff could believe him. He had, after all, given them added responsibilities. In an attempt to placate the volunteers he instituted a series of committees. Whenever a staff person was to be hired for the project, a committee consisting of Ottawa staff and volunteers of the project where the staff person was needed was formed. The volunteers were elected by their project. This pleased some of them, but not completely. The committee only recommended three names to the executive director. The three people would be interviewed by the executive group and by Vidal. The final selection would be made by him. The fact that he never went against a committee recommendation was inconsequential. The volunteers saw him holding on to the ultimate power and that was enough to turn them off.

The same procedure was kept with other committees — Vidal having the power to accept or reject recommendations. Another wrinkle was added, though, that upset them even more. The volunteers for committees such as planning and budgeting were handpicked by Ottawa staff. Vidal said it was a reward system. Volunteers who did good work would sit on the committees. This did nothing to build a belief that he supported participatory democracy.

Despite negative attitudes and some problems, the committees did a reasonable job. One outstanding example was a committee formed to write a brief for the Senate Committee on Poverty.

Visit the poor, talk with them, listen to them, said the Company. The committee tended to ignore this advice and later was thrown into conflict wherever it travelled. For once, the Company had been right and the press noticed. The Company's brief was praised, quoted from, and generally regarded as the best brief to be presented to the committee.

Claude Vidal helped present the brief to the committee. It was a rare public appearance for him. Since he took over the Company in December he had been silent, doing his job and accepting abuse. As time progressed he expected things to improve. They did the reverse. As his first three months as boss ended he received a letter from staff person Bert Deveux of Cape Breton Island. That letter accurately presents the amount of bad feelings Vidal had generated — feelings that would grow with intensity until the parliamentary inquiry in November the same year.

Deveux's letter was in reply to a letter that Vidal had sent to him. The issue was the volunteer association and Deveux's willingness to pay the travelling expenses for his volunteers who wanted to attend association meetings.

Vidal wrote to Deveux in his usual pragmatic way:

"There is an off-project travel policy created by my predecessors; it reads as follows:

" 'All staff and volunteers and consultants must receive written authority from the executive director or his designate before travelling outside their normal project or headquarters area. Expenses incurred will not be reimbursed unless a copy of this written authority is attached to the request for reimbursement.'

"Stewart Goodings did not delegate the authority to approve off-project travel; and, for the time being, I have not delegated this authority . . . . All travel outside defined project areas requires my prior written approval . . . . "

Deveux's reply was carried in its entirety in the Company's internal newsletter and ran for four pages. It carries in it all of the assorted complaints about the Vidal and transmits a genuine, common feeling.

"Your reprimand is so totally irrelevant and betrays such a crude understanding of what the CYC is all about, that I hesitate to even acknowledge it. But, I will try," Deveux began.

"First, it is unnecessary for you to throw policy at me. I became suspicious of policy seven years ago while working for the Department of Justice at Dorchester Penitentiary. It was there I witnessed two 15-year old boys being paddled by perverted guards. One of the two boys was forced to watch the other being paddled and, as he watched, he began to cry and then to vomit, and finally he fainted. The one being paddled was pleading for mercy, saying 'pretty please' and everything else he could possibly think of to persuade the Warden to stop the guards. But no! After every crack, the Warden would repeat, *'It is the policy of this institution,* etc. etc. Are you sorry?' Crack! . . . .

"My purchase order 11138, for the record, is for Dave Henry's air fare to Port Arthur to attend the Volunteer Co-ordination Committee meeting. If I had been in your shoes several weeks ago when the volunteers were planning the meeting, I would have okayed their expenses on the spot rather than make them beg, and then hearing the 'crack' from administration, namely Glen. It seems mighty peculiar to me that you can travel, . . . that seemingly everyone else in the Company can travel, but that volunteers can't without hearing the crack of the paddle.

Deveux then turned his attention to the Company's administration.

"Since last summer, I've had expenditures for this project questioned, cross-questioned and questioned again.

"Not by program people — who might be in a position to evaluate an expenditure — but by people in administration who have never visited the field, who do not understand what the Company is about . . . .

"This project has never been fully responsible for its budget. It has to justify its every expenditure to Glen and to you. Its ludicrous that you should ask for suggestions (as to how money can be saved). You are in healthy control of the situation. You control our budget. You have the say in whether we may spend . . . . Crack! It is the policy of . . . . "

Vidal did not get angry with Deveux. The staff member was not fired. But Vidal did not really understand why a decision based on policy should meet with such resentment.

21

The Volunteers and the Permanent Council

On Thursday, April 17th, 1969, Claude Vidal, flanked by the rest of the executive group, appeared before the standing Parliamentary committee on broadcasting, films and assistance to the arts. The appearance was in connection with the Company's budget estimates for the coming year.

Vidal presented an optimistic picture. He talked about the administrative changes that were going on, and about the growth of the Company. The deep internal warfare was not mentioned, nor was the controversy surrounding the appointment of the permanent council.

"Right now we are reaching, after our third year of operation, a sort of more permanent establishment of the Company," Vidal said. "And again this is important because for the first time the Company will have its council. It will be its council of volunteers, and it will be our volunteers who finally will decide what will be the future of the Company."

The previous November when the provisional council had agreed to step down, the volunteers had drawn up a set of election procedures. These procedures were forwarded to the council and approved in January. The responsibility then was passed on to Doug Ward. Ward was to prepare a document explaining why the permanent council was needed, and to forward that explanation, plus the election procedures, to the Secretary of State. If he approved of the proposed procedures, they would then be forwarded to the appropriate cabinet committee for study. Once past here, they were as good as accepted and the election could take place.

Ward got the affair off to a smashing start by sending a totally unacceptable explanation to the Secretary of State's office. It was only a couple of pages and hardly touched on the real problems in the Company — the problems were one important reason for having a permanent body. It was hoped that a permanent council could resolve issues that the provisional council had proved incapable of solving.

The Secretary of State's office sent the explanation back, and Vidal put his staff to work on it. Within a week they had re-written Ward's explanation and had it accepted by Pelletier.

The staff's arguments in favor of a permanent council were convincing. They explained that the Company would function best when a circle of accountability was established — volunteers would be responsible to field staff, field staff to the executive director, the director to a council elected by the volunteers. At present this circle did not exist. The provisional council was accountable to no one, and since it hardly met anyway, the director was also accountable to no one.

The documents were then forwarded to a cabinet committee. The committee did not like certain features of the election procedure. The procedure, for example, called for the elections to be held on a national basis. The committee recommended that the elections be held regionally.

Those recommendations were sent to the Company's provisional council in late spring. The council met on June 3rd and approved them. It would be another two months before the election was held and another four months before the council would actually meet.

The above complicated series of events is what actually took place. The government is a notoriously slow body and faster action could hardly have been expected. But the volunteers had wanted control by spring and could see no earthly reason for such a delay.

The staff did not help matters.

In February, Bernie Muzeen said that the Governor-General was on a tour of the Caribbean. Since Mr. Michener was governor-in-council, Muzeen said, nothing could be done until he got back. It was a ridiculous thing to say and the volunteers reacted as could be expected. They accused the staff of holding the entire thing up.

Jim Littleton reported that Ward had failed to submit an outline of the election procedure to the cabinet, and the Company, as a result, lost its place on the agenda.

After a while the volunteers didn't care who was doing what. They wanted their election and the cry from the field became incessantly demanding. Staff members started phoning the Secretary of State's office to find out what was holding things up. It turned out that there were doubts about the switch to a permanent council. The doubts were finally overcome.

On July 22nd, the ballots cast by the volunteers were counted in Ottawa. Ten people were to be elected by the volunteers. The additional five council members would be hand-picked by the government. The staff were relieved by the volunteer choices. It had been expected that many more anti-Vidal people would have been elected than actually were. At the time, though, the staff didn't know they had miscalculated.

Representing British Columbia on the new council would be Rob Wood, a volunteer, and Bill Horswill, a community person. The Ottawa staff regarded both as being on the fence. They expected them to be moderates and not necessarily members of the get-Vidal force.

The Prairies and the Northwest Territories presented a similar duet — Roy Daniels, a Yellowknife volunteer, and

Jack Johnson, a Calgary lawyer who had just recently become a radical.

Ontario selected Millie Barrett and Mickey Posluns. Barrett was a grandmother and a volunteer on the Northwestern Ontario project. She hated Vidal and one of her first aims was to see him fired. Posluns was no fan of the executive director's either, but the Ottawa-based volunteer could be counted on to be more reasonable.

Comcord handpicked the three elected council members from Quebec. Jean Roy, a bearded, scholarly man, not known for his frankness; Marcel Desjardins of Trois Rivieres, tall, dark and brutally honest and dedicated; and Julien Tourigny, a lively, likeable man. The three of them were the unknown factors on council. It was expected that they would push for autonomy in Quebec. It was also expected that they would continue to exhibit the sophistication of their Quebec colleagues and not push too hard at Vidal.

The Maritimes sent its radical — Skip Hambling. The son of the city of Ottawa's legal representative, Hambling had been carrying on a vicious feud with Vidal and administrator Glen Brown for months. He could be expected to join Millie Barrett in crying for the quick removal of Vidal.

Although the election was held in July, the council would not get a chance to formally meet until the beginning of October. It would take the government that long to appoint its representatives. In the meantime, the relationships between Vidal and the staff, Vidal and the volunteers, and Vidal and Quebec would become more strained. As they did, some people would rub their hands in anticipation of the first council meeting. Others would grimace and wish the whole thing would go away.

22
Vidal and the Staff

Claude Vidal was not a man who people could feel close to. He never seemed to be frank and friendly, and in a Company that gave great importance to such attributes this created a measure of distrust.

In the middle of 1969, Vidal ran headlong into a scrap with his Ottawa program staff. He had few supporters among the field staff; and even among Ottawa senior staff, where he was held in the highest regard, people still had doubts about his intentions and had no tight ties with him. In the spring, for example, Manon Vennat resigned as his executive assistant. In June, Glen Brown informed Vidal that he wanted to leave as well. Neither Vennat nor Brown disliked Vidal. They were simply fed up with the Company and he was not a strong enough force to hold them in the organization.

Exemplifying the difference between Vidal and past directors was his tough attitude towards office discipline. Stewart Goodings and Alan Clarke worked very long days themselves, but let their staff come and go as they pleased. This system had its disadvantages, but it was not totally abused by the staff. In addition, it helped create a small feeling of trust between the director and his staff. People did not feel that Big Brother was watching them.

Vidal decided the system had to stop. The Company receptionist was supplied with instructions to keep track of the meanderings of all of the staff, no matter how senior. The receptionist worked in secret for a while and the first hints of the new system's existence began when memos from Vidal arrived in certain offices. The memos were asking for explanations for staff members arriving late or seemingly not at all. The system caused some resentment, especially when some staff members arrived at work before the receptionist, but were marked absent or late because they didn't pass by her desk. Vidal, though, wouldn't listen to such explanations.

Among the field staff, the bitter feeling that Bert Deveux on Cape Breton Island had for Vidal has already been documented. Ron Christiansen of Northwestern Ontario was another who felt the same way.

The National Staff Co-ordinating Committee had had field support. The volunteers' attempt at creating a volunteer association was also supported by many of them. A typical field staff opinion at this time would have been this letter sent to the Company-at-large by Marilyn Assheton-Smith. Marilyn was the staff member on the Northwest Territories and Lesser Slave Lake projects. A former nurse, she had joined the Company about a year before Vidal. Always a moderate, she helped forge one of the Company's finest national projects in the Territories, but did so quietly and without pushing herself into the limelight. She used this same quiet approach when dealing with Ottawa. She never made excessive demands or used threats.

Her letter is a reaction to Bert Deveux's denunciation of Claude Vidal:

"First of all, there is so much in Bert's letter that I agree with that I feel I should simply say yes — oh, yes — and let it go at that. But there is something else Bert that I must react to.

"I went through months — years, I think — in CYC with no policy. That also can be cruel and evil . . . . Decisions go unmade until people give up in despair and defeat."

But as for total obedience to all policies, she turns thumbs down:

"It was clearly stated at the Montreal staff meeting that the travel policy was a very bad policy controlling but not placing responsibilities on projects . . . Glen thought the solution was to define the project area any way he liked — surely playing unreasonably to make a bad policy fit the work."

From here, Marilyn goes on to say that other complaints by Bert are correct — that some members of the Ottawa staff are incompetent and totally unaware of the field. She ends not by defending Vidal, however, but by lambasting Deveux for not making the staff co-ordinating committee work.

The attacks and conflicts that Vidal engaged in with his field staff was a minor element in the Company at this time. A major event was warming up in Ottawa — one that would help to undermine the director even further, and ruin some of his chances at co-operating with the highest level in the Company.

In the early days of the Company when programs were more centralized, the Ottawa program staff was used constantly to evaluate projects and to set up new ones. Once Alan Clarke decentralized, a good many of the program department's uses vanished.

Stewart Goodings took over the department when he became executive director. It had three main members, Jim Littleton, Cam Mackie and Charles (Chuck) Long. These three were still there when Vidal came in, but Goodings continued to report to Vidal on program affairs until he left.

During the first months of Vidal's term he used the three men to patch up problems that developed on projects with no staff members, and he eventually assigned them to look after non-staffed projects from Ottawa. Long took care of Northwestern Saskatchewan and the North American Indian Travelling College. Mackie looked in on Toronto Youth and two single volunteer placements in Toronto. Littleton's role was more confusing since he was spending the majority of his time organizing against the executive director. About the only project anyone was sure he was connected to was the National Film Board-CYC Indian film crew.

In the spring, Cam Mackie left the Company to join the Department of Health and Welfare, leaving Littleton and Long to contend with Vidal.

Littleton despised the director, and was doing everything he could to get Vidal removed from that position. Long had no liking for the director, either, but contented himself with trying to do a good job.

The problem between Vidal and the two program people was basic. They would take his recommendations only to have them ignored. They realized that program planning was needed, as well as the instituting of new projects. They tried to force these two issues. Vidal would have little to do with them. They realized that the program department needed redefining and they, personally, needed new job descriptions. Vidal did not seem anxious to discuss either matter with them.

Vidal's attitude was understandable to a point. He had given Littleton assignments only to discover that they had not been carried out properly. He knew that Littleton was visiting projects across the country rallying support for his anti-Vidal stand. When he asked Littleton for written reports about these trips, he received on several occasions rude replies stating that written reports were a waste of time. The Company was too much of a bureaucracy, Littleton took one project tour that cost more than $1,000. When Vidal asked for a report and didn't get it, Jim Littleton was marked for extinction.

It is easy to see why Vidal didn't trust Littleton. Who would trust a man whose sole aim was to drive you out of your job? But Vidal's apparent distrust of Long was not so understandable.

Long was an American, from the hilly country of southern Ohio. Thin and bearded, he had walked into the

Company office a year before and asked for a job. His qualifications were impressive. In addition to an Australian university degree and a solid activist background in that country, he had served as a co-ordinator for Volunteers In Service to America (VISTA) in the Appalachians. The Company hired him as a consultant and put him to work evaluating the Keelerville project. His evaluation was presented to council soon afterward and was received with raves. He was soon hired as a staff member.

No one ever questioned Long's diligence or competence, and most people had difficulty comprehending the problems he said he was having with Vidal. There could be several reasons for the difficulties. Vidal did not like to treat anyone differently and he treated Long as he treated Littleton — which is rather unfair in view of the different circumstances.

The real feud, though, was between Littleton and Vidal.

It became obvious to everyone in late spring that something had to give. Littleton was being openly abusive and vindictive towards Vidal.

Littleton's complaints against Vidal were that the executive director knew nothing about field conditions and was making decisions about the field without consultation; that the director was acting in an authoritarian and non-democratic fashion; and that the director was killing the Company's radical projects to appease the government. His complaints are not without an element of truth. Neither were they completely accurate. Littleton's feelings were so intense that he showed none of the objectivity that a staff member like Marilyn Assheton-Smith could provide.

Vidal's senior staff kept urging him to do something about Littleton. There would never be any peace and quiet in the field until Littleton was gone, they said. He listened but refused to act until late spring.

He first attempted to fire Littleton. Vidal asked a senior

staff member to draft a letter to Littleton for him. The letter asked Littleton to leave the Company and listed as reasons were the assignments given by Vidal that had not been carried out properly.

The director carried the letter around in his pocket for weeks, but finally decided not to send it. He was not sure that he had proper grounds for firing Littleton. Instead, he decided on a subtler strategy.

He would obliterate the entire programs department of Long and Littleton. In this way he could avoid any messy insinuations about Littleton's competence and hopefully also avoid reaction from Littleton's supporters.

The provisional council had a meeting scheduled for the last weekend in May in Toronto. The three members of the personnel committee, R.A.J. Phillips, Doug Ward and Maurice Cloutier, a volunteer from the Montreal ACEF project, would be in attendance. Vidal asked the three members to meet with him over lunch, at which time he would present his plan and seek the committee's approval.

The following Monday Vidal informed his executive group members that the personnel committee had agreed with him. The program department would go.

On June 22nd, Long and Littleton received notices from the director. He told them that the programs department had ended and gave them seven days to apply for another field staff position in the Company. If they did not do that successfully, they could look for employment elsewhere.

Chuck Long was insulted. He felt he had been doing a good job for the Company and deserved better treatment than the arrival of a registered letter asking him to leave. He knew that Vidal wanted to get rid of Littleton and even understood why. But he did not think that he should have received a letter identical to that of Littleton. Long resigned, anxious to get away from the Company and Claude Vidal.

If Vidal thought that Littleton would follow a similar pattern, he was in for an unpleasant surprise.

Within days of the director's move, stories appeared in Ottawa papers, and the voice of Jim Littleton was heard on countless radio stations. His message was clear.

Claude Vidal was trying to rid the Company of its radical people and projects, Littleton said. He was being fired because he was a radical and opposed the dictatorial methods of the executive director. Projects like Northwestern Ontario were being manipulated to appease the government.

Littleton's charges could hardly be substantiated with facts, but that didn't seem to matter. The media were more than willing to listen to him.

Vidal decided to let Littleton run his course, gambling that people would stop listening eventually.

Littleton not only attacked Vidal from outside the Company, he also made an attempt to rally projects and volunteers behind him and against Vidal. It met with some success. Willie Dunn, a volunteer with the CYC-NFB Indian film crew, wrote to indicate his project's support for Littleton. The Toronto Youth, the Cape Breton and the Northwestern Ontario projects also let it be known that they supported the staff member. That support did nothing to change Vidal's mind, but that wasn't Littleton's target anyway. He wanted to impress the new council with his case.

After he received his letter, Littleton asked the provisional council's interim program committee for permission to have a hearing from the new council. As a staff member, he had the right to appeal the decision of the executive director before the council or a committee of council. The request was denied.

Littleton, however, refused to resign. He said he would not rest until he received a fair hearing from the new council and, indeed, he would not. For a time, he would not even budge from his Company office. Vidal finally forced him out of the office, but not out of the Company. Littleton would keep fighting and organizing until his hearing.

The staff member had reasons for believing that he could win at such a hearing. This was his manifesto against Vidal's handling of the affair:

1. The allegations made by Claude Vidal against the members of the program department (that they have not developed program priorities) are completely without foundation in reality and can easily be proven so.

2. Elimination of the program department will not create more participation by the field, but will lead the way to the hiring of an executive assistant for programs who will assume dictatorial powers over the field.

3. The manner in which the decision to disband the program department was made is such that it would substantially alter the structure of the Company immediately prior to the election of the Permanent council. Not only is this in violation of the promise of the provisional council that no major changes would be made before the permanent council was elected, but it also betrays the thorough contempt which the executive director has for the volunteers and their elected council.

4. The project for which I am directly responsible, the CYC-NFB film crew, has not been consulted in any way by the executive director regarding a change in staff for them, a matter to which they take strong exception.

5. The account of the disbanding of the program department given in Newsheet was substantially censored and changed by Claude Vidal. The act again betrays his contempt for even the most basic freedoms and the right of the volunteers to information.

6. The fact that no minutes or other documentation concerning the alleged meeting of the personnel committee

of the provisional council on May 31st are available makes very questionable the entire procedure which was used in arriving at this decision.

7. The sum total of these points indicates that the entire program of the Company is being manipulated and held in contempt by the executive director and that only volunteers themselves can decide on what the just outcome should be.

Vidal didn't have to worry about most of Littleton's points and arguments, but there was one that was causing him some anxious moments. Was the personnel committee meeting to which he presented his case a legal meeting?

Since Vidal was the only staff person at that meeting it boiled down to his word versus the word of the three councillors. Maurice Cloutier supported Vidal. R.A.J. Phillips, though, was not sure whether it was a legal meeting or not — a bad blow for Vidal. An even worse blow came from the council chairman, Doug Ward. It was not a legal meeting, said the chairman.

If Ward was correct then Vidal had acted unilaterally against Littleton and Long, something he had no right to do. This would give Littleton the lever he needed to at least have a hearing. The entire episode was getting messier by the day and Vidal must have wished that he had fired Littleton.

23

Vidal and Quebec

It seems improbable that Claude Vidal should have more difficulty with the Company in Quebec than with the English-speaking staff and volunteers. But, he did.

At first, Vidal depended on his Quebec staff to keep things in line. They could not. They were hopelessly trapped between the volunteers and Ottawa and saw a good deal of value in the propositions of the volunteers. Vidal demanded that projects be evaluated or that the performances of volunteers be rated hoping that some of the bad elements in Quebec would be rooted out. He was always disappointed. Either the staff would ignore his request, or evaluate and find everything in order. Vidal knew that not everything was okay. There was nothing he could do about it though.

The Committee of Co-ordination in Quebec ran the operation. The staff saw no point in fighting with it, the staff would be sure to lose. The majority of Quebec volunteers were represented on Comcord, and accepted Comcord as the top decision-making body as far as they were concerned.

How powerful was Comcord? In a document entitled "A preliminary report on a self-determining organizational structure for Quebec" the aims of the body were spelled out.

"We believe that the Company should tend towards administration and a policy-making which correspond as closely as possible to the know-how accumulated in the field. The essence of the law creating the Company seems to us an indication that while the volunteers are working in the field, they should also run the Company. The Quebec volunteers have already started moving in this direction and they have given themselves a tool for self-administration," the document begins.

It then defines Comcord as: " . . . the structure that runs the Company in Quebec: technical administration; administration of the programs and moneys; and finally a policy body."

Technical administration means the utilization of the material of the Company. Program and money administration is the evaluation of projects, the choice of new projects, and the assignment of financial resources.

This was the difference between the English-speaking volunteers and those in Quebec. While the English fought with Vidal, the Quebecois by-passed him and set up a body. That body was recognized by all the volunteers in Quebec — this gave it power that no official sanction or ignoring could diminish.

The volunteers covered for each other in Quebec. Since Comcord had control and Comcord was a volunteer organization, the volunteers were well taken care of. A few volunteers were deselected by the organization, but they were the hopeless incompetents or the federalists. The separatists that Vidal knew and was afraid of were left alone. So were projects that Vidal was certain were no more than FLP cells.

During the summer, Vidal made repeated trips to the Quebec projects. He used to come unannounced in order to see things as they would normally be. On these trips he met the volunteers and spent many hours chatting with them. The chats fed his suspicions. They were added to by friends in Montreal. Vidal was soon certain that he knew which projects were FLP cells and which were working for the Company. He also knew which volunteers did not belong in the Company. It only led to greater frustrations.

There was no way he could act on his suspicions without

the proof coming from his staff in Quebec. All the Company could do was cover up until the new council convened. Vidal would take his charges to it and hope that some action would result.

It took a lot of fast talking to cover up all of the Company's activities during the first nine months of 1969 in Quebec.

In January, the CYC was pinpointed as an active participator in a rebellious demonstration against the Murray Hill Limousine Co. It was true that Company volunteers had taken part. It was also true that the cabbies who led the demonstration were sharing an office with some Company volunteers. The CYC said that the volunteers had taken part on their own time. They were not acting in the name of the Company. It made little difference to the Montreal police.

The following month, Prime Minister Trudeau visited an area in Montreal where the Company had a project. He was late for a meeting with some community people and was treated rudely when he finally arrived. The Company was blamed for organizing the demonstration against the PM. Lucien Saulnier, the executive committee chairman of the city of Montreal, went as far as to make charges of separatism against the Company. At the time, no one paid him much attention. The same charges in the fall, however, would almost destroy the Company.

The worst crisis came at the time of the McGill demonstration. The press made a mistake here. They got one sensational story against the Company, but it turned out to be false. They missed others.

The McGill demonstration was planned to force the university to become a French-speaking institution. It was to be the largest demonstration of its kind ever held in Quebec and months were spent preparing for it. The Company did its part. Mario Bachand, one of Quebec's better-known separatists and a Company volunteer, left his project to help plan the demonstration. From all accounts he was the principal organizer. This went relatively unnoticed, except in Ottawa. Vidal knew what Bachand's involvement was.

The demonstration was scheduled for Friday, March 28th. Vidal stayed in Montreal that day, wanting to be close to things in case the Company became badly involved. The march was carried live on the radio and the Ottawa staff and Vidal listened to the entire proceedings. It went off smoothly and everyone relaxed, a little too soon.

The first radio bulletin said that three CYC volunteers had been arrested in Joliette and that a box of nail-studded asbestos balls had been found on Company property.

From here, the story continued to skid downhill. Bit by bit, police errors were caught and corrected until the final story version was reached. Three youths, not connected to the CYC, had been arrested. The nail-studded asbestos balls were found under the stairs of the building the CYC rented part of in Joliette. No mention was made of the fact that other people rented the building, including the CNTU.

As with most things, the Company got an unfair shake from the incident. Canadian Press sent its first wire story about the affair stating that the three youths were CYC volunteers. If a correction went out, not many newspapers bothered to carry it.

In the midst of this slanted, anti-Company information several important points were missed.

No one seemed to notice that a Company car led the march on McGill, complete with placards and a speaker. No one noticed that CYC volunteers were among the prime organizers during the demonstration. No one knew that a lot of the placards had been printed at CYC expense, or that the sticks for the placards were purchased with CYC funds.

Vidal knew, but there was nothing he could do about it. He could not even touch Bachand. The police, however, could. Things began to get sticky for Mario in Montreal later in the spring. He finally fled to Cuba, still incidentally as a CYC volunteer. After he had been off the project for a month for no reason (he was in Cuba), his contract was halted.

Peter Katadotis seemed incapable of helping Vidal in Quebec. There was even a question as to whether he wanted to. Since the occupation of the Montreal office in December, Katadotis had been wary of putting too much down on paper. He may have been afraid that his documentation would fall into the hands of the volunteers. He may also have not wanted to co-operate with Vidal. In any event, Vidal decided the time had come for a full-time co-ordinator in Quebec — someone he could trust.

A selection committee was formed and more than 70 applications sifted through. The top choice was Pierre Renaud. His name was forwarded to Vidal for approval.

The questions in Vidal's mind were: could Renaud function in Quebec without being intimidated by the volunteers? would he be willing to work with Ottawa? Renaud gave his assurances and was hired on a one-year contract.

Counted as a negligible factor by Vidal was Renaud's past. When younger, Renaud had been a member of the RIN. He had taken part in an unsuccessful armed robbery attempt on a movie house on Jean Talon Ave. in Montreal. He had been given a suspended sentence. Since then, Renaud had joined the Company and served capably for several years, in a staff role. He told Vidal that his FLP days were over. Vidal believed him, as he should have, for Renaud was an open person. Little more was mentioned about his background.

Renaud seemed to try harder than Katadotis in Quebec. He was in closer contact with Ottawa and, in fact, was brought onto the executive group as a member — this was Vidal's way of identifying Renaud with Ottawa.

The relationship between Renaud and Vidal was never

one of complete trust. From the day that Renaud was hired to run Quebec, Vidal subjected him to a series of subtle tests. Questions would be asked that Vidal already knew the answers to. Vidal would ask him to try to get rid of volunteers and projects. Renaud never let on that he was upset about this. Completely amiable, he never seemed to fight or argue with Vidal.

But in the long run, the insertion of Renaud did not erase the problems. He just made things more tolerable, for a time. It was not his fault that Quebec eventaully erupted. It is unlikely that any man could have cleaned up Quebec without drastic measures — measures that Vidal was unwilling to take. Besides, Pierre Renaud was not by any stretch of the imagination a federalist. He may not have agreed with the more militant volunteers, but he was not willing to be tagged as Ottawa's man in Quebec. Comcord existed and Renaud had to co-operate with the organization.

The separatist issue in the Company in the middle of 1969 was dealt with on a sophisticated level. The issue had been with the Company for a long time and gradually a philosophy had developed.

The Company did not care what political organizations the volunteers or staff belonged to, as long as that affiliation did not interfere with the aims, objectives and everyday work of the Company. Defining this much further is impossible. A member of the Parti Quebecois could work for the Company in the field and meet the Company's qualifications. Those qualifications (creating social change) could easily manufacture an atmosphere favorable to the more progressive separatist groups.

Although it has never been stated clearly before, the Company in Quebec did indeed use political affiliations as one measure of a potential volunteer's ability. The rationale was that the Company needs concerned, bright, committed young people. The majority of young people in Quebec who met these demands had separatist leanings. This was accepted as a fact of life, an uncomfortable fact, but still one that could not be discarded.

So it came as no surprise to Ottawa staff when they took part on selection committees to find that many questions were political. The Company considered hiring an information officer for Quebec at one stage of the year and a competition was held. Two Ottawa staff, Pierre Renaud and two Quebec volunteers formed the selection team. Inevitably, each candidate for the post was asked about his or her view on federalism. Only those who opposed federalism were given any serious consideration. The Ottawa staff did not find this strange.

24

The Completion of the Permanent Council

By September, 1969, the Company of Young Canadians had reached the point where a miracle was needed. The opposition to Vidal — some English-speaking staff and volunteers, some Quebec staff and volunteers — was becoming increasingly more strident in its attacks. He was in as bad a position as ever. The provisional council would make no major policy decisions, leaving Vidal to administer with half-policies, no policies and policies that were possible to interpret several ways. He needed clarification on several points. He needed approval to disband projects. He wanted new policies to make administration more efficient. None of these objectives could be reached until the permanent council began to meet.

Because this situation existed — Vidal having to work in a vacuum created by others — the volunteers resented him. They saw him as a dictator. They hoped that his apparent power would be broken once the permanent council was officially formed.

It seems strange that the two groups, so opposed to one another, would each count on one body to alleviate their problems. Vidal was sure that the council would not be irresponsible. He had faith in the electoral process and did not see how even radicals could ignore administrative necessities. The volunteers considered the council to be their council. Their demands would be met, of that they were sure.

The election of the ten volunteer-elected members in July was a good sign for both parties. They thought that the government would appoint its five members soon after. The government, though, decided to wait. August passed and so did most of September before action was finally taken. That action was forced by the impatience of the elected members.

Early in September the elected members tried to hold a meeting on their own. Skip Hambling, Millie Barrett, Rob Wood and Jean Roy arrived in Ottawa to establish a date and set an agenda. It was an unofficial meeting, of course, and Vidal refused to acknowledge it. Doug Ward, the provisional council chairman, got the hint, though and decided the time had come to force the government's hand.

Ward called a weekend executive committee meeting of the provisional council for September 13th and 14th. He invited the ten elected members to take part as guests. This, he said, would be a chance for the old council to pass on words of advice to the new.

Vidal took the meeting seriously. He and his staff spent days compiling a lengthy list of policies that the Company needed. The list covered every department and if the policy recommendations were acted on, the Company would have benefitted greatly. The executive committee and the ten elected members, though, were in no mood for such things.

The main goal of the weekend was to force the government to appoint its five members to the permanent council.

The ten elected members and the executive committee agreed on a strategy. If the government did not name its appointees by October 4th, then another executive committee meeting would be called with the ten elected members. This would be a decision-making meeting and the group would have the powers of the council.

Ward stated this bluntly September 14th in a memo to Vidal. He also gave an idea of the sort of documentation that would be needed in October in case the government did not come through. The list gives some idea of the feeling towards Vidal.

Some of the items Ward mentioned are:

A.   Personnel policy. In this interim period there is a great need for the executive director to act in close association with the governing body on matters of personnel. This issue will be brought up and the relations between you and the remaining personnel committee and the executive committee will be clarified.

B.   Jim Littleton Issue. The executive committee requests from you a report in detail on the laying-off of Jim Littleton. In addition, Mr. Littleton will be in touch with you to request specific documents which he might prepare his report on this matter, also for translation and presentation. We ask you to make available to him all documents to which he had access rightfully under our employ, for use within this office only.

C.   Administration. The executive committee will discuss the merits of a freeze on major administrative changes, and we want your opinions on this matter.

D.   Program Department. We will discuss the phasing out of the program department for the first time, and request a report from you on this matter.

In addition, Ward said that all documents that arrived for presentation by September 22nd had to be translated into both languages by September 27th. This was an impossible task for the Company's sole translator, but was the least of Vidal's problems.

Ward's memo was an insult to Vidal. So was the treatment he had received in the press after the executive committee meeting.

The executive committee meeting had not gone well. Vidal had presented his report outlining policy needs and had taken three hours to complete it. The report had been only in English and the Quebec representatives demanded that it be also tabled in French. After a short discussion, Vidal agreed to translate it into French for them. It was understood that from here on all documents would be in both languages or they would not be discussed. There was no doubt that the Quebecois were serious.

The content of Vidal's report and his presentation of it were strongly criticized by some elected members, but the criticisms were not delivered to him in person. They came via a Canadian Press wire story.

"Claude Vidal's position as executive director of the Company of Young Canadians appeared shaky yesterday following a weekend meeting of the Company's newly-elected directors," the story began.

It then went on to recount his delivery of the policy report, and ran quotes from several members about the report.

" . . . a deliberately, incomprehensible mish-mash of words," said Millie Barrett of Northwestern Ontario. "It was an Uncle Tom act. I have no doubt that Vidal has to go."

Skip Hambling from Cape Breton was just as definite. He doubted that there was "one person on that council who really wants to maintain Vidal as director."

The reaction to Vidal's report was not justified. It was a concise analysis of the Company and a list of corrective measures that the Company had to take. Vidal even presented his personal philosophy of social change for the councillors to examine. The philosophy was unimpeachable. It was as radical as any that the volunteers held — all the right words, participation, self-determination, were used. Vidal even commented on the charge that he was trying to eliminate radical projects and volunteers. He called himself "an opponent of incompetence", not of radicalism.

The councillors like Hambling and Barrett were not interested, however, in Vidal's personal beliefs or an analysis of the CYC, no matter how honest or valuable. They were reacting against him for the imagined or real sins he had committed in previous months. No amount of good faith on his part would change their minds. It was unfortunate that their attack was not made to his face. It was also rather tragic that Doug Ward did not deem it fit to support his choice as executive director.

The Canadian Press story and Ward's memo infuriated Vidal. Ward had discounted the personnel committee meeting that Vidal thought had given him the authority to wipe out the program department. Not only had he done that, he had instructed Vidal to let Littleton back into the office and give the staff member access to all documentation that he required to build a case against the executive director. This was no way to support your director and Vidal wrote a strong letter to Ward about the memo and the Canadian Press story.

" . . . I do regret the type of articles which have been published in most English-speaking newspapers. I sat through a whole day at this meeting and never had the slightest impression of being under fire! I hope that you and your colleagues of the executive committee are going to correct through the Canadian Press the impressions that two of your guests . . . have created. In the past it seems to me that the administrators of the Company (the council) had always hid away from the responsibilities and left the executive director holding the bucket! If you and your colleagues have any sense of decency, I hope that you will see to it that corrections appear in all newspapers. At no time during the part of the meeting which I attended, or even in the chairman's remarks was there the slightest idea that I was under fire from any group.

" . . . relating to the personnel policy, I would like to state that interim period or not, I have always consulted the personnel committee of the Company as records will indicate. Do you need a report confirming the fact that I work in this manner? . . . "

"Concerning the program department, all I could produce is the document I had already presented to the personnel committee and what is in my report . . .

"As for procedure establishing dates for the evaluation of projects, this is already under way, but again I would like you to be a little more specific. What do you really want?"

This was the angriest letter that Ottawa senior staff can remember Vidal writing. He felt that Ward was playing games, taking sides after determining which side was the strongest. The volunteers were bugging Ward about Vidal and the permanent council. Ward reacted to the pressure. This tendency of Ward's to give in to pressure had been seen before when Alan Clarke was caught in the Beliveau affair. Rather than support his director, the chairman of the council preferred to let Clarke hang. Now, rather than support Vidal and the recommendations Vidal brought forward, Ward went with the volunteers and left Vidal in limbo.

In late September, the government finally announced the five people it would appoint to the Company's governing council. This nullified Ward's intent to constitute his executive committee and the ten elected members as the power body, which is what the strategy had planned for.

The elected members were glad that they could now meet and the dates of October 4th, 5th and 6th were set aside for the first council gathering. They were not expecting to get along too well with the appointed members. Regarded as government lackeys by the elected members, the appointees would have to earn trust. The appointees' job wasn't made any easier by a newspaper story which ran coast-to-coast before the council met.

The *Globe and Mail* quoted Secretary of State Gerard Pelletier as saying that the CYC would not be permitted to engage in separatist activity. To underline his point, Pelletier was quoted as saying:

"Mr. Axworthy is in control now and he is beginning to use his influence on the Company. I think you will see the activities of the Company stabilized in the very near future."

Lloyd Axworthy, formerly executive assistant to Paul Hellyer when Hellyer was transport minister, was one of the government's appointees. He would be only one vote in 15 and for Pelletier to suggest Axworthy was in control was stupid and certain to whip up resentment among the elected council members. It did.

A lengthy, anti-government press release was written by some elected members and sent to Canadian Press. Luckily, CP checked with the Ottawa office and the release was torpedoed. The simple fact was that Pelletier had been badly misquoted.

According to Paul Dunn, CP's Ottawa bureau chief, Pelletier said that all of the council appointees were exceptional and their influence would be felt on the council. A reporter recognized Axworthy's name and reported that his influence would be great.

The fact that so obvious a misquote could be believed by the elected members points out how paranoid they had become. If their rebuttal had been printed, it would most certainly have not improved already crumbling Company-government relations.

The government's appointees were in reality an exceptional group. In addition to Axworthy, who was director of the Institute of Urban Studies at the University of Winnipeg, the government picked Jeannette Corbiere of Toronto, the youth director of the Canadian Indian Centre and a former Company field worker; Michael Kirby of Halifax, a professor of applied mathematics and business administration at Dalhousie University; Sean Sullivan of Vancouver, a former president of the student government at the University of British Columbia; and Jean Thibault, a legal adviser to the Confederation of National Trade Unions in Quebec City.

The elected members initially saw them all as Liberals and not to be counted upon to understand the volunteer situation. The matter of alienating the appointees did not have that much relevance to the elected members. They were in the majority.

The vision that the permanent council would re-unite the Company was vanishing. A line in the Company's internal newsletter referring to the Pelletier misquote summed the situation up best: "These things happen — but why do they always happen to us?" Why indeed? Could the Company do nothing properly?

25

The First Meeting

The scene is the conference room at CYC Ottawa head-quarters.

It is Saturday, October 4th, 1969, and the Company of Young Canadians is having its first permanent council meeting. A revolution of sorts is expected, and the conference room, with its sparseness, sets a tone befitting Che or Lenin, two heroes of the Company's left.

The press would be at the meeting, by invitation. The council's first agenda item would be a discussion on whether the press should be allowed to cover council meetings. It was expected that the answer would be yes, and the press had already been invited. They would be a curious lot, seeing the inside workings of the Company for the first time. They would be easy to pick out, as well, dressing far less flamboyantly than Company members.

The meeting would be an important event in the life of Jim Littleton, still trying to beat Claude Vidal. He had been given a place on the agenda and had spent weeks preparing his report. He was hopeful that the volunteer council would support him against Vidal — already some of them had made that commitment.

Another of Vidal's more blatantly open enemies would be present at the meeting as well. Bert Deveux had flown in from Cape Breton to plead for the help of council. He wanted the council to authorize things his project needed, like more volunteers and a car. If the council approved, it would be a slap at Vidal, for Deveux was under his authority. Deveux also wanted the chance to assault Vidal verbally before the council and press.

The subject of Deveux's hostility knew that he was not in for an easy time at the meeting, but it didn't seem to concern him greatly. Cool as usual, Claude Vidal had spent a good deal of time planning his approach to the meeting.

The appointed members must have had some reservations about walking into that first meeting. Jean Thibault, the Quebec City union lawyer, had made his entry easier by meeting with the volunteers in Montreal prior to his arrival in Ottawa. Jeannette Corbiere, being a Company veteran, at least knew what to expect. But for Michael Kirby, Sean Sullivan and Lloyd Axworthy, the Company would be a new experience.

The elected councillors were an excitable lot. For about a year, most of them had been fighting Claude Vidal and the old council. They were for the most part the Company's radicals and rhetoricians and they had an objective — revolution within the Company. The balance of power had to be swung from Vidal to them. They had control and intended to use it. Vidal would do as he was told. This first meeting would be an indication of the new order, and the new order intended to make clear its feelings.

There would be one more group at the meeting — a disinterested, often bored group. The Company was bilingual and its meetings were held in both official languages. Since not all councillors were bilingual, simultaneous translation was used. The translators sat in a glass enclosed office at the far end of the room. From here, they would try to catch, assimilate and then translate the words of council. These words were sometimes profane, sometimes obscene and often difficult to understand. The Company had a language all its own at times — the language of the new left. This council would add another, a neat combination of Marxist-Leninist clichés.

This was the scene. Now on with the play.

It began with a bang — a discussion on the admissability of the news media to council meetings. The appointed members, most notably Axworthy and Sullivan, were against it. Both of them had had experience with the media before and had found that they tended to sensationalize things. In the case of the Company this had certainly been the case, they said.

Skip Hambling presented the main case for those in favor. The Company is for the people, he stated, and the people have a right to know what's going on.

Hambling, finger pointing and hair waving as he spoke, was extreme in both his defence of the news media and in his attack on the members. The press was allowed to attend.

That was the only major decision made on that first day. The rest of the time was spent trying to define the Company of Young Canadians, and the roles of the different groups within the Company. It was an interesting experience for the press, which probably never realized just how diverse the Company was.

Sean Sullivan and Lloyd Axworthy, equally pragmatic, suggested that the council should be dealing with policies, that the director should be implementing the policies, and that the Company should be a social change organization.

The elected members, mainly Hambling, Millie Barrett and the Quebec representatives, rose up in anger. One even tore up a Company policy book to show his displeasure with such things.

All policies of the Company are useless, they declared. The only reality is the volunteers and the field. The council must ignore all past policies. It must create new ones for the volunteers. The bureaucratic staff must go.

The debate went around in circles for hours with seemingly no end and no agreement. Everyone wanted to speak and everyone did. The press sat and listened, at first in wonderment, but later sad-eyed, obviously not pleased that there were two more days of this to come.

Indeed, the press did get a repeat performance for two more days, but at least there was a little humour to brighten things up.

On one occasion, a note that appointed members were passing around to each other was intercepted by an elected member. Believing that council members should have no secrets from each other he opened the note and read it. He exploded in anger.

The note asked if Sean Sullivan, Lloyd Axworthy and Michael Kirby wished to have lunch with Robert Rabinovitch, the special assistant to Secretary of State Gerard Pelletier.

The elected member from Quebec termed such action traitorous. The Company wanted nothing to do with the government. The elected members then debated upon whether or not the appointed members should be allowed to have lunch with such officials.

The appointed members and the news men found this response hard to take seriously, but the anger was no joke. It was deadly serious. The elected councillors were aghast that anyone in the Company would want anything to do with the government, the enemy of the people.

The elected members were a serious bunch. They truly believed that the government was the enemy, and that the appointed members were there to do the bidding of the government. Not all of the elected members thought this way of course, but enough of them to form a majority did.

One of them was Marcel Desjardins from Trois Rivieres, a 34-year old volunteer. Prior to joining the Company, Desjardins had held a multitude of jobs — everything from insurance brokering to delivering milk. He had been in many different organizations — the Ordre de Jacques Cartier, the Liberal Party and the RIN, to name a few. Desjardins never got past the ninth grade in school, but continued his education in the streets. He was a strong-speaking man and, with his large, hook nose and black beetle eyebrows, was also a fierce-looking one. Desjardins believed in community organization and had little time for anything else. He had little faith in governments or institutions. His world was the street and he wanted the CYC to accept that as the only real world.

Jack Johnson was one of the rare breed – a late-blooming radical. Thin, balding and wearing glasses, Johnson did not present an overpowering picture. His training as a lawyer, however, had given him a nimble tongue and mind. He used them to pull all the different shades of an argument together into one large proposition at council meetings. During that first meeting, Johnson stood with the radicals. He had just resigned from his conservative law firm in Calgary to start his own firm, and had months earlier resigned from his position as vice-president of the Alberta Liberal Party, cutting most of his ties with his background. Johnson wanted to build a new Canada in a new way and thought the CYC was one tool that could be used. He had, at first, as little use for staff and the government as the volunteer radicals. Eventually, however, he was to modify this opinion.

One cannot speak of elected members without mentioning three other names – Skip Hambling, Millie Barrett and Jean Roy.

Hambling was a bit of a mystery. The son of the city of Ottawa's solicitor, Hambling had obviously cut most of the ties with his family and old friends – they were perhaps too middle class for his liking. He had gone to university in the Maritimes and earned a B.A. in English.

Hambling joined the Company in 1968 as a volunteer on Cape Breton Island. From that lonely outpost he fought a long, literate battle with Glen Brown, the Company's financial administrator. Hambling's letters to Brown and his subsequent letter of resignation in the middle of 1969, were literary masterpieces. He talked in the same colourful style. Nothing was too radical for Hambling. He claimed to be for and with the people, and was a strong advocate of Leninism.

Mrs. Barrett was a good friend of Hambling's. They saw eye to eye on nearly everything. Only their backgrounds and mannerisms were different. Both despised the staff. Both disliked the government and the appointed members. Both wanted the volunteers to control every part of the Company. But, while Hambling came from a well-off family, Barrett used to state that she was born in a log shack in the bush of northern Ontario. At the age of 46, Barrett had been around for a lot longer than Hambling; she was even a grandmother. Toughened as a political and community organizer, she was no slouch at pouring abuse on the head of Claude Vidal. But unfortunately, while Hambling had staying power and could continue for hours, Barrett would occasionally break into tears. This is usually regarded as a woman's prerogative, but no one really thought of Barrett as that kind of woman. She was no fluffy charmer, but a plainly dressed woman with short hair and a rough tongue.

Behind his back, Ottawa staff called Jean Roy "Pere Roy". It was not his long hair and beard, or even his penchant for sandals that inspired this nickname. It was his knack of speaking too simply and slowly, while saying even the most outrageous things. Roy was an elected member from Montreal and the real leader of the three Quebec representatives. He was a leader in Comcord, and in Quebec as a whole. Vidal never trusted him, probably with good reason. Roy was a planner and a schemer. He never did anything without considering the consequences. His background, like that of Desjardins, was varied. He had been a lumberman, an underground worker, an army clerk, a sculptor and a writer by the time he joined the Company at the age of 29.

Roy was one of the councillors who took strong exception to the note passing between the appointed members. It seems like a childish thing to take offence at, but one should remember that for most of the elected members it was their first opportunity at running something as large as the Company. All of them had come in with preconceived ideas — namely that the appointed members were Liberal stooges — and grasped at anything that could substantiate their ideas, no matter how silly and inconsequential.

Having thus proved their willingness to go after the appointed members, the elected members then turned their attention to rules, procedures and the executive director.

The rules and procedures were given short shrift. It was decided that the council would operate in a truly democratic fashion. It would not elect a chairman or vice-chairman. Jean Grenier, the animateur, would chair their meetings for a while. This would leave all councillors free to take part in debates without having to worry about the influence of the chair. A council with no leader was indeed democratic, but it also led to verbal anarchy.

Claude Vidal sat patiently through most of the meeting, taking no part and ignoring the swipes that Barrett, Hambling and others took at him. When the time came to discuss the Jim Littleton affair, however, he moved closer to the table.

Littleton had done his homework well and presented his case against the executive director convincingly. His most effective argument was that Vidal had acted unilaterally in disbanding the programs department. He produced statements from Doug Ward and R.A.J. Phillips to back him up. Ward said there was no personnel committee meeting. Phillips said he wasn't sure whether or not there had been one.

Vidal's turn came and he didn't fight too hard. He simply

pointed to the documentation that had been presented to the committee.

The council debated for some time. Hambling and Barrett, of course, demanded that Littleton be reinstated and Vidal be disciplined. The others were not so sure, but eventually reached a compromise.

Jim Littleton, they said, had the right to have his case re-examined. An ad-hoc committee — Sean Sullivan, Jack Johnson and Millie Barrett — was established to do just that. In the interim, Littleton would be paid.

It was a slap at Vidal. Council had ignored the requests of Axworthy and Sullivan that the council support its director. It had decided on the side of Littleton this time.

This meeting was the fulfillment of the Company's legislation — it was the Company of Young Canadians with its structure complete, the CYC at its best. But what had the meeting really accomplished?

The staff considered it a calamity and criticized the council in the Company's internal newsletter. The councillors had spent nearly the entire three days in angry, philosophical discussions. The policies that the Company so desperately needed, the decisions that had to be made, and the final showdown between the staff and elected councillors had all been bypassed. In terms of Company progress not an inch had been gained as far as the staff were concerned; no problems had been solved.

The elected councillors left the meeting in fair spirits. They had managed to get a few good shots off at Claude Vidal and were sure they would have other opportunities. The English-speaking radicals were especially pleased that the Quebec representatives, a question mark until the meeting, were on their side. That supplied a hard-core of five to seven votes. This would be enough to change the direction of the Company in due time.

Time, everyone said, was needed. The Company during the last year had been torn apart through internal squabbling. The two main warring factions were now facing each other at council meetings and nothing would be resolved quickly. In order for the council to develop and the problems to be ironed out, time would be needed.

The press was not so tolerant. The reporters had been forced to sit through three days of interminable discussions. Tired by it, they snatched at the lively, gossipy, sometimes silly things and ignored the philosophical ramblings. The council, as a result, looked foolish in the eyes of the public. This, after all, was the Company's first chance to govern itself and the public was interested in how it would do. The reports from the meeting did nothing to enhance the image of the new council.

Time, everyone said to the critics, it will take time, but time was running out.

26

Montreal Explodes

The picture that has been presented of the Company of Young Canadians thus far is not a pleasant one in many ways. The Company since its formation in 1966 had been a perpetual-crisis organization.

The Company's first permanent council meeting ended on October 6, 1969. It had been a flop. The children didn't seem to know or care. On the following day, the 7th, they were back at work doing what they were paid to do, and doing what the Company of Young Canadians was intended to do.

In Fort Rae, a small settlement of shacks in the Northwest Territories, Steve Iveson was chatting with the Indian residents about the problems of the area. Iveson had been there for more than a year and was accepted as one of the people.

In Toronto, Maggi Redmonds was at work at 999 Queen Street, an Ontario mental hospital. Maggi was a go-between for patients and medical staff. It was a new concept in health care and one that had been working well. She, too, had been doing this kind of work for more than a year.

Steve Iveson and Maggi Redmonds were not exceptions in the Company. For as long as the Company had been in existence there had been people like them. People who put their communities ahead of internal strife and lack of democracy. Their non-involvement in Company affairs had saved them some personal grief, but it also had left them open to attacks whenever the Company as a whole was skewered.

The Company used the Iveson's and Redmond's. It used

them as examples of what the Company could be, to divert attention from what the Company really was. These volunteers were the only reason for keeping the Company alive. The Company repaid them with national fiascos and disasters.

Each disaster set back community work. Each undermined months of trust-building. The volunteers wanted no more of them.

The staff, more than anyone else, were also acutely aware that the CYC could not survive another major crisis. Each crisis over the three years had weakened the Company, and made it harder to survive the next. The Company had no credibility, save for its few volunteers. The Company did not have many supporters. It had to hold onto those it had and build a new trust among Canadians.

The one weak area in staff projections was Quebec.

English-speaking Canada had never been as volatile as Quebec. The volunteers tended to work more quietly and were less concerned with political issues. Vidal could act here without worrying about national repercussions.

Quebec was something else. The last time Ottawa had tried to rid Quebec of its volatile element, an occupation of the Montreal office had developed. If it tried again something far worse might be the result. Vidal did not and could not take the risk. He had to wait. He had to let things he disagreed with continue.

No one was suggesting for a moment that the Company should not engage in controversial activities. The volunteers and the staff both agreed that the Company was an agent for social change, that in order to be effective it had to become involved in political and social controversy.

The Company was not secretive about this. It stated this belief openly and bluntly on many occasions, and included it in its annual report for 1968-1969:

"Our job is to facilitate social change. This is done by making people aware of their rights and helping them to organize to take full advantage of the democratic system in order to achieve their rights. It is important to emphasize that the Company at no time decides what a community will or won't do. We believe that people in a community are fully aware of what their problems and needs are. Our job is to help them come together to solve their problems and fulfill their needs.

"There are several hard facts that the Company has accepted about social change. Four of the most important are: social change automatically has political implications; social change cannot be achieved without organization at the community level; volunteers must put the community's needs ahead of their own ideologies; social change involves tension, emotion and friction. The last three facts are usually accepted but few wish to accept the first. Yet politics are invariably connected with change, whether at the civic, provincial or federal levels."

Claude Vidal added one other statement to this.

"Volunteers, above all, must be competent."

This philosophy was workable and defendable as long as it was adhered to. If a volunteer organized citizens concerned about urban renewal and those citizens, on their own accord, marched on a city council, the Company could easily support and justify the volunteer's role. He was, after all, only helping the citizens. He was not a leader and he was not forcing solutions upon them.

The Company was open about its objectives and methods of work. It told the government and the public, in its annual report, what to expect. No one reacted. Just as long as the Company was quiet and responsible, it could say and do what it wanted.

That is, until Black Tuesday.

The day after the Company's permanent council ended its meeting — the day that Company volunteers in English-speaking Canada were peacefully promoting change — the city of Montreal blew apart.

For months the police of that city had been negotiating for a salary increase. The increase would bring them up to parity with their equivalents in Toronto, and the parity, in view of Montreal's high crime rate, seemed justified. The city was in debt, however, and the administration was in no mood for spending more money. The police finally took action.

They walked off their beats on October 7 and left the city unguarded.

Banks closed, fearful that they would be robbed. Stores did the same. As many people as possible stayed off the streets to avoid the lawless.

The city was relatively peaceful until dark came, but with the night came the burners and looters. They marched down Montreal's main streets in large gangs, breaking store windows and taking what merchandise they wanted. Others were not so interested in material benefits. They saw an opportunity to advance another battle, one that had been raging for more than a year between them and Murray Hill Limousine Services Ltd.

Murray Hill had exclusive taxi and bus rights at Montreal International Airport just outside the city. The other cabbies resented this and were trying to break the monopoly.

The main thrust against Murray Hill was led by a group called the Mouvement de Liberation du Taxi. This was a militant body and had, before the police strike, held numerous demonstrations against Murray Hill and destroyed Murray Hill property. Some Company volunteers had taken part in a few of these demonstrations and many were avid supporters of the Mouvement.

Black Tuesday was the perfect opportunity for the Mouvement to strike hard at Murray Hill. Members loaded into cars and headed for the limousine company's main garage. The company must have been expecting trouble, for the garage was well-manned when the cars arrived.

Within minutes, gun shots were being exchanged between the two groups. Some came from inside the garage, others from rooftops across the street. Caught in the middle was Corporal Robert Dumas of the Quebec Provincial Police.

He was shot in the back and killed.

While the shooting went on, Murray Hill buses and property were set on fire.

For the next few days, Montreal was an armed camp. Soldiers patrolled the downtown area keeping citizens moving, not letting any crowds congregate in any one spot. The police were back on the job by then, but city officials, under a national microscope, were taking no chances that civil disorder might reappear.

Bad news began to come to Ottawa from Pierre Renaud in Montreal.

Montreal police and the QPP were raiding CYCer's homes, and CYC offices. By Renaud's count more than 25 dwellings had already been searched, including his and that of Jean Roy, the council member.

The Ottawa office stiffened, waiting for the worst. By late Friday night, October 10th, nothing had developed and everyone relaxed. The weekend would be a welcome break from the pressure.

Lucien Saulnier, however, did not want anyone to relax.

On Saturday night, the executive committee chairman for the city of Montreal held a press conference and appealed to Prime Minister Trudeau to institute a Royal Commission into the activities of the CYC. In the meantime, he asked that the government cut off the flow of public funds to the Company.

He charged that CYC volunteer ranks in Quebec had been infiltrated by convicted terrorists and Communist agitators bent on destroying democratic governments.

Flanked by Mayor Jean Drapeau and Police Director J.P. Gilbert, he continued on to say that the city had masses of documentary evidence linking some of the CYC volunteers with groups financed by foreign countries in Communist bloc.

Becoming more specific, the executive committee chairman then listed some of the Company's sins: Several of the CYC members in Montreal had been convicted of FLQ terrorist activities after the first wave of bombings in 1963. A printing press belonging to the Company had been used the week before to print thousands of leaflets urging students and workers to take part in a Friday night demonstration organized by the Front de Liberation Populaire. Police had found firearms in a raid on October 9th at an office used by the organizers of a CYC project. CYC volunteers helped to organize protest marches and class boycotts by college and university students the previous year. Piles of Communist propaganda and revolutionary instructions on how to make Molotov cocktails, bombs and other weapons had been found in CYC offices.

The story first broke as Claude Vidal was preparing to go out with his wife in Montreal. His main public relations man was milking cows at a farm outside of Ottawa. Both men were contacted by the CBC for comments and were requested to appear on Weekend, a new CBC show getting its first airing that night. Vidal decided to let his information man handle it and called him. Both men were calm. Saulnier had not done as much damage as they had expected.

The Company had been afraid that it would be linked definitely with bombing or terrorist activity in the Montreal area. Anything less than that was getting off easy.

Saulnier's charges were still serious, however. The very timing and slant of Saulnier's attack was enough.

There was no love between Montreal's city administration and the Company. For about a year there had been an increasingly bitter fight between the Drapeau-Saulnier regime and Company-led forces in Montreal. It started with the Company taking part in a protest demonstration against

Prime Minister Trudeau in Petite Bourgogne in the city. This was embarrassing for the mayor. Next, a noisy citizen's delegation, Company-inspired, broke up a city council meeting. And finally, the Company helped to establish anti-Drapeau committees in Montreal slum districts, including St. Henri, Milton Park and Mercier. This was hardly the way to gain the affection of the civic leaders in Montreal.

The anti-Drapeau committees were not hard to organize. Montreal was having more than its share of financial problems. Expo, the subway and other costly ventures had put the city deep in the red and citizens were complaining that Drapeau made money available for such playthings, but was neglecting such crucial needs as adequate housing.

This is not to say that the city administration did not have the right to attack the Company in Quebec. For some time Montreal, city police and the QPP had been gathering documentation on the CYC's activities and, once previously, Lucien Saulnier had levelled similar charges at the Company. But now with the nation's eyes on Montreal, he had a much more attentive audience.

The CYC executive director and the director of information decided to accuse Saulnier of using the Company as a red herring to deflect criticism from his own administration. The committee chairman's direct charges would have to be answered more specifically, of course, and this the Company would attempt to do as honestly as possible.

On television that night the director of information sat on a panel that included William Kelly, just recently retired from the RCMP. Kelly had been head of the RCMP's anti-spy, anti-subversion ring. During the warm-up prior to going on the air, the information man was asked bluntly whether the Company had hired former terrorists in Quebec. He and Kelly answered yes almost simultaneously. It was obvious that the Company's secrets were not so secret after all, if even the RCMP was involved.

The red herring routine was gone through swiftly and then the information man returned to his home to spend the weekend on the phone with newsmen. Canadian newspapers were pulling out all the stops in their coverage of the Company.

On Monday morning, October 13, the Ottawa staff gathered to discuss plans. The plans had to be limited as the permanent council would no doubt want to play an active part in deciding what path to follow. All the staff could do was keep things in one piece until the council met.

"Let's at least be honest," Vidal told his co-workers. "Don't try to cover up anything."

The staff then adjourned to watch the game being played, with the Company as the ball. Newsmen, Lucien Saulnier and Gerard Pelletier were the main participants.

Pelletier rejected the idea for a Royal Commission in the press, but said that RCMP officers were investigating the Company in Montreal.

Saulnier continued to step up his attack.

He said that the organization, supported by government tax money, was working actively to: encourage methods of action which rapidly develop into a revolutionary test of strength; encourage the occupation of industrial plants during strikes in order to create head-on collisions; distribute written information on Communist activities in other countries.

The newspapers, meanwhile, were having a field day.

"Provincial Police Director Maurice St. Pierre flew to Quebec City shortly before dawn today for a meeting with Justice Minister Remi Paul and other members of the provincial cabinet," *The Montreal Star* reported on October 14.

The front-page story then said the cause of the secret mission was "to report to the provincial authorities on investigations into the activities of the Company of Young Canadians."

St. Pierre took with him a file on the CYC compiled by

the combined anti-subversive squad, composed of members of the QPP, the RCMP and Montreal police. It was the first time that anyone had ever heard of a combined anti-subversive squad, and some people openly doubted its existence. There was no question, however, that the police had a file on the Company. During the weekend of the 11th, 14 more homes had been raided and 27 people associated with the Company had been taken into custody for questioning. If it was a red herring, it was a damn impressive one.

From Ottawa, the Company admitted that former terrorists had been hired by the Company. Then, speaking about Pierre Renaud specifically, defended the choice.

In Montreal, Bernard Mataign, a Company volunteer and an executive member of the Front de Liberation Populaire, one of the left-wing separatist parties that Saulnier had attacked, was also doing a lot of talking. He seemed to undo everything that Ottawa was attempting to do.

"Bernard Mataign, 25, a member of the Company of Young Canadians, openly stated Monday night that he is 'an independist' and that 'there are many like me working for the Company in Montreal'," The *Toronto Daily Star* reported.

Mataign was one of the main targets of the Montreal police. Convicted in 1964 for illegal possession of dynamite, he was one of the better known separatists in Montreal. Stewart Goodings had tried to get rid of him in late 1968, but failed. The Company was now paying for that failure. For no matter how reformed Mataign may have been, and there were doubts about that, his casual acceptance of separatism shocked many English-speaking Canadians.

As if Mataign's statements were not enough, word was received from Montreal that Louis-Phillipe Aubert, another volunteer Goodings had tried to deselect, had been tagged as a material witness in the shooting-death of Corporal Robert Dumas.

Aubert had been at the Murray Hill garage the night of the shooting. He had arrived with other men in a CYC car. When police searched the automobile they found guns. When questioned about the guns, Aubert is reported to have said that they were "to defend CYC property".

It was just as well that Aubert's guns, however innocent, were not reported, for editorial opinion about the Company was unfavorable enough.

The Toronto *Globe and Mail* was one example.

Even if the Company of Young Canadians were disbanded tomorrow, the City of Montreal would still have enough troubles of its own making to engage the full attention of its leaders. The dramatic attack on the Company by executive committee chairman Lucien Saulnier, backed by Mayor Jean Drapeau and police director J.P. Gilbert, was probably intended, at least in part, to direct attention away from the failures of the municipal government. We trust the people of Montreal will not be diverted.

Nevertheless, the CYC should be disbanded.

. . . There was nothing indigenous about the CYC, it had no grass roots, it was not an expression of Canadian youth which the Government recognized and fostered. It was simply an expedient.

Its history had been a history of one indiscretion after another. Nobody ever managed to give it a real reason for being. What the Government did give it was money; and it has spent its time finding what were generally unacceptable ways to spend the money.

The members psychoanalyzed each other. They developed a nice taste for automobiles. They promoted each other to well-paid posts as consultants. The Quebec division discovered that everything from the national body was distasteful, except the money. Almost everywhere else the members seemed to feel that their mandate was to annoy. After each mistake they were given another chance. But patience ends.

Some good work was done, but this was almost entirely the result of workers in the field, far from head office, using their own initiative and often at considerable personal sacrifice . . . .

The Company has made itself hospitable to those who preach revolution, violence, separation. It is not a recipe for action that we should be financing from public revenue. There are other, more solidly built agencies — and agencies, too, which involve youth — which can do the valid work of the CYC; they should be handed it.

As for the CYC — the Government is practicing strict economy; there is no money it could more properly save than the $2-million annual CYC budget.

This sentiment was expressed by most of Canada's daily newspapers. Their patience was indeed exhausted by the antics of the Company. As Claude Vidal and others in the Company had guessed before the explosion in Montreal, the Company could not afford another crisis. Now that one was upon them they would do their best to keep the Company alive, if only for the good work that even the *Globe and Mail* had to recognize. At this stage, no one knew if that could be done. The government had reiterated its unwillingness to have a Royal Commission into Company activities. The sages, however, did not discount the possibility of an inquiry.

It would all really depend on the council meeting scheduled for the weekend of October 18. If the Company could move decisively on its own to wipe out the undesirable elements in Quebec, then the government might stay out. This was the hope of the senior staff and of the appointed members. Whether the Company would move, though, was up to the elected members of the council. In office for less than three weeks, they were already under the gun. Their reaction would determine the fate of the Company.

27

The Council's Response

The CYC crisis experts were confident that the Company could pull its way out of the Montreal mess.

Lucien Saulnier's charges, they reasoned, were accurate on the point of separatism, but exaggerated when he started to talk about Communism and national, or provincial, conspiracies. The government would not dare to act on such innuendos without appearing to be witch-hunting.

Prime Minister Trudeau and Secretary of State Pelletier were also exceedingly liberal. Both had accepted the concept of the Company as being radical, and both surely realized that this would have political implications. They would not move in on the Company for tangling with Drapeau and Saulnier, especially since the two civic politicians' motives were so suspect.

Finally, the permanent council of the Company was only two weeks old. The government, after creating the council, would have to give it a chance to solve the problem in Montreal. They were sure that, given this chance, the council would respond positively.

On October 18th, the council met once more in the smoke-filled conference room. The atmosphere was electric and gave one the impression that big decisions were to be made. The press thought so too and were there in large numbers. The Company, always a source of interest to them, was becoming an obsession.

To the outsider, Quebec seemed to be an issue that would draw the Company together. It even seemed that way to some staff and council members. There was surely no way that the council and staff could remain divided on something so basic to the future of the Company.

Claude Vidal was concerned about Quebec along with everyone else, but he was concerned about something else as well. The council's decision on Jim Littleton at its previous meeting had disturbed him. He decided to try to regain some ground at this meeting. He wanted to test council, as if Quebec were not test enough. It was a crucial decision for him to make.

With everyone poised for discussion on Quebec, the executive director presented a letter to council, addressed to the council secretary, questioning the legality of the October 4th to 6th meeting.

Vidal had consulted with the Company lawyers and had doubts that the council could legally operate without having a duly-elected chairman and vice-chairman.

The council erupted.

The radical members accused the director of harassing and obstructing the council and of failing to respect its authority. Even the moderates were angry and lectured Vidal on the inappropriateness of his letter.

To advance the meeting, though, the council decided that it would elect a chairman and vice-chairman before the weekend was over. The council could then approve, retroactively, all previous decisions.

Skip Hambling stormed out of the meeting in disgust. He had wanted Vidal's resignation.

A newspaperman approached a senior staff member.

"What the hell is going on here?" he asked. "Doesn't the Company know what happened in Quebec?"

The Company did know and moved on to discuss the situation. The press, much to their displeasure, were asked to leave during the discussion in order to prevent any prejudicial reporting against people involved in the upheavals. The reporters adjourned to the Company's reception room.

Pierre Renaud delivered his analysis of the situation. He

spoke of the police strike, the riots, the Murray Hill fiasco, and of Louis-Phillipe Aubert's involvement. He also generally listed which volunteers were and which were not separatists, and hinted that some of those mentioned by the press would be resigning.

It was now up to the council.

The council decided it would establish a policy for the Company to follow. That policy was simply a restating of one that the Company had been following. The new version read:

"Because the objectives of the Company of Young Canadians are to assist the powerless and voiceless to participate fully in society, it is inevitable that, in the course of their employment, Company personnel will on occasion find themselves in conflict with particular political, social or economic structures. Such conflicts are acceptable provided that they are in legitimate pursuance of the goals of a particular CYC project. The goals of these projects are defined by the Company staff and volunteers, subject to final approval and periodic evaluation by the council.

"It is accepted that volunteers have their personal political convictions but neither the volunteers, nor the projects in which they work, should be involved in direct partisan political activity. The role of the volunteer is to assist people to organize themselves to act on their own behalf. It is neither practical nor desirable for the Company to censor the private political convictions of a volunteer. Nevertheless, because the public acts of a volunteer reflect on the entire Company, any volunteer who wishes to carry his private political convictions to the point of active partisan political involvement will be asked to resign."

This is a curiously naive policy and leaves at least one important question unanswered.

As Arthur Blakely of the *Montreal Gazette* pointed out, "there is no recognition of the hard fact that the former (members of standard Canadian political parties) are content to operate under the accepted political ground rules of Canadian society. The Maoists, Communists and separatists, neither accept that society in its present form, nor the ground rules it has seen fit to adopt".

There was also no recognition that the FLP and other left-wing separatist groups demand total allegiance to their cause. A volunteer with the CYC who was a member of the FLP would pay lip service to the Company, but serve the FLP. He might not be overtly politically active but his objectives would be those of the FLP.

What a solution to a pressing problem! The Company is accused of being separatist-dominated in Quebec, and the Company responds by saying that this kind of action cannot be tolerated and that the volunteers in Quebec, the separatists, have the responsibility of ferreting out the bad influences.

If this was not included in the policy, it became clear in the aftermath, when council decided what to do about St. Henri, the project of Louis-Phillipe Aubert.

The council requested that Pierre Renaud and the St. Henri volunteers, presumably Aubert as well as his wife, examine the necessity of deselection of volunteers on that project. Their recommendations would be submitted to the council, but not before going through Comcord.

Jean Roy must have been pleased with the council's decisions. The entire Company was being threatened by Quebec, but the council was refusing to sacrifice that province's autonomy for the good of the rest of the Company.

Why, one must ask, did the rest of the council go along with Quebec on this issue?

Claude Vidal was not unhappy with the final decision of council. It was becoming obvious to him and to other senior staff that the council was not serious about cleaning up the difficulties in the Company. In their minds, a parliamentary inquiry would now not be such a bad thing. That impression was transmitted quietly and probably without Vidal's knowledge to Pelletier's office. The final split had occurred. Vidal would now try to make it wider by placing more pressure upon the council, by irritating it even further.

The future of the Company looked bleak to some as the council meeting ended. Not all Company people, though, were pessimistic. Jack Johnson, the Calgary lawyer, had been elected council chairman. He believed that the policy was workable and that the Company had presented an image of responsibility. Quiet, determined, and the image of responsibility, Johnson read the policy to the news media. He did an excellent job, and anyone watching television that night could not have mistaken him for any left-wing fanatic. He made promises that the Company, given the necessary time, would right itself. These were promises that he would never be able to keep.

Sitting by Johnson that night as he read his statement was Jean Roy. Smiling and content, Roy offered advice to Johnson and even stepped in to help in French. He deserved to be there. His newly won post of vice-chairman of council entitled him to that.

His presence was one final reminder to the government, and to the city of Montreal, that the Company had not taken the charges seriously. Was not Roy one of the men linked to the subversive tactics? Had he not won a smashing victory for the autonomous Quebec cause in Canada's capital?

One can almost hear Alan Clarke speaking in the background.

"Discipline," he once said, "is not a word included in our vocabulary."

28
The Government Steps In

The charges levelled at the CYC by Lucien Saulnier had been extreme enough to catch the entire country's attention. They had also won him the support, when facing the federal government, of the mayors of more than a dozen cities and towns in Quebec. The government might be able to say no to Saulnier and Drapeau, but could it also ignore Granby, La Tuque, Lauzon, Amqui, Matane, Riviere Du Loup and Val d'Or?

On October 22nd, Gerard Pelletier rose in the Commons to announce that the Standing Committee on Broadcasting, Films and Assistance to the Arts would conduct an inquiry into the operations of the CYC. No one was surprised.

It was understood that the inquiry would lead to changes in the Company. Pelletier himself said that the government wants "the exceptional liberty" of the Company reduced.

Oddly enough, Pelletier's announcement did not rate headline coverage in the daily newspapers the next day. Not that people were losing interest in the Company. Headline coverage was given to a more sensational Company disclosure.

In Montreal on the night of October 22, T.R. Anthony Malcolm, vice-president of the Quebec section of the Liberal Federation of Canada, and co-chairman of the anti-separatist Canada Committee, gave a speech to the Town of Mount Royal Women's Club.

Where he got the information contained in his speech is not known. Many Company people felt that it was planted by the federal Liberals to reinforce their decision to hold an inquiry. Others thought that the QPP or the Montreal police gave it to Malcolm to back up the Saulnier-Drapeau team. Where it came from doesn't really matter, it was devastating enough without the source being revealed.

Subversive elements which have infiltrated the Company of Young Canadians and the Parti Quebecois were getting financial and material help from Cuba, Algeria and the Soviet Union, he charged.

Malcolm, a lawyer, then listed the names of 27 people whom he alleged were subversives. Of the 27, 18 had worked or were working for the CYC. This was more than even the Company had counted.

Malcolm was particularly hard on Mario Bachand, Bernard Blondin, Louis Beaulieu, Bernard Mataign and Louis-Phillipe Aubert.

"Bachand," he said, "formed part of the first FLQ movement in 1963 and was condemned for bombing attempts in the city of Montreal, became a volunteer with the CYC after release from prison.

"He put his training with the Company of Young Canadians to good use in forming the Comite Independant Socialiste — one of the two founding organizations of the present FLP.

"This was achieved together with Bernard Blondin and Louis Beaulieu. The premises which they occupy at 2100 St. Denis St. is paid for at the rate of $60 a month by the Company of Young Canadians," Malcolm said.

Malcolm went on to accuse the following CYC members:

"Bernard Mataign, convicted of possession of dynamite in 1965, is one of the present directors of the executive of the Front de Liberation Populaire and a volunteer in the Company of Young Canadians; printer and distributer of the revolutionary newspaper *La Masse*.

"Louis-Phillipe Aubert, one of the directors of the FLP

acts as a director of the workers committee of St. Henri for the CYC. He was also found guilty of the possession of dynamite in 1965 with Mataigne.

"Pierre Renaud, one of the principal directors of the CYC in Quebec. He is in charge of three major projects; former candidate for the RIN and a member of the FLQ-Valliere-Gagnon group, condemned for armed robbery of a movie house on Jean Talon Street.

"Bernard Fauteux, who directed three projects of the CYC and received a salary of $7,000 a year. He also drove a Volvo paid for by the government of Canada.

"Jacques Geoffroy, the brother of Pierre Paul Geoffroy, a convicted terrorist. He is a volunteer of the CYC in St. Jerome. He writes for the revolutionary papers *La Masse* and *LeRezo*.

"Jean Roy, Jean Pierre Potvin, Raymond Barbeau, Michel Benoit, Claude Lariviere, Gilles Prud'homme and Jacques Larue-Langlois, all former or present members of the CYC."

Everyone thought that Claude Vidal would be upset by Malcolm's speech. The executive director, however, took things in his stride.

He was not unhappy that the inquiry had been called. This would, at least, force the Company to clean house and give him an opportunity to present the Company's problems to a group that was willing to listen, and had the power to act. This would probably mean that Vidal would break from the Company's council and put his own neck on the line.

This was something he had done before in Quebec and was quite willing to do again. He had been through two inquiries in his native province and had performed admirably at both. There was no reason to believe that he would not manage to survive yet another.

As for Malcolm's charges? Malcolm provided Vidal with

information that he didn't have, or reinforced information that he already held. The charges would prove, in the long run, to be more useful than damaging.

There was not that much time to worry about Malcolm at this stage. The inquiry had already been called by Pelletier, and on Friday, October 24th, the parliamentary committee received its order of reference. The order was large.

The committee was to consider the legislative framework, organization and operations of the Company of Young Canadians. It was given until December 5th, just over a month, to examine the three years of the Company and to make a final report to the Commons. That gave the Company little time for preparation, and the committee not much more time to arrive at some logical conclusions.

But before the committee would get a chance to meet, the council of the Company would hold another meeting. This one would be in Montreal, and it would be the last rational attempt to hold the Company together.

29
The Toronto Youth Project

The volunteers and the field operations of the Company of Young Canadians were disturbed very little by the announcement of an inquiry. Nor did the apparent mediocrity of their elected council disturb them. Through crisis after crisis the volunteers had carried on in their communities either doing their good work or continuing their bad. Nothing seemed to stop them. This was unfortunate for Claude Vidal, and the council.

The council did not want Claude Vidal to have anything to do with the projects. The field was their area of priority and they wanted to make decisions without obstructions from the executive director. Vidal did not see his role as one of an obstructionist, and refused to give up the responsibility for projects that the act and the Company's policy clearly stated he had. This brought Vidal and the council into further conflict.

At an earlier meeting, the permanent council had instructed Vidal to maintain the status quo on all projects. At the same time, it told him that all existing policies were to remain and be used until the council had time to change them. This put the director in a difficult position. If he saw the need to change a project, he had the authority under the Company's policies. But the council had instructed him to maintain the status quo. Which decision took priority? Vidal decided he would have to forego the status quo as far as Toronto Youth was concerned.

There were only two volunteers left on Toronto Youth — David Gardner and Larry Williams, both Americans.

For months, Richard Lightbown, a very capable, if somewhat square, staff member, had been trying to find out what the project was doing. All he could find out was that Williams and Gardner were living on Toronto Island in a sort of commune. There they were pursuing studies in hydroponics — a science concerning soil-less plant production. This was hardly the type of project that the CYC should have been involved in.

The two volunteers refused to acknowledge Lightbown's existence, even though he was the staff person responsible for them. It was also evident that they were misusing Company funds and government equipment at an alarming rate.

The volunteers, in fact, furnished the office of *Harbinger,* a Toronto underground newspaper, with government equipment, and were using Company phones to call people in areas such as Hollywood and Baltimore.

Lightbown at the end of October had had enough. He saw no useful end for the project or the volunteers and recommended to Claude Vidal that the project be closed and the volunteers deselected. Vidal accepted his recommendation and initiated deselection procedures, and just in time.

Within days, one exploit of the two volunteers was revealed on the front page of the Toronto *Globe and Mail.*

They had used government envelopes with illegal postage paid stickers to mail out copies of *Harbinger.*

The Toronto Youth issue found its way onto the council agenda for the weekend meeting in Montreal of November 1st, 2nd and 3rd. It was a heavy agenda and chairman Jack Johnson wanted to complete it. His feeling was that the council, by getting down to hard policy decisions, could prove to the government that it was responsible and deserving of government support. Johnson was appearing before the parliamentary committee on November 4th as the first witness and wanted to take a list of policy decisions with him.

Toronto Youth, however, was not the only important

item to be discussed that weekend by the council. There were other projects with problems that would have to be solved; there were evaluation and administrative policies to consider; and there was Jim Littleton.

At its first meeting, when council had reinstated Littleton, Vidal had interpreted this reinstatement his own way and refused to let Littleton into the Company office or to use Company materials. At its second meeting Vidal questioned the legality of the first meeting, council objected to the director's treatment of Jim Littleton, but eventually backed down and placed the errant staff member on a forced leave of absence. Now, the ad hoc committee that was investigating the Littleton episode had completed its report for presentation to this, the third meeting.

The meeting was held at the University Settlement Centre in the Milton Park area of Montreal. The council showed up in force, as did the volunteers whose projects were to be discussed. For once the press stayed away and William Morris of the Toronto *Globe and Mail* was the only reporter present.

Jack Johnson realized the importance of this meeting and opened it with a short speech.

"We are trying to prove ourselves responsible. Let's get on with the agenda and make some decisions," he said.

The first day was spent dissecting the Cape Breton project. It was a long, arduous and frustrating process. Skip Hambling presented a report that called for expansion of the Cape Breton project and expansion into other parts of the Maritimes. He suggested that the Ottawa office should have no authority or involvement in any of this.

The staff fought back. They did not want Cape Breton or the Maritimes to expand under the direction of Bert Deveux and his volunteers. Documents were presented that accurately presented the financial position of the project — it was not good, particularly in the areas of transportation and communications.

To further insure that Cape Breton would not be supported, and as indication of their willingness to mix it up with council members, the staff circulated, especially to the Quebec councillors, a copy of a story that Skip Hambling had given to the Canadian University Press.

In it, Hambling accused Vidal of quashing radical, English-speaking projects and then said:

"Yet radicals, and that means separatists, in Quebec projects are not hassled — that's partly because we flagellate ourselves with liberal self guilt over Canada's special problem."

Cape Breton was given nothing and lost nothing. Council, instead, decided to do an evaluation. Since there was no evaluation procedure, and more time would have to be spent to arrive at one, it was decided to wait until Monday.

Saturday's meeting ended with a happy staff. They had blocked Cape Breton and hopefully broken the Hambling-Quebec alliance. The real test, however, would be coming on Sunday with Toronto Youth, Jim Littleton, Toronto Development and the inquiry due for discussion.

When staff and councillors arrived for the new day's activities, they found the Toronto volunteers already firmly in place. These volunteers were typical of the Company's image — long-hair, unkempt, and mouthy.

They were grouped together in one corner of the meeting room, burning incense and drinking a special kind of tea. If their appearance and habits were distracting, their conduct was downright alarming.

As the meeting began, they started passing notes to council members, their form of lobbying for their project. As it continued they became more bold. Council members and staff were dragged from the room to listen to a lecture on the wonders of health food and the miracle of hydroponics. The volunteers then began to cheer and boo councillor's statements, and would occasionally rush up to the council table to whisper words of encouragement or censure in councillor's ears.

Claude Vidal and his staff watched in wonder.

The staff presented its case for closing the Toronto Youth Project. The floor was then turned over to the volunteers. Larry Williams squatted Indian style on a chair and proceeded to harangue the staff and remind the volunteer councillors about who had elected them.

When the time came for a decision, it happened. Unbelievably, the council voted to keep the project until an evaluation could be done. Claude Vidal, his staff, the more moderate council members, and William Morris of the *Globe and Mail* sat with their mouths open. How in God's name, they wondered, could the council justify an action as ludicrous as this?

It was not difficult.

The council, said Jean Roy, had ordered the status quo to be maintained on all projects. Vidal had acted illegally, and had in fact mocked the authority of council, by deselecting these volunteers. The fact that they were so clearly not suited for the Company didn't matter at all.

Then to add madness to stupidity, Roy proposed that the Ottawa administration be censured for its actions.

This vote was tied, but the damage had been done.

It is difficult to fault Vidal in this case. The evidence against the Toronto Youth project was so overwhelmingly damning that nobody with self-respect could have voted to maintain it, not even until an evaluation was done. What had caused the council to be so blind?

It wasn't all of the council, of course. Lloyd Axworthy, Sean Sullivan and a few other moderates wanted the project killed. With them on this issue, and leaving the ranks of the self-defined radicals, was Jack Johnson. Desperately trying to boost the already riddled credibility of the council, Johnson had seen this meeting as a sort of last chance. A believer in competence he saw only one choice that could be made concerning Toronto Youth and was stunned when the volunteer councillors voted to keep it. The added shock of the motion of censure against Claude Vidal opened his eyes to many things.

The Toronto Youth decision climaxed the meeting. There were other decisions made and some policies established, but none had such impact.

Jim Littleton was finally ousted from the Company. The ad hoc committee that investigated his case voted two to one that he should leave. Millie Barrett presented the minority report. Despite the decision, and council's approval, Claude Vidal was still rudely treated for his handling of the entire affair.

Another group which called itself the Southern Ontario Region, presented a manifesto calling for its independence. Among other things, the region wanted the right to hire its own staff. The Quebecois dismissed it out of hand. After working for a year on Comcord, they were not willing to look at a document that had been drawn up over a few weeks. The region was told to bring more information.

The Toronto Development project refused to present a report on its activities since the Ontario Region manifesto had been ignored, but still demanded that its staff member, the unfortunate Dick Lightbown, be removed. The council ordered another evaluation.

Comcord emerged once more from the bushes to present its case for decentralization of the Company. This time it was warmly received. An ad hoc group held a spontaneous meeting one night to bash out a report on decentralization for the entire Company. It effectively shut the executive director out of the picture, and left the Company totally in the hands of the volunteers and projects. In the light of the Toronto Youth project, it did not appear to be a wise move. No final decision was taken, however. Decentralization would be discussed again before anything was done.

And finally, the council approved an evaluation procedure on the last day of the meeting. The procedure was invoked to cover the projects that already had presented reports to council at that meeting. That the procedure was loaded — the volunteers on the projects concerned would be evaluating themselves with some outside help — didn't seem to concern many people.

As the meeting dragged to a close on Monday, November 3rd, it was obvious, at least to an outsider, that the Company was in trouble. As usual the Company did not agree. So used to looking inward and separating itself from the rest of society, the Company accepted even the most horrendous occurances as normal. William Morris of the *Globe and Mail* did not have the same gift.

On Monday, his reporting of the council meeting was scathing. He emphasized the Toronto Youth decision and branded the council as irresponsible.

On Tuesday, November 4, the opening day of the inquiry, he expanded his article verbally on CBC Radio. Here, he was even less kind towards the council.

His criticisms were accepted with glee by the staff. The worse the council looked, the better their own chances before the inquiry.

The volunteer council members gave Morris very little attention. He was, after all, an establishment member and had no understanding of social change and the role of the volunteer. They forgot that the rest of the country was in the same position as Morris.

And then there was Jack Johnson. He had tried during the meeting to bring some semblance of order to it and, except for the last day, had failed. He hoped that the decisions made that last day would have a positive effect. It was wishful thinking.

Many council members felt that the Company could

weather any storm; that their boldness and political ideal-ism could not be shattered by mere MPs. They did not count on the fact that their harsh treatment of Claude Vidal would be their undoing; that the man they had mocked and ridiculed would have his day.

In reality, the majority of council members were not even seriously concerned about the inquiry. The proof of that had come during the council meeting.

Jack Johnson had raised the issue and requested that the discussion surrounding the Company's attitude towards the inquiry be gone over behind closed doors. His request was denied. Johnson then refused to discuss what exactly he would say to the parliamentary committee and the problem was allowed to drop.

Johnson would attend the inquiry the next day in the company of Jean Roy and Claude Vidal.

The Company was coming to an end and true to form, refused to recognize the problem as one worthy of dis-cussion.

30
The Forgotten Volunteers

As the politicians gathered in the transportation hearings room in the Centre Block of Canada's House of Commons on November 4th to gather evidence and deliver judgements on the Company of Young Canadians; as the press took their positions alongside, with pens poised to note the havoc in the agency that none of them understood; as Jack Johnson and Jean Roy sat down to defend the two months they had been in power, and to ignore the other three years; as Claude Vidal sat with them, preparing his own version of those two months, and the previous nine months; a cynic might have asked what these people had to do with the Company of Young Canadians?

Canada's more liberal newspapers and magazines, a minority, had been asking that question and answering it for some time. The answer was a definite "nothing". The Company of Young Canadians was in the field.

"Don't throw out the good with the bad," *Time* had cried on October 24th.

The magazine had then related stories of volunteer success after volunteer success and then added, "Despite some remarkable successes, the CYC's volunteers have often run into such strenuous opposition that they could hardly be blamed if they chucked it all."

The inquiry would have been the ideal time to consider the volunteers. Wouldn't it be marvellous for the MPs to visit projects and see the Company in action, someone suggested. That had been suggested before but few MPs, even the critics, had dared venture onto CYC projects.

Perhaps they were afraid that the stereotyped image of a volunteer — long-hair, untamed, revolutionary — would turn out to be correct and they would be driven away with stones.

This time the suggestion was taken more seriously. If the parliamentary committee was to have an accurate picture of the Company it would undoubtedly have to visit the projects.

The MPs would never make it, though. Their drive for information was muffled by the complexity they found just in Ottawa, by their own predetermined opinions, and by the ridiculous time limitation of one month.

For their part, the volunteers didn't particularly want to be bothered by the MPs anyway. Over the years they had developed an attitude towards Ottawa staff, towards the governing council and towards the government — let them alone, they all do what they want anyway, just keep working in the communities where things are real and honest.

What would the MPs have found in the field if they had gone to visit the volunteers?

The tenure of Claude Vidal had not brought the volunteers any closer to the Company staff, nor had it changed existing projects or added any new ones, with the exception of Winnipeg. This permitted the field to have continuity, and for some projects to delve more deeply into problems.

In Calgary, Elaine Husband had developed a tough team of volunteers and several concerned community groups into an organization called NOW — No Other Way. NOW was tackling the self-complacency of Canada's largest American city and, with the Company's help, was winning.

Calgary is one of Canada's richest cities on a per capita basis. It is an oil city and since the oil industry is an American prerogative, more than 100,000 Americans live there.

For years, Calgary was dominated by its nouveau-riche. These people, the McMahons and Bells, along with other businessmen, were the city's heroes. This meant, in practical terms, a conservative-oriented city council and mayor, and a general ignoring of social problems.

Bernie Muzeen, when he was a volunteer in Calgary, sparked the first awakening of the people. When he left, Elaine Husband, Mark de Haas, Harvey Cohen and Phil Lalonde, carried on to expand his base. The city would never be the same.

The first issue was housing and the target was Prime Minister Trudeau. In the city to address a $50-a plate supper meeting of oilmen, the Prime Minister declined an invitation to meet with NOW. The organization decided to run a competitive banquet.

NOW's banquet cost 50 cents and consisted of hot dogs and other non-gourmet delights and more than a thousand people attended. Pat Mahoney, the Liberal MP from Calgary, even appeared to apologize for the Prime Minister's inability to appear.

Unimpressed by Mahoney's speech, the banquet crowd marched to the Calgary Stampede grounds to confront the PM as he went into the rich people's do.

When Trudeau arrived he was rather ceremoniously presented with a dead mouse and implored to do something about Calgary's housing situation. He listened and said all good things take time. After addressing the crowd he went inside to talk to the money-men.

The confrontation with the Prime Minister was aired on television coast-to-coast. And although nothing concrete resulted immediately, the rest of Canada now knew that Calgary had its problems, and more people in Calgary began to realize it too. NOW had had its first taste of conservative blood.

The next target was welfare and the Calgary *Herald*. People receive welfare in Calgary, just like in any other city, but Calgary didn't like to talk about it because it presented an unfavorable image. The Calgary *Herald*, one of the country's least dynamic and most conservative news-papers, generally supported this stand. This made it all the more surprising when Merv Anderson, the paper's city editor, gave reporter Jacques Hamilton the go-ahead to do a feature on welfare.

Hamilton spent weeks interviewing people and studying statistics. He then wrote a series of articles. The series found its way into the upper echelons of the paper and was killed, presumably for showing that welfare did exist in Calgary. NOW moved into action.

Pickets were set up outside the newspaper offices and NOW condemned the paper for suppressing information. When this had no affect, NOW had the most damning parts of Hamilton's articles reprinted on leaflets. When the city of Calgary held its annual Calgary Stampede Parade, and thousands of visitors were in the city, these leaflets were distributed along the parade route.

The paper finally backed down.

Actions like this, and others, gradually began to make Calgarians believe that their city did have problems. The mayor, Jack Leslie, a real-estate man, tried to explain them away. It was to no avail. When election day came, a liberal, Rod Sykes, handily trounced Leslie for the highest office in the city.

In the space of three years, Calgary had been changed. Elaine Husband and the CYC have to be given a good deal of the credit.

Few other projects in the Company had such a wide influence, but, many others were promoting change success-fully.

In the Northwest Territories, for example, Company volunteers attacked small, isolated injustices and won some important victories.

Laura Dexter, a tall, stringy girl from Nova Scotia, orig-inally came to the Territories as editor of Yellowknife's weekly newspaper, the *News of the North*. In this role she came into contact with Company people, and soon became involved in the issues that the Company was pushing. Her involvement grew to such an extent that she soon left her job to become a Company volunteer.

She went to work in Yellowknife's Indian Village, a settlement a few miles from the city. The village was an eyesore to white residents and they preferred to ignore its existence. They also ignored the inhabitants and their children.

Education is important in the north. This is the way that native children can break away from the poverty of their background. This is the way they can be assimilated. The assimilation might work if there were jobs for the children when they finished school. Inevitably there are none, and the children, now well-educated, return to their villages and soon learn to hate them.

What the white man's schools do, in effect, is break down the Indian family structure. By sending the Indian children away from their homes to school, the children never learn the important values in their own society. They are taught white values and white ways. When white society rejects them, they return to the Indian society and are lost there amid values they have never learned.

The Indian Village was treated no differently than other Indian communities. The children went to school in Yellowknife. Laura Dexter talked to the Indian people about this and discovered that they disliked this as much as she did. They decided to do something about it.

Making use of her contacts at the paper and at CBC Radio, Laura soon made the plight of the Indian Village clear. All she needed now was action from the residents of the Indian Village. She started to organize through the chief. Meetings were held and the problem discussed. The Indians, without her coaching, decided to approach the Territorial government.

Their approaches did not meet with much success and

Laura went back to the press and radio.

Eventually, the government capitulated. The village would have its school.

Unimportant as this may seem to most people, to the Indians it was a victory of the utmost magnitude.

While Laura Dexter was working quietly in the Indian Village on one part of the education problem, Steve Iveson, a red-haired Montrealer, was tackling more directly and controversially another part.

Akaitcho Hall is a government school in Yellowknife and more than 200 young people, boys and girls between the ages of 14 and 24, were staying there, nearly all of them Indians.

Steve Iveson stayed at the residence on occasion and began to notice more than one thing wrong with it. He decided to act.

Over a short period of time, Iveson talked with students, with their families and with residents of the area about the school. From these conversations he wrote a report that eventually found its way into the hands of David Lewis, the Toronto NDP member of parliament. Lewis used the report to slam the Department of Indian Affairs and Northern Development, and no wonder.

In it, Iveson described the regulations that had been imposed on the residents. They would have made the member of a fascist youth club uncomfortable.

The only form of affection that would be permitted in Akaitcho Hall was hand-holding.

Students could not visit homes in Old Town Yellowknife, an Indian section.

Students could not visit their own homes without paternal permission.

Students could not question teachers.

The list went on and on for about 10 pages. These pages had to be memorized by each new house resident. He was given a page at a time, and when he had memorized one perfectly, was given one more.

While Lewis was criticizing the school, and the press was joining in, the government was fuming that the Company hadn't delivered the report into its hands. Perhaps Iveson was afraid that no action would have resulted.

As it happened there was lots of action, both in Yellowknife and in Ottawa.

The school superintendent worked quickly to revise his medieval regulations. A copy of a summary was sent to Northern Affairs Minister Jean Chretien. The superintendent also pressured a student into circulating a petition at the school to ensure Chretien that nothing was amiss.

Other students realized what was going on and refused to sign. Instead, they held a meeting and agreed that no telegram or petition should be sent criticizing David Lewis. This did not deter the superintendent — a telegram was sent anyway with 150 signatures listed.

Two girls, wanting to encourage Lewis in his investigation, organized the students to send a second telegram refuting the first. Both were expelled from the school, supposedly for using obscene language during their confrontation with the superintendent.

By this time, nearly all of Yellowknife was into the act. The citizens were outraged that conditions as described actually did exist at the school. They added their voices to those of the students. The result was predictable — the school rules were changed.

Here once again is the Company initiating action. Here is the Company sticking its neck out to battle an injustice. And here is the Company winning.

Calgary and the Northwest Territories were not the only outstanding projects during 1969. They do stand out, though, because their actions had public repercussions.

Pat Fergusson in Vancouver working on the city's skid

row with rubbies and prostitutes would never have a success that large. Her successes were smaller, but just as important on an individual basis. Every prostitute that she convinced to take voluntary venereal disease check-ups was a victory. Every drunk that she helped dry out made her worth her salary a hundred times over.

Ian Crawford in Maeve Hancey's old work area – the Orchard Park public housing project – was just as involved. He helped set up a "free store", a place where people could trade things they no longer wanted. He was in on the lobbying that resulted in city council approving a community hall for the area.

Then there's Buddy Sault and his Indian volunteers in Northwestern Ontario. Not quite so radical or racial now, they were looking in 1969 at industry and trying to get a lumber mill started as well as getting donations to start up a larger fishing business for Indians.

There are others as well. Vic Cathers in Lesser Slave Lake with volunteers like Rose Auger, a thoroughly troublesome, honest and dedicated Indian woman. At this lake they were organizing meetings, bringing in experts, holding creative classes for children, and uniting communities to fight poverty by bringing in industry.

The ACEF project in Montreal was no longer just dealing with consumer budgetting, but attacking finance companies that were charging interest rates of 50 to 100 per cent, protesting price increases in such necessities as milk, and organizing community co-operatives to bring money into the community, supply capital and create jobs.

All of these projects were giving something to Canadians that they had lacked before – pride. They were showing that someone cared enough to live with people who were having problems, to talk with them and, ultimately, to fight with them. Many of the battles were small, almost invisible when contrasted to the problems of Canada the nation, but as each small problem was solved, and other

Canadians saw that the system could be made to work, the larger problems facing Canada were reduced by some minute fraction.

The hope of social change is that the minute fractions will eventually form something larger. That, as more and more people become committed to change, a snowball will develop, a ball that grows larger by the week until it can't be ignored any longer. The Company volunteers were the start. As layers formed around them the volunteers would be difficult to find, but they were there all the same.

In 1966, for example, urban renewal was regarded as the right and proper thing. As the scabs on the urban renewal process became more visible, people began to see that some better process must be available. The exposing of those scabs took place all across Canada and, in nearly every early instance, the CYC was involved. Once it was accepted that urban renewal was not so holy, the Company's contribution was quickly forgotten. And the rhetoric that the Company used to attack the process, rhetoric that the Company was criticized for, was now being widely used by politicians and other concerned citizens.

In many ways the Company's best volunteers were always ahead of the rest of society. The volunteers were preaching participation long before the government caught on to it and made it a meaningless word. The volunteers were organizing citizen's groups two years before the country was deluged with citizen participation. The volunteers were setting examples, being shot down for their brashness, and then seeing the very people who criticized them pick up the examples to use for themselves.

That, one must imagine, is the price one pays for individualism, non-conformity and originality.

The Company and its projects were not all sweetness and progress in 1969. The constant bickering between Claude Vidal and the volunteers, and between the staff and Vidal took its price. Not many projects died, unlike former years, but enough were pushed to a point of ineffectiveness.

There was Northwestern Saskatchewan, where the volunteers, solidly on the side of the Indians, were virtually driven out of two small towns by hostile whites, led by their priest; the white project in Northwestern Ontario, killed by lack of funds, poor management, an inability to cooperate with the Indian project in the same area, and an unwillingness to heed Claude Vidal; Toronto Youth, already documented; Toronto Development, torn apart by a desire to help Italians while refusing to admit that anyone but the volunteers could have the right answers; Cape Breton, weakened by continual fighting with Ottawa administration and by its own ineptitude at keeping volunteers on the project for more than six months; and Vancouver Youth, where the volunteers would not admit that administration was needed when it came to running a school.

Despite these failures, 1969 had been an amazing year for the Company. Buffeted by external pressures, nearly destroyed by internal fighting, humiliated in Quebec, and now the whipping-boy for Mayor Jean Drapeau and Executive Committee Chairman Lucien Saulnier, the Company, one should say the volunteers, had still managed to carry on in more than a token way.

If the MPs and press who were taking the Company apart in Ottawa had only left their caves for a week they might have seen some of the Company's accomplishments.

The inquiry was on. Its verdict already tucked away in someone's brain. The volunteers would not be consulted about their own fate, for after all, what did they know? What could they offer?

31
The Inquiry

The twenty members of the Standing Committee on Broadcasting, Films and Assistance to the Arts were no better and no worse than any other group of MPs. They had their biases in either direction, of course, and many of them had already made up their minds on the question at hand. All they needed now was to uncover the information they required to reinforce the opinions they already held about the Company of Young Canadians. It would not be difficult.

The inquiry into the CYC was a big event. Since the first day of its existence, the Company had been an irritant to many MPs, the press and the public. Finally, all three groups had a chance to find out how the Company worked, where it had gone wrong and where it had succeeded.

If this had been done six months before the Drapeau-Saulnier charges the Company would not have received half the attention it was getting now. The charges made for drama and for tremendous interest.

The chairman of the broadcasting committee was John Reid, a northern Ontario MP. Reputedly a tough chairman, and not one to let things get out of control, Reid had been absent the last time the Company had appeared before his committee. He was absent again when the inquiry began. Taking his place was Pierre De Bane, a Quebec MP. Rather young and excitable, De Bane was a thoroughly likeable person. He had a difficult job to do. However would he be up to it?

The committee as an entirety was undefinable. By some stroke of fate, it appeared to have most of Canada's minority groups represented on it. Lincoln Alexander, the black Tory from Hamilton, Len Marchand, an Indian and Liberal from Kamloops-Caribou, Phil Givens, Jewish, Liberal and the former Mayor of Toronto, all sat on it.

Others who were known to Company people were Walter Dinsdale, a former Tory cabinet minister, now just another Manitoba MP; Patrick Nowlan, another Tory, this time from Nova Scotia; Keith Penner, a Liberal from Northern Ontario; and Steve Paproski, a former football player turned politician, representing Edmonton and the Conservative Party.

On November 4th the chairman and vice-chairman of the CYC council were scheduled to appear before this committee in the afternoon. The morning was spent reviewing the committee's membership and what could be expected.

Not totally politically naive, the Company expected the Tories to be opposed to its continued existence, no matter what evidence was presented. The NDP, it was thought, would take the other extreme view and try to keep the Company no matter what. The key to the inquiry was the Liberals, particularly the Quebec Liberals. Normally a quiet bunch, they were irate at the Company's alleged activities in their home province and were expected to be tough. The Company would have to convince them that things were not entirely black.

This was made quite clear when Jack Johnson, Mickey Posluns, Jean Roy and Claude Vidal lunched prior to the first session with Pierre De Bane and the committee counsel, Claude-Armand Sheppard of Montreal, a short, stout lawyer appointed especially for the inquiry.

De Bane and Sheppard fired questions at Johnson and Roy throughout the meal about the Company's structure, organization and activities in Quebec. Claude Vidal sat listening, neither contradicting or approving the answers. His chance would come later.

The lunch ended soon enough for the men to make

their way to the railway committee room. It was packed by the press and curious onlookers. The MPs began to straggle in one or two at a time.

Looking around the committee room at that time was like reliving the history of the Company. Sitting among the onlookers were Alan Clarke, Bill McWhinney and Jim Littleton. The only major figure missing was Stewart Goodings, at work in Kenya for CUSO. Clarke, McWhinney and Littleton would all get a chance to testify at the inquiry, and at least one would be supplying information for parties to use against Claude Vidal.

Pierre De Bane eventually gavelled the meeting to order and prepared to introduce Johnson, Posluns, Roy and Vidal. Before he could begin, however, the Tories, ever political, held proceedings up by questioning the selection of Sheppard, the counsel, and his pay. Sheppard was receiving in the neighbourhood of $100 a day for his services, plus expenses, plus overtime. The Liberals swept the affair aside and turned to the Company.

The inquiry was on.

Rather nervously, Jack Johnson read the council's statement. It was a rather uneven and overly optimistic document.

"Since its establishment . . . the Company of Young Canadians has had a somewhat stormy, uneven career. Unfortunately, as Shakespeare noted, 'the evil that men do lives after them, the good is oft interred with their bones' . . . . , " it began.

Johnson then told of the turmoil in the Company; the lame-duck provisional council, the delay in electing the permanent council, the council finally taking office only to be beset by old problems.

"The council has now commenced, in conjunction with both administration and field workers, a comprehensive review of the entire Company," he continued, and went on to predict that by March 31st, 1970, the Company would be operating smoothly enough for it to approach Parliament for more money.

The MPs on the committee showed no amazement at this statement, although they might well have. Here they were studying to see if the Company should even survive, and the Company chairman arrives to say that they will soon be asking for more money.

Johnson concluded by mentioning that the ten elected and five appointed members were working in relative harmony together. He quickly underlined the "relative harmony" (most MPs had heard William Morris on CBC Radio analyzing the council meeting in Montreal) by admitting that council meetings had their dramatic and stormy moments, but added that things would be better once the councillors got used to working together.

The floor was now open for questions, and the MPs moved in on the council chairman, vice-chairman and Mickey Posluns, a volunteer-elected member of council.

The questions were, for the most part, to the point and centred on such things as program priorities, criteria for volunteer selection, and how the Company stopped volunteers from imposing their wills on a community.

Johnson remained cool and answered to the best of his ability. He was obviously limited, however, by his lack of knowledge about past history, and the fact that the Company had never really spelled out its priorities. This meant that Johnson and the others had no answers to some questions. It looked like clear evasion and the MPs became agitated. They were after answers and could not accept that the Company was too complex for Johnson to digest in a month. They, as it would turn out, had the same period of time and would fall short of his understanding.

Two questions that Johnson did answer precisely, and that Vidal noted, were: "Would you like to see any changes in the Act? Do you think the Company is too divorced from the Secretary of State's office?" In both cases, the answer was a blunt no. The council, it appeared, was unrepentant.

The ghosts were next on the agenda.

Bill McWhinney, now executive assistant to Donald McDonald, head of the Privy Council, added little. What more could the MPs expect? McWhinney had only been executive director for a short time, and with the exception of Antigonish, had missed all of the Company's major crises. He was finished quickly.

Alan Clarke took longer.

Looking not much different from the day he left the Company, Clarke was grilled ruthlessly by the committee. He stood up well. Refusing to be boxed in, or wishy-washy, he defended his term as executive director with a clarity and firmness that he had sometimes lacked when he held the job. The time then came for finding reasons for the CYC's problems, and Clarke supplied some.

The government was one reason, he said, and went into detail on the Beliveau affair.

The non-support of council was another. The Beliveau affair, and the imposing of Phil Girard on the Company, were two illustrations.

Clarke had chosen well. The Tories took up his evidence and began to clamour for action. Former Prime Minister Pearson should be called, they insisted. Marc Lalonde and R.A.J. Phillips too. The Liberals beat off the Pearson attempt, but went along with Lalonde and Phillips. They would eventually appear to repudiate many of Clarke's statements. It made little difference, in any event. Government interference was of minor interest at this point.

Doug Ward appeared to defend himself and his council. He was adequate but not much more. Alan Clarke had hurt the council through his appearance, and Ward could not remove all of the stigmas that his former executive director had rightly pointed out.

The Company's auditors came, represented by Charles

Gale, the partner in charge of the Ottawa office for Touche, Ross and Company.

Gale had attended council meetings before and Company people knew what to expect from him. They knew that he would be honest, articulate and persuasive. Middle-aged and balding, Gale could never be considered leftist and, considering his profession, he could more properly be placed on the political right. Yet, he had appeared before the Company's radical permanent council and convinced them that they needed more auditing help.

This salesmanship did not let him down at the inquiry.

He told, in tactful terms of his fight with the Company to get it to adopt proper financial procedures. He described its early financial affairs and presented as an example the Company's transportation bill in 1968. The Company, he said, had spent $110,000 that year on air travel, an average of $560 for each member.

Finally, the auditor told of the recent changes in financial procedures and testified that there had been definite improvements in financial controls, but that more should be done.

Unimportant as Gale's testimony would be in the long run, it did at least present an accurate picture of one part of the Company that had been concerning the MPs. The same could not be said for the appearances of Jim Lotz, Guy Beaugrand-Champagne, Donald Hamilton, or Jim Littleton.

Littleton was continuing his fight with Vidal. What was driving him on, one could only guess, but it was certainly strong. Having lost with the council, and with the press, the red-haired, red-bearded former staff member, was now taking his cause into the inquiry.

From the questions that first the Tories, then the NDP and then Keith Penner of the Liberals asked the executive director when he appeared before them, it was obvious that Littleton was feeding information, his own brand, to the MPs. The Tories, anxious for any evidence that would hurt the Company, appeared to use him more than the others, and even had Littleton called as witness.

Why the committee called Jim Lotz and Guy Beaugrand-Champagne to testify was never fully understood by Company people. The committee decided after opening the inquiry that it would not have time to visit Company projects. In order, however, to understand the process of social change, and the ability of the Company to use that process, it called in these two supposed experts to give their opinions.

Lotz was a research professor in community development and an associate director of the Canadian Research Centre for Anthropology at St. Paul's University in Ottawa. He had published many papers on community development and was held in high esteem by John Reid, the committee chairman. Most Company people assumed that Reid's opinion of Lotz was the main reason for the invitation to him. As far as Company people were concerned, Lotz had a lot to learn about community development.

Beaugrand-Champagne had at least worked for the Company on contract for a while. No one doubted his competency, but at best his presence was a poor substitute for the knowledge that the committee could have picked up during personal visits to Company projects.

The testimony of Donald Hamilton was in keeping with the political overtones of the inquiry. Hamilton was executive assistant to Premier Harry Strom of Alberta, but had previously headed the Alberta Service Corps, a volunteer organization keenly devoted to the service role.

As these witnesses paraded in front of the committee, one could imagine that the inquiry was low-key. In fact, it was not. It is just that these witnesses were lost before and during the testimony of Claude Vidal and the Drapeau-Saulnier forces.

32

Vidal and Renaud Testify

Since his appointment as Director of the Company of Young Canadians, Vidal had been fighting a lonely battle against what he considered to be the errors of the Company. Up until October, he fought the volunteers and staff on the grounds of effectiveness and competency. He demanded a lot from them, and they gave him abuse and radical rhetoric in return. He eventually came to realize that he could not change the Company to fit the legislation that had created it. His reasons were complex and will be gone into later in detail but, basically, he believed that the legislation had flaws — flaws that allowed irresponsibility to grow, and supplied no safeguards against irresponsibility.

When the permanent council was created, Vidal hoped for a while that it might overcome the flaws and take the hard stand that he thought was needed. The council did not. Instead it accentuated the Company's problems — it drove staff and volunteers further apart; it became a destructive, rather than a unifying force. Vidal eventually came to regard the powers of the council, and the make-up of the council, as additional flaws in the Company's legislation.

No one could deny, least of all Vidal, that he had played his part in the battles that were tearing the Company apart. His refusal to moderate some stands, his seeming disregard for personal feelings, his deliberate testing of the council, which included his challenging its authority, had all contributed to the Company's ills.

All of that was behind now. Vidal, during his year as director, had observed what he thought were the sources of the Company's problems. When he appeared before the parliamentary inquiry, he decided to act to correct the wrongs. If this meant further alienating volunteers, and trying to ruin the credibility of the council, so be it. Things had gone too far for him to turn back. He believed what he thought was right and would not hold back. It was, admittedly, a gamble. If he lost and the Company and council remained unaltered, it was difficult to see how he could survive as director. If he won, however, the Company would virtually be his to redirect.

His chore was not an easy one. He had to point out the Company's failings, but at the same time show its strengths. He was after balance, enough weaknesses to warrant change, enough strength to justify keeping the organization.

Vidal and his staff would appear on five different occasions as witnesses before the parliamentary committee.

The first meeting was on November 7th and lasted for only a few hours. It was important, however, for Vidal clearly broke from his boss, the council.

In his opening statement, the executive director said: " . . . in my opinion the Company of Young Canadians can be an effective organization, one with the ability to involve young people in the problems facing this country and with the potential for helping to solve these problems.

"I say *can be,* however, for at present I believe the Company is a long way from attaining this objective."

Vidal then outlined generally the Company's habit of getting into problems, and commented that the administration was always blamed for them. He promptly switched the discussion to the Company's structure and detailed how it was supposed to work. Was it working? No, he said, and listed eight reasons: there is no definition of volunteer and the very concept of volunteerism in the CYC; there are no clearly defined lines of authority and responsibility; the Company's council seems incapable of differentiating between management decisions and policy decisions; there is no clear definition of the relations between the three levels in the Company; the Company has never set a program objective from which priorities and criteria can clearly emerge; the Company has never had a full set of policies; the concept of participation has never been sufficiently explained, or indeed resolved; the role of the executive director is not defined anywhere but in Bill C–174. There has never been a description of the duties and responsibilities of the director at the council level.

"I can give specific examples of these points if requested . . . " he continued, but went on to explain what the eight points meant in the day-to-day operation of the Company.

"All three levels in the Company believe they have the power to make decisions and often each attempts to impose its decision. The result is anger, mistrust, frustration and lack of co-operation. And, ironically, often a decision which belongs at one level is passed on to another. When the buck stops there and a decision is made the consequences are predictable – if the decision is favorable to a project, for example, nothing is said; if the decision is not favorable, then the administration is accused of being autocratic and a witch-hunt begins within the Company. So the present state of affairs can be summed up as everyone trying to make decisions or everyone trying to avoid making one decision. I can't see how the Company can continue in this way. In fact, the first three years of the Company's existence prove this."

For further elaboration of the Company's ills, Vidal then tabled the policy paper he had presented to the council in September, the paper that had been ignored.

By the time he was finished, the Company people present who were not loyal to Vidal had rushed to the nearest telephones. They phoned volunteers and council members with the news of Vidal's statement. It had been a stunner.

It was evident he was going to try to destroy the council.

Claude Vidal had burned the bridges behind him. There was no way he could go back.

The MPs were in no way interested in helping him.

J. Patrick Nowlan, the Nova Scotia Tory, was the first questioner. A large, hulking man, Nowlan wasted little time on courtesies. He was after the real truth about the Company of Young Canadians and bored in on Vidal.

Nowlan started on the Jim Littleton issue and then swung over to Quebec. He stayed on Quebec.

He asked question after question on Pierre Renaud — how he was hired? did Vidal know about his past? was he still with the Company?

Vidal answered each question as best he could, but was obviously having difficulty with the English language. He would misinterpret some of Nowlan's questions and give long-winded answers that did not answer the question in the first place. Nowlan became irritated. The hearing was not going as well as Vidal had hoped.

Nowlan finally gave up and other MPs took their shots at the director. The most prominent was Douglas Hogarth, a Liberal from British Columbia. Hogarth used his training as a criminal lawyer well. His subject, too, was Quebec.

What did Vidal do about Saulnier's complaints? Had any volunteers been fired? What was the chain of command in Quebec?

The director and his staff tried to answer the questions. They tried to explain the complicated history of Quebec in ten minutes. It was impossible. What they did manage, however, was to make clear that Claude Vidal had no authority in Quebec.

Several other problems were raised at that first session as well; problems that Vidal and others tried to solve before he would have to return before the committee on November 13th.

Because of the time limitations, the MPs were trying to

ask as many questions as they could in ten minutes. They were also trying to cover the three years of the Company in that short time. As a result, the questioning was often disjointed with no logical follow-through. Vidal was having enough problems with the language, and interpreting questions posed in English, without this additional burden being placed on him.

The lack of order in the questioning meant that the director had to skip from Quebec to Jim Littleton in seconds, all the time remembering dates, names and places. If the Company had been a slow-moving organization this might not have been difficult, but with so many events overlapping one another, it was easy for the director to make mistakes.

Vidal was also expected to be well-versed in Company history. He was, but not to the extent that some MPs demanded. One even asked him about a young girl that had attended one of the Company's first training sessions. The girl had not been selected a volunteer and had never worked for the Company. Still, Vidal was supposed to know something about this incident.

Realizing that if the questioning continued through other sessions as it had at the first the committee would never get an entire picture of the Company and its operations, Vidal went to Pierre De Bane with a proposal. He suggested that the acting chairman list five subject areas. The MPs could question the director on one area at a time. When that area had been covered, they could move on to the next. In this way, in-depth information could be transmitted and probably a greater understanding of the Company would result.

The young Liberal agreed with Vidal and the procedure was put, unsuccessfully as it turned out, into effect.

Despite Vidal's troubles before the committee, his attitude and performance behind the scenes was continuing to astound his staff.

He and acting committee chairman De Bane were quite

close. Vidal was going to De Bane's office before each
session, and usually after, for talks, and soon the Liberal
seemed converted to Vidal's way of thinking. De Bane's
office was Vidal's semi-official office. The director kept his
documentation there, his personal belongings there, and
used the office for phone calls and the like.

This person to person lobbying was Vidal's forte. Just
as he convinced De Bane of the rightness of his actions, so
he too eventually would swing several other MPs solidly in
line with him.

The director did not do this alone, of course. His staff
knew some MPs and spent a considerable amount of time
with them. And then there was the Company's and/or
Vidal's powerful ally — the Secretary of State.

Vidal's opponents in the Company had always sworn
that the director was the government's man, that Gerard
Pelletier had almost hand-picked him for his post. This was
untrue. But after Vidal was installed as director, he and
Pelletier maintained a close relationship — something that
would have shocked Alan Clarke and scandalized the
volunteers. This relationship came in handy during the
inquiry.

Bob Rabinovitch, Pelletier's special assistant, sat in on
most of the inquiry hearings. He was there, of course, to
make sure that his minister was well protected, but also to
help Vidal and the Company.

If the presence and help of Rabinovitch wasn't enough
of an indicator of the support of the Secretary of State,
Pelletier himself appeared before the parliamentary committee. His testimony, which included a number of changes he
would like to see in the act, was remarkably similar to
that of the executive director's and left no doubt as to
whose side Pelletier was on.

At first, even with Pelletier's support, the Company and
Claude Vidal were in no way assured of surviving the inquiry.
But as the inquiry progressed, it became evident that a
decision had been made. Only some new, startling informa-

tion from the Drapeau-Saulnier group or a major blunder on the part of Vidal could change things.

On November 13th, a Thursday, Vidal and his staff appeared again before the committee. This turned out to be a marathon sitting, with the Company people being subjected to morning, afternoon and evening grillings.

The director kept trying to get his opinion across: the Company was worthwhile, but changes were needed. He kept showing the areas where the Company was lacking and describing the results of the weaknesses. The results were apparent.

This was a far better session than the first. The questioning was still disjointed, repetitive and blurry, but the staff were using the questions for leaps into long explanations, explanations that covered more points than had been requested.

De Bane's plan of going at the Company area by area was announced. It did little good. The first area was supposed to be programs. Somehow, the MPs linked everything else up with programs, especially anything controversial.

The presence of the press in such numbers was an irresistible lure to most MPs. If they could dig up something controversial they would be assured of national coverage. In this way, the folks back home could see what a fine job they were doing. After a while this became so obvious that the press began to wonder who the MP's questions were aimed at — the people at home or the witnesses.

It was not unusual, for example, to see an MP question Vidal and then hurry outside the committee room to give an interview to a newsman. Vidal, of course, was stuck inside, unable to give his version. Not that he would have anyway. The director was still refusing to talk to the press. He left that to his staff, but instructed them to get working. He wasn't about to let the MPs crucify the Company for their own personal vanity.

Vanity is the right word. There was even one occasion

when one MP entered the committee room with TV make-up on.

On November 14th, Vidal appeared for the third time in front of the committee. This was a short meeting and was most unsatisfactory. The ground that the staff felt they had gained the previous day was lost as the MPs continued to repeat themselves and play to the gallery. They were still on the program area. Vidal began to fear that they would never touch on the other four subjects.

At the Company's next appearance on November 18th two rays of sunshine appeared – John Reid and Pierre Renaud.

Pierre De Bane had been doing an adequate job as chairman, but his obvious inexperience and his unwillingness to be tough had not speeded proceedings. Reid would now take over the chair and bring back the formality that had been missing. This would also free De Bane to question witnesses – something he was remarkably good at. In fact, De Bane's performance during the coming week would be one main reason that the Company managed to survive the inquiry. When Jim Littleton tried to throw doubts on the testimony of Claude Vidal, it was De Bane who came charging to the rescue. When Vidal was trying to explain his problems, it was De Bane who asked the leading questions. And when Lucien Saulnier appeared before the committee, it was De Bane who helped make the executive committee chairman look like an out-of-touch old man.

Pierre Renaud's appearance was a blessing for the Company. Throughout previous testimony, the young staff member had been sort of a bogey-man. This was the terrible person, the MPs implied, who was convicted of terrorist activities. This was the man Vidal had hired, and now had the audacity to defend. Either spurred on by the publicity that Renaud's appearance would get, or by a genuine interest in finding some facts, the committee invited Renaud to give evidence.

Only 25 years old, Renaud had been thrust from the anonymity of a staff role in Quebec into leadership in that province. Once promoted he had been forced to work on a tight-rope, balancing between Quebec and Ottawa, trying to please both and move the Company forward. Even Vidal admitted that he had done well.

Now even more pressure was on him.

His personal life had been exposed, sometimes incorrectly, and he had been painted as a destructive monster, out to ruin the province of Quebec. As if that were not enough, he was now expected to prove that he was not a monster before a parliamentary committee, a committee that had not been kind to the Company and certainly would be no more kind to one of the alleged cancers that was supposedly destroying the fabric of Canadian life.

There was another pressure on Renaud as well, one that Vidal and the Company did not mention.

The Quebec director was one of the key witnesses in the Valliere-Gagnon trial that was being held in Montreal. The two Quebecois were leading separatists and had been jailed for their activities. The trial that was going on was a re-trial and one of the utmost importance in Quebec.

Fortunately, the Valliere-Gagnon trial was never mentioned. Knowledge that he was a witness would only have given the gossip-mongers more ammunition to fire at him.

Renaud's performance was of the greatest importance to Vidal. If the staff member did well and came across as a responsible, dedicated young man, then the committee could only acknowledge that Vidal had not been irresponsible when he hired him. If Renaud did poorly, the committee would look less favorably upon Vidal.

Vidal need not have worried.

For two and one-half hours, Renaud stood the committee on its head.

Half-an-hour was spent by committee members fighting among each other as to which questions could be asked

Renaud, and which could not. He sat silently watching the performance with a tight, small smile on his face. He was prepared to answer any question and didn't see what the fuss was about.

It was all a charade, anyway. No ruling from the chair would prevent an MP from asking any question. If one was ruled out of order, they would change the wording and try again.

Doug Hogarth, the B.C. Liberal, was the first questioner, but like Renaud, was forced to wait until everyone was satisfied.

"This is the dandiest bingo game I have ever been involved in," he said.

When the procedural difficulties were finally cleared away, Hogarth zoomed in on Renaud in no uncertain way.

"At the time you joined the CYC, or at any time you were a member of it, were you a member of the RIN?" he asked.

"I have never been a member of the RIN," Renaud responded.

The MPs took Renaud through the entire list of charges against him and his fellow Quebecois. He answered calmly and precisely, never wavering, never unsure.

Yes, he said, he had been involved in terrorist activities of a political nature.

Yes, other former terrorists had been with the Company and still were.

No, he no longer believed or followed those pursuits. To his knowledge, the others didn't either.

He was so believable, so confident, that the MPs even began to ask questions in a manner of total respect. Renaud didn't seem to care. His demeanour never changed.

When Renaud finished answering questions some facts were quite evident to all.

Lucien Saulnier had not been totally wrong as far as his specific charges were concerned. His conclusions from those charges, and the implications they had on people like Pierre Renaud, would now, however, be questioned.

Claude Vidal had also been telling the truth. No one had ever really doubted that, but the MPs could not help worrying about his sometimes roundabout way of saying things. It was also obvious that Vidal had no control in Quebec, but by hiring Renaud had tried to bring some authority to the province.

As for Pierre Renaud, he had wowed the MPs and the press. His low-key, articulate answers were so impressive that Phil Givens, the Toronto Liberal, was heard to remark, "I wouldn't mind having that boy for a son."

The Company's star was on the rise. On his fifth appearance, Claude Vidal would try to push it higher.

Vidal was scheduled to appear before the committee one more time, on Tuesday, November 18th. He decided the time had come to strike. The committee had not gone into the field, so Vidal would bring the Company's understanding of its role to the committee. The committee had not dug deeply enough into structural problems, so he would outline the problems and the chaos that resulted. The committee had not discussed changes in the Act with him to any great length, so he would present the changes he wanted. A total picture had not been presented. Vidal was going to present the total picture and sink or swim with it.

John Reid was approached with the idea and agreed that a paper could be presented. He suggested that it be done at the night meeting on the 18th.

When Claude Vidal and his staff entered the committee room that day not many people knew what they were carrying. The press, somewhat tired at having to cover the director again, and waiting for Saulnier and Drapeau, were not too interested. The MPs were so familiar with Vidal that they expected no radical departure from his usual calm, reasoned, and occasionally somewhat mystifying statements.

The Secretary of State, though, had been warned in

advance through his special assistant. Rabinovitch had read a rough draft of the document and recommended a couple of changes. His advice was heeded. The changes in no way took the guts out of Vidal's statement.

The document was distributed for the MPs to read as the meeting began.

Patrick Nowlan found the document to be "either the frankest or the most provocative document that has been presented before a parliamentary committee".

One Quebec MP said it was "insulting".

Speaking about the role of the Company, Vidal made it clear that the Company was radical and should remain radical, using quotes from Prime Minister Trudeau and Secretary of State Pelletier to support this stand. The quotes did not have as much effect as the document's own disarming honesty.

"The role we have described for the Company of Young Canadians is a valid one. If the actions and foresight of our legislators matched the rhetoric of our legislators then there would be no need for the Company of Young Canadians. But, gentlemen, poverty, discrimination, poor housing, alienation of youth and unequal opportunity still exist in this country. Someone has to deal with them . . . . We must continue to do that. If we don't, then the Company of Young Canadians is not worth keeping around, even as a token gesture," it read.

If this was not enough to upset the MPs, the document went after them again:

"We would like to mention that Prime Minister Trudeau has publicly accepted the Company being 'a thorn in the side of the establishment'. And, we doubt that there is a body in Canada that can be more properly called the establishment than the House of Commons, unless of course it is the Senate, but we consider that to be the retired establishment. But, inevitably, and it is most understandable, most MPs are extremely thin skinned when their competence or concern for their constituents is questioned."

From here, the document analyzed the structure of the Company and repeated the same eight failings that Vidal had mentioned on his first visit. This time, however, he was not waiting for MPs to ask for examples of the failings. The examples were included.

The Toronto Youth project was raised as an example of the blurred lines of authority. Council was criticized for meddling in management affairs, and accused of not knowing the difference between management and policy decisions, or if it did know, of not caring. The example here was Jean Roy's assertion that he was "responsible for the CYC's internal affairs". Comcord was finally fully explained. The groups objectives and methods of operating were laid on the table. The lack of policy was examined.

Finally, changes in the Act were suggested. Here was proof of Vidal's break with the council.

"At present, five members are appointed by the Governor-in-Council and ten members are elected by the volunteers. Of the ten elected, eight are or were volunteers. This, admittedly, brings the field focus into play at the highest level, but it also tends to blur the perspective and mar the objectivity of the Council. Volunteers on council, for example, tend to be protective of their own particular projects.

" . . . We believe there is a need to broaden the representation on council in order for the Company to see itself in a more objective light; in order for the Company to look at itself in perspective with the rest of the country; and in order for the Company to make use of the many talented and concerned people who are presently outside our tiny borders."

The document then recommended that the government continue to appoint five members to council; that the volunteers elect five members, but not volunteers; and that the five remaining members be chosen from interest groups, such as educators.

Other changes were recommended – changes that would

place the volunteers and staff more firmly under the control of the director, restrict council's actions to setting and approving policy, and ensure that consultants be responsible solely to the director.

If the parliamentary committee ever accepted the recommendations, the council would be finished. The executive director would be in control.

When that fifth and final session ended, Claude Vidal and his staff retreated gratefully to the background. They had done all they could to forward their arguments and their positions. Now they had to defend them against the onslaught of Lucien Saulnier and Jean Drapeau. This is where Claude Vidal's real strength, his back room maneuvering, would be tested.

33

Montreal Loses

For two days in late November of 1969, the city of Montreal tried to convince a committee of the Parliament of Canada that the country was being threatened by a large contingent of subversives.

The evidence that the city presented had been seized mainly during raids on premises rented, occupied or leased by the Company of Young Canadians or workers with the Company.

This link, the city argued, proved that the federal government was financing the subversion itself through its support of the Company of Young Canadians. It therefore demanded a Royal Commission to investigate the subversive elements at work in Canada.

It was an exciting and emotional two days.

On the morning of November 27th, Lucien Saulnier, Executive Committee Chairman of the city; Jean Drapeau, its mayor; Police Chief J.P. Gilbert; Michel Cote, Montreal's chief city attorney; and Jules Allard, the joint legal adviser to the Montreal police department, filed into the committee room to give their testimony.

Saulnier, Allard and Cote would be the only witnesses. Mayor Drapeau and Gilbert were there to support them with the prestige of their offices.

The committee room, in fact the entire West Block, was well guarded. The mayor and Saulnier had brought along their own body guards, and the federal government had added extra security police. There would be no disruptions at this meeting. Neither would there be any of the public allowed.

The police net was there for a purpose. Committee chairman Reid and others were afraid that CYC volunteers might show up and create a disturbance. They wanted Drapeau and Saulnier to be safe in Ottawa.

As it turned out, five volunteers from Quebec did show up. When refused admittance at the West Block door, they threatened to demonstrate. Bernie Muzeen, the Company's operations officer, talked them out of it. The Company didn't need any more problems.

There was no justification, however, for turning back Pierre Renaud and two other Company officials at the door. Renaud and one of the others had testified at the inquiry, but could not convince the guards of their identity.

"Get identification cards," they were told. They rushed back to the Ottawa office, got their cards and were then let in.

When they came back later that same day, though, for the second sitting, even the identification cards didn't help. The guards would not let them in. Angry and frustrated, the CYC'ers complained to some newsmen. The newsmen helpfully took them up to the committee room via the tunnel that connects the Centre Block to the West Block.

The security precautions that were taken helped to create an atmosphere of danger. One felt that Saulnier, Drapeau and friends were taking their lives in their hands by even agreeing to appear before the committee. In reality, they were probably the two safest men in Ottawa.

To make sure that they understood, the Company staff who were allowed in were making the rounds of the press table, talking to the reporters they knew. The strategy on this first day was straightforward. If Saulnier or Cote said anything inaccurate or far-fetched, the Company people would head for the nearest reporter. By catching these small items they might create a few seeds of doubt about the testimony. Every doubt, no matter how small, would be useful.

Finally the Montreal group was in the room and moving towards the witness chairs. Saulnier, tall and austere in a gray suit, his face grim; Cote, just as large and dressed almost the same, curly hair and a small moustache; Drapeau, the most easily recognized, but the hardest to find, his bald head, glasses and moustache being obscured by his larger cohorts and his police escort.

The first day of the hearing belonged to them.

Lucien Saulnier re-read the press release that had started the affair, and added to it. Old though it was, it still created a stir in the room. The time had come for the charges to be substantiated. Michel Cote began. For the entire morning session he presented the city's case. No questions were allowed. He started the afternoon session and it took him almost 5 p.m. to finish.

Michel Cote had presented an overwhelming case, in terms of documentation, against the CYC. The city's argument, as he carefully pointed out, was not contained in any one document. It tied together hundreds of documents and pictures into one general conclusion. That conclusion was that the CYC had been engaging in subversive activities.

For the most part there were no surprises in the city's evidence.

The volunteers who Vidal himself had admitted were separatists, the volunteers he had been trying to get rid of, were named and their crimes listed. There were pictures of CYC'ers taking part in demonstrations, of CYC Volvos leading the McGill march. There were revolutionary documents seized on CYC-connected premises, documents that called for revolution, that outlined ways of making molotov cocktails and other insidious weapons, that spoke of connections with Cuba, that linked the Company to separatist organizations, that connected some CYC volunteers to disturbances in Montreal, that showed some volunteers trying to undermine the Drapeau-Saulnier administration.

Most of the documents had been seized in places such as the office of the Workers Committee of St. Henri, where Louis-Phillipe Aubert was working for the Company, or Atelier-Communication in Montreal, where council vice-chairman, Jean Roy, was a volunteer.

The evidence against Atelier was the most surprising to Claude Vidal. He had always had his hunches about Roy. He suspected for example, that Atelier was printing a lot of revolutionary documents, but had never been able to confirm them. The city of Montreal did that for him, and also gave him another stunning bit of news. Atelier was registered as a business in Montreal. A CYC project registered as a business was, to Vidal, as close to vested interests as one could get.

The rest of Cote's evidence, however, did not add much to the information that the director had. It showed that a small group of volunteers, perhaps only seven or eight, had been using the Company to further their own ends and the ends of other organizations. The entire Company across the country or even in Quebec could not be dragged into it.

The city of Montreal would claim that these seven or eight volunteers were the surface element, that there were more. This was difficult to prove. They would also claim that these volunteers were part of a larger subversive group. This too would be difficult to prove.

But they were interesting charges and the Montreal accusers were not men to be taken lightly.

Cote's presentation impressed many of the MPs but left a good number unconvinced. They challenged Saulnier and Cote at the evening session.

The challenge, basically, was that Cote and Saulnier had presented a case against only seven or eight volunteers.

These volunteers were disturbing the city of Montreal and not the entire country. There was no reason to have a Royal Commission.

Cote and Saulnier, sure of their ground, stood firm. They reiterated the seriousness of the volunteers' actions and played a trump card.

The documentation that had been presented was insignificant compared to the pile that was still in Montreal. Cote would later say that only five per cent of the seized documents had been gone through. If a Royal Commission was called, the rest could be turned over to it.

Doug Hogarth was the principle questioner that evening. Tough and honest as always, he bored into the main points of the evidence. There was one exchange between him and Cote that made the Montreal lawyer look evasive.

"How many members of the CYC — arising out of all the difficulties, all the civil disorder you have had in Montreal — were charged and convicted for being in an unlawful assembly or inciting a riot or being in a riot in the city of Montreal?" the B.C. Liberal asked.

"Charged is one thing and . . . . " said Cote.

"I said charged and convicted," replied Hogarth.

" . . . convicted is another, especially when bench warrants are pending on people in Cuba," said the Montreal lawyer.

"Well . . . . " Hogarth said.

"So we cannot convict them," the lawyer continued.

"No, I appreciate that," Hogarth went on. "I want charged and convicted."

"During the demonstrations generally, the CYC volunteers are not arrested. May I explain why? If one reads the plan and one sees how this movement of masses — we have seen it. I have been on the street for I do not know how many dozens of demonstrations in order to look at them and see how they are held, and those who hold flags and lead them are never the ones arrested at the end because they disappear when the violence begins," Cote explained.

"Mr. Cote, you are an experienced Crown prosecutor. You have photographs of people who are obviously participating in unlawful assembly. I want to know how many people were charged and convicted," Hogarth said.

"I will have to check the record for that," the lawyer said.

"You should know that," retorted the MP.

"Your question was very narrow . . . . " was part of Cote's reply.

Narrow or not, Hogarth's line of questioning was important for the Company. He wanted facts and figures, not just suppositions. The failure of Cote to provide them on this occasion did not help his credibility, but did not fluster him. The Montrealers were professionals. They would not lose their cool. They would not be baited into anger. Not that night anyway.

The following day was as different from that night as the CYC from the Red Cross.

Claude Vidal had been busy for one thing. He and Pierre De Bane worked on a list of questions that would be asked of the executive committee chairman. The questions were designed to get Saulnier talking about the city, about its handling of youth and minority groups. They were nice questions, humble questions and, hopefully, questions that would point out that the city administration's view of youth was somewhat restricted.

The session started as it ended, with the Montreal group in command of the situation. Cote and Saulnier were confident, almost arrogant. They answered crisply and concisely, always coming back to their request for a Royal Commission.

Then Harold Stafford got under their skins.

A large-faced man, Stafford was a Liberal from southwestern Ontario. He had not taken a great part in the inquiry up to this point, but nevertheless plunged ahead.

He talked about the slums in Montreal and the need for help; help, he thought, the CYC could supply.

Saulnier, tight-lipped, said the city was doing a fine job by itself. No other government at any level could work as fast.

The newsmen took notes. They knew, if Saulnier didn't, that slum discontent was a major sore point among Montreal residents.

Blithely, Stafford then went into the police strike. He asked what had provoked it.

The chairman cut him off. It was too late. The question had been asked and had irritated.

Stafford's closing assault was no kinder. He virtually accused Saulnier of using the CYC as a smoke-screen to cover up the illegal police strike.

Pierre De Bane was next, and he was masterful. Carefully and respectfully he asked Saulnier questions about the city of Montreal. What had the city done to enable young people to put their idealism to good use?

"Well, in the field of urban renewal, we have established offices in districts where the people in charge of municipal efforts are in daily contact with the population, and I want to bear witness to the wonderful self-sacrifice of these employees, who do far more than their duty requires them to do towards giving the efforts, which we make to improve physical housing conditions . . . . " the executive committee chairman explained.

He then added that Montreal had the most active, the most up-to-date and best equipped municipal park service in all of North America.

Newsmen looked at each other in surprise. Some MPs who knew Montreal were wondering if Saulnier was talking about the city they knew. In the field of urban renewal, as an example, the city administration had been harshly condemned by more than one citizens' group for its alleged autocratic methods.

While Saulnier presented his rosy picture of Montreal he never smiled. The inquiry was serious business. Michel Cote didn't smile, either, when he stepped in to expand on what the city was doing for youth. By the time he finished, however, a good many other people thought his example quite humorous.

Cote talked about motorcycle gangs in Montreal and how they used to have a bad reputation. The police department had worked with them and nowadays, the lawyer said, they have a fine reputation.

"We even have a policeman who wears a leather jacket, the way they do, and rides a red motorcycle," he confided.

The chuckles coming from the press section were almost audible. The city administration's attitude towards youth to most of them was typified by the policeman on the red motorcycle, quite out of date and very paternalistic.

Bud Osler, in a series of sophisticated questions that linked poverty, poor housing and discrimination to social unrest, tried to point this out more definitely. Would the city of Montreal not solve its problems by getting rid of the sources of unrest, instead of getting rid of the CYC? He also mentioned the poor communications between governments and people all across the country.

"I state again that this is not the case in the city of Montreal. The communications are extremely good with all citizens," Saulnier said.

Phil Givens provoked Cote one step further.

He began by remarking that for just one night's work, and considering that the documentation was only five per cent of the total, Michel Cote had presented a masterful chronological dossier to the committee. Then he added:

"I wonder, Mr. Cote, whether you are really being frank with the committee. I mean, this was intended to be a very serious presentation. You are here; Mr. Saulnier is here; my old friend His Worship the Mayor is here; so you came here really to impress us and yet notwithstanding the masterful dossier and the case that you presented yesterday I am puzzled by the fact that I really heard nothing new in the past day and a half.

No one was prepared for Cote's reaction.

He screamed at Givens, finger pointing, "One thing, Mr. Chairman, I would like to know whether or not the honourable member asked me the question, whether or not I had been frank." His voice rose even higher, " . . . I would like to hear an answer to that right now."

It was no way to speak to a Member of Parliament. It also shattered the cool, responsible image that Cote had been so careful to keep intact. He was finished, and so was the inquiry.

The Cote-Saulnier evidence was the cause of the inquiry, and had been the centre point for it. If the two men could have convinced the MPs that the disturbances in Montreal were part of a national subversive movement, a movement which the Company was an important part of, then undoubtedly the CYC would have been finished. They failed to do this, however, and in the process failed to destroy the Company.

What had the inquiry accomplished?

It gave Claude Vidal his chance to outline the problems of the Company, and to recommend changes. It gave him a chance that he would not have had any other way.

Some MPs had a chance to go on television and to have their quotes carried in newspapers from coast to coast.

It supplied the press with an abundance of news stories.

And lastly, it proved that the Company of Young Canadians was a mess. The only problem was that that fact had been known before the inquiry began.

34

The Verdict

So many people had contributed, deliberately or uncon-
sciously, to the chaos in the CYC that it was impossible to
determine who had been responsible for what.

This did not make it easy for the parliamentary committee that had to make recommendations on the fate of the
Company, but at least it did put things on an intellectual,
rather than a personal, level.

The committee started to have in-camera meetings almost
as soon as the inquiry ended.

Some of the MPs had made their minds up before the
inquiry even began as to what should be done about the
Company.

The Tories, for example, led by Pat Nowlan and Lincoln
Alexander had been bullish, almost totally hostile, to witnesses who represented the Company. With Saulnier and
Cote, they had been the reverse. It was as if they came into
the inquiry with the idea that the Company should be killed
and all they had to do was find the proof.

There were a few exceptions among the Conservatives.
Walter Dinsdale had been kind on occasion and had appeared genuinely interested in the work of the volunteers. In
the end, though, he would go with Nowlan and Alexander.

The NDP supported the Company throughout. It would
have gone against the party's social conscience to have done
anything else. So no matter what personal opinions David
Orlikow and Mark Rose, the two NDP'ers on the committee

held, and at times they seemed to think the same as the Tories, the Company could expect NDP support.

The key, of course, was the Liberal party.

During the inquiry it became obvious that the Company had the support of the Secretary of State, Gerard Pelletier. This meant that a good part of the cabinet would also go along with retaining the CYC. The standing committee's recommendations would be going to cabinet for approval. Could they possibly cause trouble? It seemed unlikely.

This is not to say that the Liberal members of the committee would have gone against the Company. But there were some who had no fondness for the CYC.

The Quebec members, with the exception of Pierre De Bane, were not happy with the Company's actions in their home province. They had grilled and attacked Company members as much as anyone. Claude Vidal hoped they would be held in line.

Even John Reid, the committee chairman, was not an advocate of the Company.

A newsman told one Company staff member that Reid would kill the Company if it was left up to him to decide. Then who *was* for the Company?

Basically a small group of enlightened Liberals: Phil Givens, Doug Hogarth, Bud Osler and Pierre De Bane.

Givens was the former mayor of Toronto. This does not necessarily provide anyone with special insight, but in Givens' case, it did. Listening to him during the inquiry and speaking with him privately, Company staff soon learned that Givens understood the need for a CYC. It was all tied in with his understanding of urban problems and the troubles of youth.

A believer in participatory democracy, Givens preached for greater communications among citizens. To solve problems, he said, you have to talk about them.

Doug Hogarth did not treat the Company as kindly as Givens, but that was his way.

Abrasive, demanding and honest, Hogarth pounded away at the situation in the Company, trying to get at the truth. But, unlike Nowlan, he could be satisfied with an answer and refused to play favorites. This attitude quickly won him the respect of the Company staff, and of the newsmen.

And when Hogarth finally came down on the side of the Company, most people saw it as an honest decision: one that Hogarth himself was sure was correct.

The other two Liberals, De Bane and Osler, came from different backgrounds and approached the Company in different manners. They both did a lot to help the Company make a presentable showing at the inquiry.

Tall and lean, Bud Osler is a member of one of Canada's most illustrious families. A writer and historian, Osler had a keen, analytical mind.

More than anyone, Osler understood the structure of the Company and where it went wrong. He understood the complex nature of social change and why it is necessary. He could accept that politicians needed prodding, that citizens had to become more involved. He understood it all so well that when his time came to ask questions at sessions, the Company people would smile with relief. They knew that his questions would be to the point.

Pierre De Bane was thoroughly likeable. That he was bright was important, but it was his attractiveness that the Company appreciated.

Throughout the inquiry he was always there to lend a hand; to clarify some obscure point; to help defend Vidal against Littleton's attacks; to assist Vidal when the director was a witness; and, finally, to be just about the only friendly face in the room when things were at their blackest.

However, despite the personal opinions of the MPs, the

decision of what to do about the CYC was eventually reduced to the common denominator – politics.

The Tories were against the Company.

The Liberals were for the Company, but wanted changes.

The NDP were for the Company with no changes.

The ayes had it.

On the date required, John Reid presented the committee's report to the House.

Only seven pages in length, the committee's report did not illuminate the scope of the hearings. It seemed to cop out when it came time for hard recommendations, the main reason for the inquiry.

The committee, notwithstanding the Company's "obvious accomplishments and successes", said it was gravely disturbed by many aspects of the legislation, organization and operations of the Company.

It listed lack of administrative procedures; questionable financial procedures; the apparent infiltration of the Company in one region of the country by subversive elements; overt acts of partisan politics by volunteers in other regions; and the inability of the executive director to perform his duties, as its main concerns.

These concerns, the report said, resulted from numerous factors. Its list closely resembled the one that Vidal had presented.

Having thus outlined the faults of the CYC, the committee then turned around to say that the original concepts and objectives of the Company could still be realized. But that this could not be done without substantial changes in the legislative framework, organization and operations of the Company.

The committee then recommended that the Company be placed under trusteeship for a year; this, it said, would allow the Minister and the Company to have consultations before any changes were implemented.

All changes recommended to the House were amazingly

similar to those that Vidal had recommended to the committee.

The membership on the council was questioned; further definition of the executive director's and council's roles was needed; the contractual status of the volunteers should be reviewed; the books should be audited by the Auditor-General.

As for Saulnier?

He lost. The committee recommended that the city of Montreal's evidence and representations be given further study by the appropriate federal cabinet minister, a long way short of a Royal Commission.

This report, not surprisingly, did not please anyone.

The Company staff were unhappy for several reasons. The council was still alive and would remain in action until the Minister saw fit to introduce changes in the legislation. All of the other changes were also at the discretion of the Minister and would have to be worked out in detail by his staff. Why, the CYC staff asked, couldn't the committee have done that? Why did it have to sluff off the responsibility onto the Minister? They could see time being wasted and they had very little time. The council was due to meet again in December, and the staff wanted to go in with a strong hand. The committee report denied them that. The proposed trusteeship also would take away Claude Vidal's opportunity to clean up the Company himself. In addition, it would add another structure to the already structure-ridden Company' with the council still intact, Vidal would have to work through them and the trustee. Things were complicated and bitter enough without that.

The trustee proposal did not sit well with the Secretary of State or with council chairman Jack Johnson, for different reasons of course.

Having backed Claude Vidal thus far, the minister's office was prepared to go all of the way with him. The trustees might be helpful, but a year was too long to wait for more decisive action regarding the Company. The government wanted action now, and since the committee hadn't taken it, the Minister would. At least, he had been given a free hand by the committee. This also entailed taking all the responsiblity.

Johnson said the report was ambiguous. It, on one hand endorsed the role of the Company, but on the other provided the weapons necessary to stifle that role. It all depended, he said, on the sympathy and desires of the government.

The Trustee proposal he regarded as a travesty.

"The major specific recommendation, the trusteeship proposal, is in my opinion a personal insult to the fifteen-member governing Council of the Company. We have never had a fair chance. The government delayed our taking office for months, thereby creating an unhealthy power vacuum. We were finally allowed to take office October 4th, 1969, but less than three weeks thereafter, the government called for a Parliamentary Inquiry.

"At the inquiry itself, we were unfairly treated in several important ways. The council was the first witness and was never allowed to return thereafter to rebut our critics, or even to submit other witnesses. In a court of law, the accused is always called after the accusers but not in our case. Mr. Saulnier and his associates not only had the last word, but also had twice as much committee time as we had.

"I propose to the Parliamentary Committee that because we had just taken office, we should be given until March 31, 1970 to get our house in order. We ask no special favour, just a fair chance to prove ourselves capable and responsible. That chance is apparently to be denied us."

Johnson was wrong in the last paragraph. The council would be given one more chance to prove itself capable and responsible. A council meeting was scheduled for December 12, 13 and 14.

35

The Council's Last Stand

There had been a dream once. It may have been idealistic and naive, but at least it was there when the Company of Young Canadians needed something to aim for, when it needed something to give it hope.

The dream was a volunteer-controlled Company of Young Canadians. Canada's young people with their own organization, with their chance to prove their responsibility, their ability, their caring. Oh, there would be faults in it, of course, but they would be the faults of youth, inexperience and overzealousnous.

Yet something had gone wrong. The Company was in trouble and all of a sudden the young people, the supreme body in the Company, found themselves dying. They were less than two months old and already their elders had lost patience. Was it justified? Jack Johnson didn't think so. And the meeting of the council on December 12th, 13th and 14th was the time to prove it.

They came back to Ottawa for the meeting, back to the lair of Claude Vidal — the enemy.

They gathered in the Company's conference room on the 12th, a Friday, to move the Company forward. Only Jack Johnson and a few others seemed to realize that this wasn't just another meeting. Only Johnson seemed to realize that the inquiry had even been held. The others, especially the elected volunteers, actually appeared to think that the council would not be touched, that they were beyond the grasp of the politicians.

The onlookers, the nervous staff and the press, once again out in great numbers expecting a gigantic clash be-

tween Vidal and his foes and the death of one or the
other, listened as Jack Johnson started the meeting with a
short speech.

The government is watching, he said. The press is here.
The executive director has accused us of being many things.
Let us prove that we're not. Let us be responsible, let us
work together, let us make decisions.

If the council could accomplish this, it might restore its
credibility and gain some respect. Then, perhaps, and just
perhaps, it might give the government some thought to
continuing the council in its present form. It might give
the dream one more chance.

Lloyd Axworthy gave council its first test.

He suggested that the Company investigate thoroughly
its own operation in Quebec.

Saulnier's charges may have been red herrings, he said,
but the Company has a duty to find out for itself. It
should appoint an investigating team and go to Quebec.

Jean Roy charged at him; the sovereignty of Quebec
was not to be challenged. The Company was not to investigate. His reputation already smudged by Saulnier's testimony, it was easy to understand why Roy took that stand.
It is not so easy to explain why he was so well supported.
But he was. The recommendation never came to a vote.

Not many things came to a vote that Friday.

Every possible excuse to attack Claude Vidal was implemented.

Many of the councillors were furious with Vidal, with the
government, and with the inquiry. They began to lash out
in an almost irrational way. The rhetoric belonged to
anarchists, Marxists, extremists. Axworthy, Johnson and
Sean Sullivan tried to tone things down. It was useless.

The press watched, and the press got dragged in. It was
inevitable.

John Drewery of the CBC found himself being insulted

by two Toronto volunteers. He forgot his passive newsman's role.

"What kind of idiots are these people?" he asked a staff person. "I feel sorry for Vidal. I can understand why he said what he did at the inquiry."

Drewery said some nasty things that night on the national news. He even managed to out-do Claude Vidal.

Meanwhile, Jack Johnson and a few other council members were pretending that Friday had never happened.

While being interviewed by the news media, Johnson went as far to say that there was no schism on the council, and that the body could work responsibly. He would be regretting those words within twenty-four hours.

Roy Daniels, the volunteer member from the Northwest Territories, wasn't about to wait for twenty-four hours. On Friday, he announced his resignation from the council. He told the gathering that he was sick of listening to them. He was going back to the field where things were real.

He also accused the Quebec members of being racists; the accusation resulting from the fact that there was not one Indian project in Quebec. The Quebecois didn't want one. Quebec was for the French.

Despite Daniels' resignation and Drewery's denunciation of the council, Saturday dawned and the council re-grouped for another effort. It was a three-day meeting and two good days could offset the bad beginning, Johnson reasoned.

The meeting started with Johnson once again giving his speech. He was desperate by now. After committing himself publicly the night before, he did not want to be dragged into the muck.

The first topic on the agenda was the Toronto Youth project.

The council had ordered an evaluation of the project at its last meeting and had appointed council member Mickey Posluns to carry it out. He presented his report.

The project, he revealed, would not accept a consultant to help him in his evaluation; the volunteers would not talk to their staff member; the volunteers didn't want to talk to him about what they were doing; they had misled the reporting team on several key points; they had made no effort to fulfill their project's approved role, working with youth.

In view of the facts, Posluns said, there was only one thing that could be done — get rid of the volunteers and the project.

The newsmen were amazed at Posluns's report. They had never imagined that projects could be that bad. They waited for the council to act.

The council voted six to four to keep the project and the volunteers.

The press gasped. The staff winced. The four councillors: Posluns, Johnson, Axworthy and Sullivan, who voted to get rid of the project, threw their hands up in disgust.

"You are irresponsible and incompetent," Posluns exploded.

He then rose from his chair and walked from the room. His resignation came a few moments later.

Claude Vidal sat motionless. He needn't have attacked the council; it was destroying itself.

Then lunchtime came and the meetings started.

The radicals went off by themselves, no doubt to discuss strategy. They seemed oblivious to the fiasco.

Jack Johnson, pale and wan, was struggling with the realization that it couldn't work; that moderation and logic meant nothing. He talked with Sullivan and Axworthy and with some staff members. What could they do?

The field, Johnson kept saying, the field, why should it suffer because of these people?

When the meeting reconvened everyone was present.

In the afternoon, Jack Johnson led things off by resigning as chairman of the council. His resignation would take effect immediately. He was also resigning as a council member effective Sunday night, December 14th.

Lloyd Axworthy then moved in an attempt to deny the radicals control.

He proposed that the council terminate its activities and ask the Secretary of State to exercise responsibility for the operations of the CYC until Parliament could restructure the Company. Jack Johnson seconded his motion.

It was defeated six to three.

Johnson, Axworthy and Sullivan stayed. They could not abandon the Company at this stage.

The abuse came once more as a result of the motion. It was growing more hysterical with each succeeding wave. Ideologies were thrown back and forth; compromises were refused. The radicals would not negotiate. Skip Hambling quoted Lenin to underline his refusal to budge.

At this point Jean Roy interceded. The Quebec volunteer seemed to be almost enjoying himself. Precisely and reasonably he suggested that the Company was in a bad position because it had no policies, neatly forgetting the policies that did exist, but which he refused to recognize. He proposed that an all-night session be held to work out policies for the Company. The radicals agreed with him. The meeting was adjourned and off they went: Roy, Hambling, Millie Barrett, Marcel Desjardins, into a world of their own.

The council reconvened the following morning at 10:45. Mickey Posluns and Roy Daniels were missing because of their resignations. Jean Thibault hadn't been there all weekend. Rob Wood had headed back to Vancouver. Michael Kirby was missing. The others showed up ready to do battle.

Roy had been doing some figuring during the night. The radicals were getting nowhere fighting at the council table.

An alternate way of running the Company had to be found.

The first step in the plan was swiftly complete: Jean Roy was elected chairman of the council.

He described his victory as a *coup d'etat*.

Rob Wood was elected vice-chairman and he accepted the post by telephone.

The radicals' plans then began to unfold, more than slightly obscured by the insults they could not resist throwing at the moderate council members, and at Claude Vidal and the administration. Vidal by this time was being blamed for everything and anything that was wrong with the CYC. He was still sitting quietly, confident that it would all be over soon.

Johnson, Axworthy and Sullivan were not so content to wait.

Every five minutes or so they would appeal for moderation, for reason, for anything other than the total madness that was prevailing.

The radicals did not swerve. They were going to take control.

Marcel Desjardins motioned that an executive committee be set up to carry all the powers of the council.

This five-member committee, Jean Roy said, would make operational decisions which the council was manifestly incapable of making. It would even change CYC policy.

That this appeared to be in defiance of the Company's constitution didn't bother him. He wanted control.

As council chairman and vice-chairman, Roy and Wood were automatically members of the executive committee. Three more had to be elected. It took almost two hours of nominations, refusals and finally begging to get the other three members. They were Skip Hambling, Millie Barrett and Jeanette Corbiere.

While the moderates were still present and the council meeting still on, Jean Roy read a policy statement which he wanted the council to accept.

It proposed three-year volunteer contracts (Roy's own two-year contract was ending and Vidal was refusing to renew it); the total decentralization of the Company's funds across the country, cutting out Ottawa and controls entirely; and withdrawing from any project which was limited to a specific minority group, such as youth, or Indians.

This last measure would have meant the disbanding of the Toronto Youth project, the same project that Roy and the radicals had so vigorously defended the previous day. They made no apologies, however, for their change of mind.

The policy was never voted on. Arguments flared once more and Roy adjourned the meeting. The executive committee then moved upstairs to finish the council agenda.

Jack Johnson, Lloyd Axworthy and Sean Sullivan moved to the other side of the city, to the office of the Secretary of State to recommend the disbanding of council and the complete control of the CYC by Parliament. This same message was repeated to the press. The press agreed wholeheartedly. So did Pelletier.

They need not have panicked. Claude Vidal was still in Ottawa and still at the office. As far as he was concerned, the executive committee was illegal and the council, through stupidness, had thrown away its right to govern. He would not obey or even listen to Jean Roy.

As proof of this, the following day he wrote to Dick Lightbown, his Toronto co-ordinator. His message was clear.

" . . . as of this date, David Gardner and Larry Williams (the two Toronto Youth volunteers) are no longer members of the Company of Young Canadians."

Jean Roy could do what he wanted. Claude Vidal was running the Company.

The government was not sitting around, either. An Act was hastily drawn up and pushed through Parliament. On December 19th, a Friday, Claude Vidal received a telegram from a lawyer in Montreal.

FURTHER TO ACT OF PARLIAMENT AND ORDER IN COUNCIL OF DECEMBER 19, 1969 I HAVE BEEN APPOINTED CONTROLLER OF THE COMPANY OF YOUNG CANADIANS. THE ACT PROVIDES THAT NO PAYMENT OF MONEY SHALL BE MADE BY THE COMPANY AND NO CONTRACT OR OTHER ARRANGEMENTS PROVIDING FOR THE PAYMENT OF MONEY BY THE COMPANY SHALL BE ENTERED INTO OR HAVE ANY FORCE OR EFFECT WITHOUT MY APPROVAL. ACCORDINGLY NO EXPENSES OR OBLIGATIONS OF ANY SORT ARE TO BE INCURRED OR AUTHORIZED PRIOR TO OUR MEETING SCHEDULED FOR MONDAY, DECEMBER 22ND.

> Max Mendlesohn,
> Controller,
> Company of Young Canadians.

With those curt statements, Max Mendlesohn signified the end of the Company of Young Canadians as it had been known. The council was dead. The goal of participation gone with it. The Company was finally and irrevocably changed. It had dared the government just once too often.

Anticipated as the news was, it still was not received with any great joy in the Company's Ottawa office. Claude Vidal was not unhappy, of course. He was sure he and Mendlesohn would work together to clean up. It was the other staff who were not quite so prepared. Who can blame them?

For years, most of them had been struggling for the kind of Company they believed in. It was the Company of Stewart Goodings; brave, idealistic, and responsible. They had stood alongside Vidal to fight for the same thing and, although they criticized the council, they still believed that the volunteers had to be involved in the running of the Company, that the Company should not become another bureaucracy.

Some of these staff members had been volunteers. Dale Seddon and Bernie Muzeen, the two operation officers, were still close to the field and to the concept of volunteerism.

Seddon, particularly, seemed to sense that the Company would never be the same — that the joy he had known as a volunteer, and the freedom, would never be available again. Usually exuberant and energetic, it was dismaying to see him drag himself around the office at the end of December.

The volunteers in the field did not feel the despondency that many staff were sharing.

Ottawa was so far removed from them. It had always been that way.

In the past, the volunteers had been subjected to four executive directors, a provisional council, a permanent council, government attacks, press attacks, and citizen outrages. They had always survived. Their work had always gone on.

Promises had been made countless times. Tricks had been played. Every kind of structure had been used on them. To the volunteers it all added up to the same thing — Ottawa, always Ottawa.

To most of them, the demise of the permanent council, their long awaited dream, and the emergence of the government's heavy hand was not much to get excited about. All of that monkeying around only meant changes in Ottawa. Ottawa was unreal anyway. The field was the Company and would always be the Company. That was where reality was. The parliamentary committee had ignored reality; the permanent council couldn't see it; the staff had never acknowledged any greater sacrifice than their own.

The volunteers didn't realize that their reality was going to be upset. That this time the change was more than an exchange between manipulators. The Company was going to be different.

36

The New CYC?

It is March, 1970, and nothing has been heard lately about the Company of Young Canadians.

The organization that for three years dominated the front pages of Canada's newspapers on a monthly basis, and during the late months of 1969 on a daily basis, is either finished or in hiding.

There is no word about clashes with governments, no news about the Company's latest stand, and little sight of the 200 or so volunteers who disrupted so much of Canada. Have the volunteers been purged? Is the Company really clean?

The cynics hoot. The Company, they claim, will always be the Company.

For once they are wrong.

Since Mendlesohn had stepped into the Company as controller in December, 1969, he had worked closely with the executive director.

Mendlesohn, small, dark and Jewish, was as pragmatic and efficient as the taller, balding Vidal. The Montreal lawyer, a bankruptcy expert, had been put into the Company to take over its finances and straighten them out. He had a free hand with any matter related to finances, and nothing in the Company was being run without cost. This gave Mendlesohn the widest of powers. He could virtually cancel volunteer contracts, disband projects and cut project budgets.

Before any of this could be done, though, Mendlesohn had to find out what the Company's financial situation was. In order to do this as quickly as possible, he froze all spending; recalled all petty cashes; and ordered activities, such as travelling, to cease. Once the situation was clear, Mendlesohn told the projects, he would re-release funds and start paying bills again.

His rationalization, and his job, however necessary, did not please the volunteers. With their petty cashes gone, they were penniless. With no travelling allowed, volunteers on isolated projects were more isolated than ever. With no bills being paid, local merchants would look unfavorably upon the volunteers.

While spending was frozen, Mendlesohn did exhaustive research into the Company's finances. He didn't like what he found. The Company was again, even under Vidal, going to overspend unless some drastic cuts were made. The good projects were going to have to suffer as much as the bad ones.

Together, Mendlesohn and Vidal agreed that some projects were to be wiped out. Their choices were not unfair. Cape Breton was demolished. St. Henri, St. Marie and a few others in Quebec were obliterated. The Vancouver Youth project's contract was not renewed.

Attention was then turned to the projects that remained and the volunteers who had survived the last year. There were only about 100 of them now, their numbers reduced by a multitude of plagues, the latest being the double-pronged assault of Claude Vidal and Max Mendlesohn.

The director was questioning at length the activities of these projects, the financial activities that is. He seemed not to care about the work the projects were doing, or how valuable that work was. The projects had first to toe the financial line.

The volunteers might have asked, who put the Company in a financial hole in the first place, staff or volunteers? Whose work kept the Company alive?

Instead, for a while, they suffered in silence and contemplated the Kremlin-like atmosphere in the new Company.

Others were watching too, some staff who had been close to Claude Vidal during the last trying year; people who had stood by him and fought with and for him.

The staff had always wondered about Claude Vidal, about that something he always held in reserve. At times they had thought the worst; that he was an autocrat, a non-feeling person, a knife at work for the government. Somehow these doubts had always vanished and they had regrouped behind him. He, apparently, did not want another regrouping.

These staff, who had shared his confidences and given him advice, were now effectively shut out of his office.

Pierre Renaud is only one example.

The Quebec staff member had performed valiantly for Vidal in Quebec. The director had acknowledged this at the inquiry. Renaud had also strengthened Vidal's hand immeasurably at the inquiry by appearing to testify. His testimony was one main reason that the Company had done so well.

Shortly after Max Mendlesohn came into the Company, Renaud left for a holiday in France. He did it badly, only giving two days notice and leaving no staff member in Quebec to replace him.

But he was physically depleted. His energy drained by the constant warfare between Quebec and Ottawa, and the pressure of being under the nation's microscope. He surely had deserved the rest.

Vidal disagreed.

Deciding that Renaud had acted irresponsibly by leaving at such a time, Vidal suspended his Quebec co-ordinator.

Renaud resigned a short time later, not having worked one more day for the CYC since the suspension.

Others did not resign so quickly or quietly. They were beginning to realize the enormity of the change taking place in the Company and wanted some moderation. Their dissatisfaction was relayed to the field and ears perked up.

Looking at their depleted resources, at the seeming harassment that they were being subjected to, at the volunteers they needed, but were being denied for fiscal reasons, a small part of the field decided it had had enough. They phoned some staff members in Ottawa to discuss strategy and decide on demands. It was decided that a national Company meeting would be the wisest move, a meeting to iron out any problems and misunderstandings in the Company. If Vidal wouldn't agree, they would approach the government.

As a test, a staff member called the Secretary of State's office. There is trouble in the field, he told Bob Rabinovitch, Pelletier's special assistant. The volunteers and staff are unhappy with the autocratic way things are being done. If Vidal wouldn't meet with them, they were going to ask for an appearance before the Broadcasting Committee to try to stop the Company's new legislation being passed.

Rabinovitch was blunt. It's too late, he said, it's too late. They can't do anything. They can't change anything. If they kick up a fuss, they'll only kill the Company.

"I don't care," Elaine Husband in Calgary said. "I'd rather have a dead Company than one like this." Peter Puxley in Yellowknife and Vic Cathers in Lesser Slave Lake, two other dissidents, and two men who Vidal himself had hired, seemed to agree with her.

The field's concerns and demands were relayed to Max Mendlesohn and Claude Vidal. Mendlesohn seemed more worried than the director about the reactions in the field. He thought that something should be done. Not Vidal. He saw the reactions as personal feelings, as misunderstandings. There was nothing he could do about them.

The staff was amazed by his attitude.

Dale Seddon and Bernie Muzeen huddled together. Because both were former volunteers, they understood full well how the projects felt. What they couldn't understand was Claude Vidal.

Claude Vidal was a professional. He was a top-notch administrator and a highly competent manager. His forte was figures, plans, structures, job descriptions, policies and all of the things that the Company had been missing. To him, the Company was almost a book-keeping problem, one that could be solved systematically, thoroughly and without any personal involvement.

He never realized that not everyone could match his professionalism. That not everyone could isolate themselves from feelings. That not everyone wanted to. And that many people did not work for the Company because of the money.

They worked for the CYC, when they could have made more money for less pain elsewhere. They naively believed in the concept of the Company. They believed in social change, in the rights of people, and in other things that smacked of personalization.

And so they rebelled. Many of the people who had supported Vidal came at him, and at the two people closest to him, Maeve Hancey and Max Mendlesohn. They pleaded the case of the field. They demanded that something be done.

Mendlesohn and Hancey did understand. Together, with the other staff, they went to Vidal. The case was presented to the director. He grudgingly gave way, but not all the way. He doubted that a meeting would accomplish much. There was still so much to do in Ottawa, and there was a problem of financing a meeting. He and Mendlesohn couldn't give the field anything anyway. They didn't know what the full picture of the Company was yet and wouldn't make any promises. He did, however, finally agree to travel west to visit the dissidents.

It was a quick tour, a day here and a day there. One of his unhappy staff members went with him. It was a reluctant show of staff solidarity. On the first night they were in the west, Vidal and the staff member sat down together to discuss the gap that had developed between them, and why the staff member was resigning.

"I find that you are too administratively concerned," the staff member said. "It isn't enough to look at figures. You have to also look at people. You have to balance."

As the staff member and Vidal visited projects, it appeared the director was making an effort to do just that. He promised the staff that a meeting would be held, perhaps in late March. It would only be for staff, though. The staff, Vidal said, should find out where they are going. They should become involved in the planning of Company priorities.

March came, and as the month dragged by, democracy within the Company, always a rare commodity, seemed to have disappeared. The staff had little power. The volunteers had none.

Vidal had made the position of the volunteers, the few who were left, clear when he had been in the west.

The staff, he told them, would be meeting to plan Company priorities. There would be no volunteers at the meeting. The volunteers would not be involved until the staff were working well together.

Some were revolted by Vidal's opinions.

Bernie Muzeen, the former volunteer, and one of Vidal's often used examples of a volunteer participating in the Company after his contract had ended, thought it wrong, totally wrong.

It was as if the concept of volunteerism that Stewart Goodings and others had stood for was dirty and shameful. Volunteers, Goodings had said, are not just cheap labor. They are people who dedicate themselves to serve. Their reward, in his mind, was the chance to participate.

Certainly some had abused that chance, but they were in a minority. They did not represent the 100 or so who were left, who were still serving, who refused to give up.

Vidal seemed to be mocking them. His insistence that the staff meet first, that the elders decide what must be done before consulting with the children, was an old-fashioned idea. The children ought to be respectful to their elders, no matter how silly they are.

Vidal was not alone in this opinion.

The government was still there in March working on new legislation for the CYC, throwing out the good with the bad.

The legislation was being changed through fear. Young people had been given a chance, the government reasoned, and had blown it. There was no thought that perhaps the chance had been an image, an image that had been denied the volunteers for years, and then turned into reality when the Company was at its blackest and failure was the certain result.

The path of the Company had been irrevocably downhill. It would not be changed. It could not be changed. Circumstances had determined what would happen. The Company's history, which most of the volunteers inherited and did not make, was against them.

The government didn't care. The volunteers had failed. They could not be entrusted with responsibility.

They would still be counted upon to do well in the field, of course. They would still be given a chance to prove that the Liberals had made a wise choice when it let the Company live. They would still be the workhorses, the miracle-makers and the doers.

In March, as Claude Vidal was making the internal autocracy vivid, the government quietly informed an uninterested nation that the CYC would be governed by an appointed council of nine members. The Council and its chairman would be government picked, and government answerable. If it did not do a good job, the government could disband it.

The executive director, too, would be chosen by the government.

The Children's Crusade that had begun with drums and

flags, hopes for a better Canada and promises of success, had ended with the same old order, the same old winners, triumphing once more.

The children had been deceived. They had been made promises that were never kept. They had been given masters who used them and led them astray. They had been frustrated and forced to desperate lengths. It's our crusade, they kept yelling. You are screwing it up. Give us the chance you promised us. No, they were told. Wait, they were told. You aren't ready, they were told. The chance was withheld and withheld until the last moment. When it came, it was only a mirage.

The Company of Young Canadians still lives. But it is a government agency. It is a bureaucracy. It no longer acknowledges the Crusade.

But somewhere in Canada there is a volunteer who does acknowledge it. He is living it daily in a slum, in an Indian community. The time will come when he will raise the standard again for other children to follow. This time, the Crusade will be of their own making and it will be impossible to deceive or stop.

This Crusade will be the Company of Young Canadians as it was meant to be, and as it should have been.

The volunteers, as they have always done, will keep the Crusade alive.

The Company of Young Canadians died in March, 1970. The Children's Crusade will carry on without it.

Epilogue

The Company of Young Canadians did effectively die in March, 1970. The government, while spouting radical justifications, provided the means by which the concept and role of the Company could be made meaningless.

That the Company should end this way is almost fitting. It did, after all, begin in the same way.

When the Company was born in 1965, perhaps a few of its architects understood what they were doing. They wanted to create an agency for change, an agency that would be apart from the government, from the establishment and from the institutions that stifle change as a means of self-preservation. They understood full well that in order to be effective, the CYC had to be apart.

These few architects shrewdly sensed changes in the air. They saw, a little before others, that young people were restless, that young people wanted to become involved and wanted responsibility. So they made a young people's agency that would be controlled by these same young people. They were giving youth the chance that no other country in the world had permitted.

The government made these ideas law, and then quickly reneged.

For despite its approval, the government was not quite convinced that young people were in fact responsible, and could be trusted. Consequently, it appointed a provisional council, consisting of some radicals, some undefinables, and some of its own, trustworthy kind, to set up the Company and administer its affairs until the young people became responsible. They forgot two things: people only become responsible when they are given responsibility, and that government appointed people are not necessarily particularly talented.

For three years, this provisional council and Company staff ran the CYC and the volunteers. They ran it badly, as Doug Ward admitted.

While the volunteers were plugging away in the field, these responsible elders were helping to throw money away, making bad decisions, and helping to make the name of the CYC a disgrace. The volunteers had to suffer for these sins.

And so the volunteers became frustrated. The things they wanted most, an efficient Ottawa office, some support, Stewart Goodings as a director, were denied them. If they had been denied by an obviously competent and reasonable body, it might have been sufferable. But the volunteers kept looking at the Company, kept seeing the mess and couldn't understand.

The press didn't understand either. The Company was a novelty, an experiment to be picked apart. And did they pick. Every piece of dirt, every farce, was reported in detail. The work of the volunteers was a lesser consideration.

The volunteers worked in the middle of this, in slums, in Indian communities, with people who needed help. The volunteers were not there to bandage wounds. They were there to get to the sources of problems. Oh they mucked it up some times. They made large mistakes. They were too extreme, or too open, or too honest. But, other times, they were magnificent.

They performed miracles. Citizens groups sprang up all over the country. People began to realize they had a voice, an opinion and should be heard. They rocked governments. They rocked dogmas. They made the words participatory democracy come true for people who had believed that you do what you are told. The volunteers worked for $225 a month and gave the government more for its money than the millions it had spent on the war on poverty, on welfare, and on countless other programs.

For their efforts, they were abused.

After three years of waiting, and three years of promises, the volunteers finally decided they had earned the right to run the Company. They had created the things that the Company and government could point to with pride. They had not created the mess.

When they made their demands, more promises were given. When the promises took too long to become true, the volunteers became bitter. The staff, the government, the establishment became their enemies. Can you blame them?

By the time they were given their chance, the Company had been going downhill for a long time. It would take an amazingly talented group of people to stop the slide and to reverse it.

The volunteers did not elect an amazingly talented group; the group was in fact not as well equipped as the people who elected them. The council was also ridden with the hatred and extremism that the years of maltreatment had been fostering.

Within three weeks of taking office, the council was finished. It ended with the inquiry.

It was an example of the political fakery that permeates so many societies. When the Company was going badly, under its provisional council, the government refused to become involved, although God knows it had reason. It took a political charge, and a charge that was not wholly substantiated, to make the government move.

The government turned the Company back over to the staff. It had held the volunteers at bay for three years. It had endured incompetence from the very people it appointed. Then it decided, after giving the young people three weeks to prove themselves, that volunteers and young people could never be given that kind of responsibility.

It then passed legislation putting the Company firmly

into the grips of Parliament, debasing the second original concept of the Company.

Social change cannot take place under government jurisdiction. Social change has political implications and what government is going to sit back and be criticized and threatened by an agency which it can control?

Gerard Pelletier may be an enlightened Secretary of State. He may resist the temptation to step in. But some day, there will be a different Secretary of State, and a different government. When that happens and the CYC steps out of line, it will all be over.

By cutting the heart out of the two concepts that made the Company of Young Canadians different, that made it unique, that made it worth keeping, the government has made it worthless.

The Company still lives, of course, on paper. And will probably continue to live. It will be an empty, hollow existence, however, one that mocks the original intent of the Company.

The Company will never be what it was intended to be. It will never be a force for change, and proof that young people can make a better world.

The sad thing is that the young people might have done it if they had been left alone. The work on the projects was theirs. The successes of the Company were their successes. But no one saw them. No one gave them the chance.

The Company of Young Canadians is a testimonial to the failures of the system that created it to deal with failures, then obstructed it at every opportunity.

The Company of Young Canadians never was a company of young Canadians.

March on children.